VOLUPTUOUS HORRORS

100 WEIRD MENACE PULP MAGAZINE COVERS 1933-1937

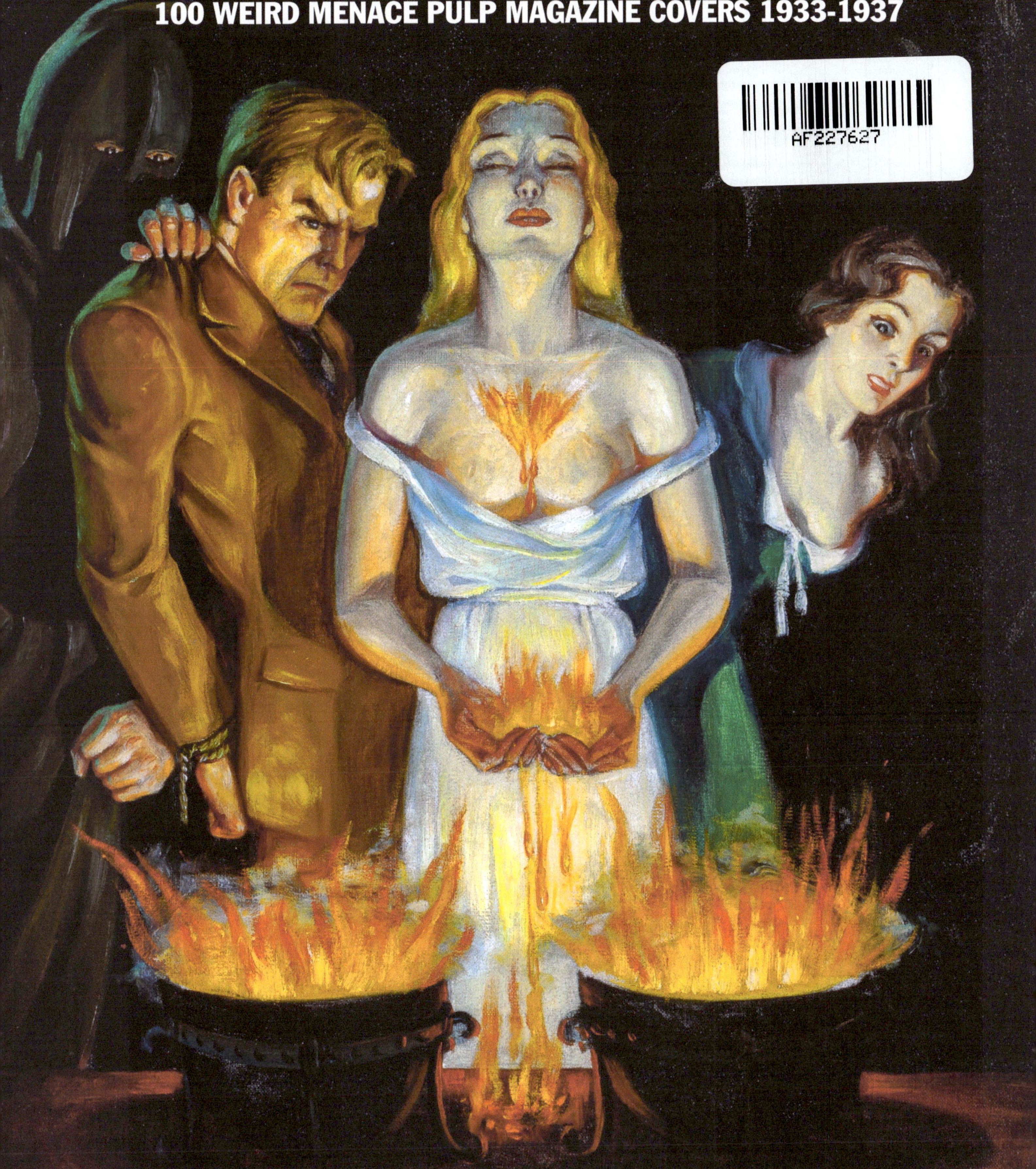

VOLUPTUOUS HORRORS

EDITED BY G.H. JANUS
ISBN 978-1-8383595-8-4
PUBLISHED BY BONEFYRE BOOKS 2023
COPYRIGHT © BONEFYRE BOOKS 2023
ALL WORLD RIGHTS RESERVED

FOREWORD

One of the first key waves of populist, or pulp, art created in American cultural history came during the period from 1933 to 1940, when a range of provocative magazines sprang up with exceptionally striking, often startling cover illustrations by some of the most imaginative artists of the time. The most controversial of these publications were those themed around "weird menace" fiction, a genre which coalesced in October 1933 with the inception of **Dime Mystery Magazine**, from Popular Publications. This watershed issue saw the magazine – previously titled **Dime Mystery Book Magazine** – shift its focus from crime to horror, with full-cover artwork by Walter M. Baumhofer showing a hooded killer forcing a woman to cut the rope holding her boyfriend from falling into a vat of flesh-eating acid. The skeleton of a previous victim, stripped clean to the bone, can be seen floating in the foreground. This shift in artwork was accompanied by a similar change in story titles, with the cover featuring "Dance Of the Skeletons". Other titles in this issue included "Monster In The Dark", "The Graveless Dead", and "Gate Of The Two Coffins". This new genre was variously described as "horror", "terror-mystery", and "the weirdest stories ever told" on **Dime Mystery** covers, with the definitive term "weird menace" first appearing on the cover of **Terror Tales** in 1937.

The covers produced for this and similar pulps were mainly centred around images of attractive young women – scantily clad in ripped dresses and underwear, or even naked – being threatened with torture, mutilation and death by an array of hooded cultists, mad doctors and other deranged psychopaths. Regular artists for these publications included Baumhofer, Tom Lovell, Rudolph Belarski, John Newton Howitt, John Drew, and John Walter Scott, all purveyors of prime voluptuous horror. Among the other weird menace pulps were **Terror Tales**, **Horror Stories**, **Mystery Tales**, **Strange Stories**, **Eerie Mysteries**, **Uncanny Tales**, and **Thrilling Mystery**, growing increasingly daring in content[1] until finally, in the early 1940s, a combination of moral backlash and the paper shortage caused by world war saw weird menace slowly disappear from the newsstands.

VOLUPTUOUS HORRORS collects 100 full-page, full-colour weird menace magazine covers from 1933-1937, presenting some of the world's most lurid and often sadistic cover designs from the golden age of pulps.

1. For example, when the February 1940 issue of **Dime Mystery** recycled cover artwork from **Horror Stories**, October 1937, the image was reworked so that the woman in peril was now naked, her modesty only shielded by steam from the vat in which she is being slowly boiled alive.

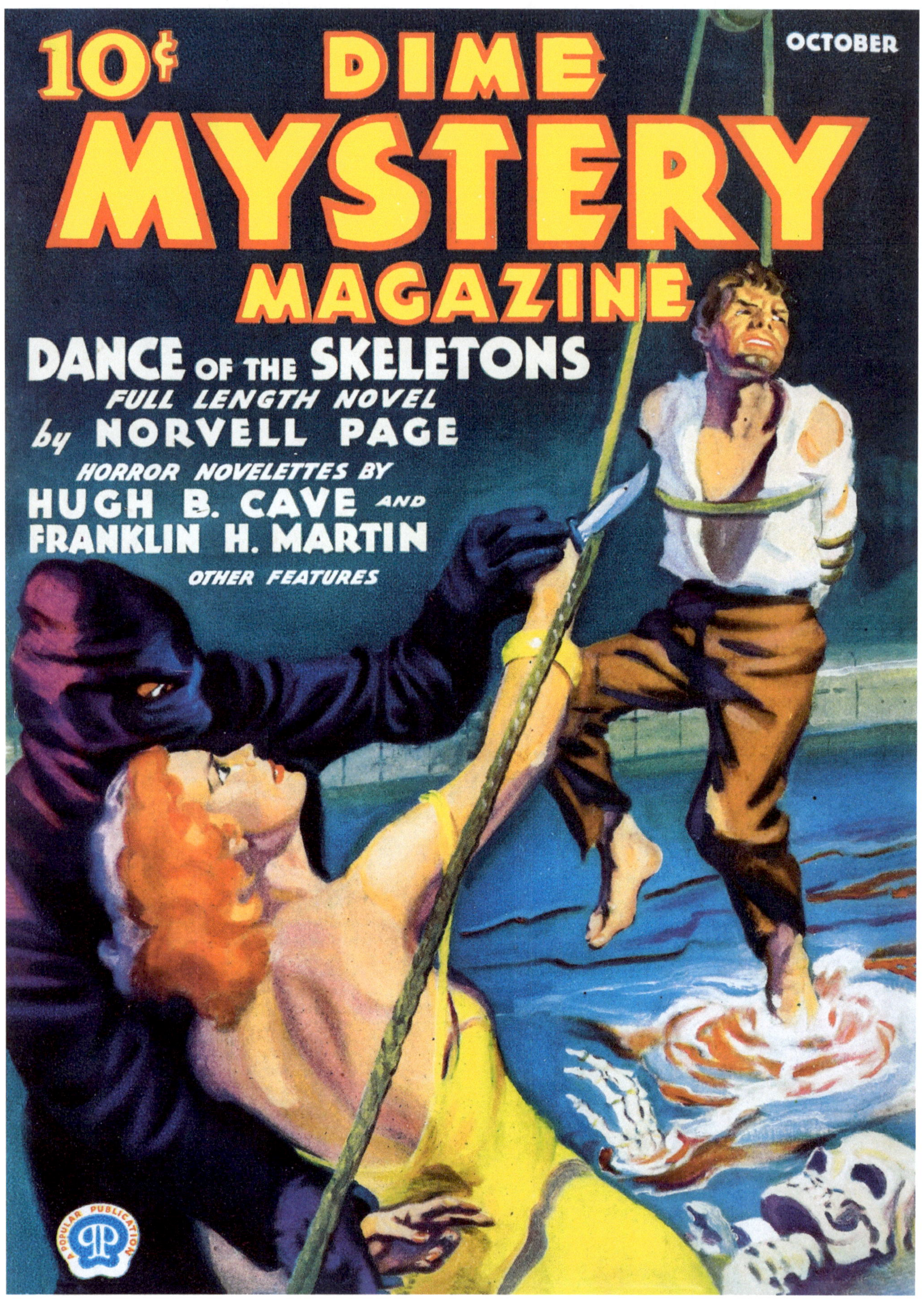

DIME MYSTERY MAGAZINE
OCTOBER 1933

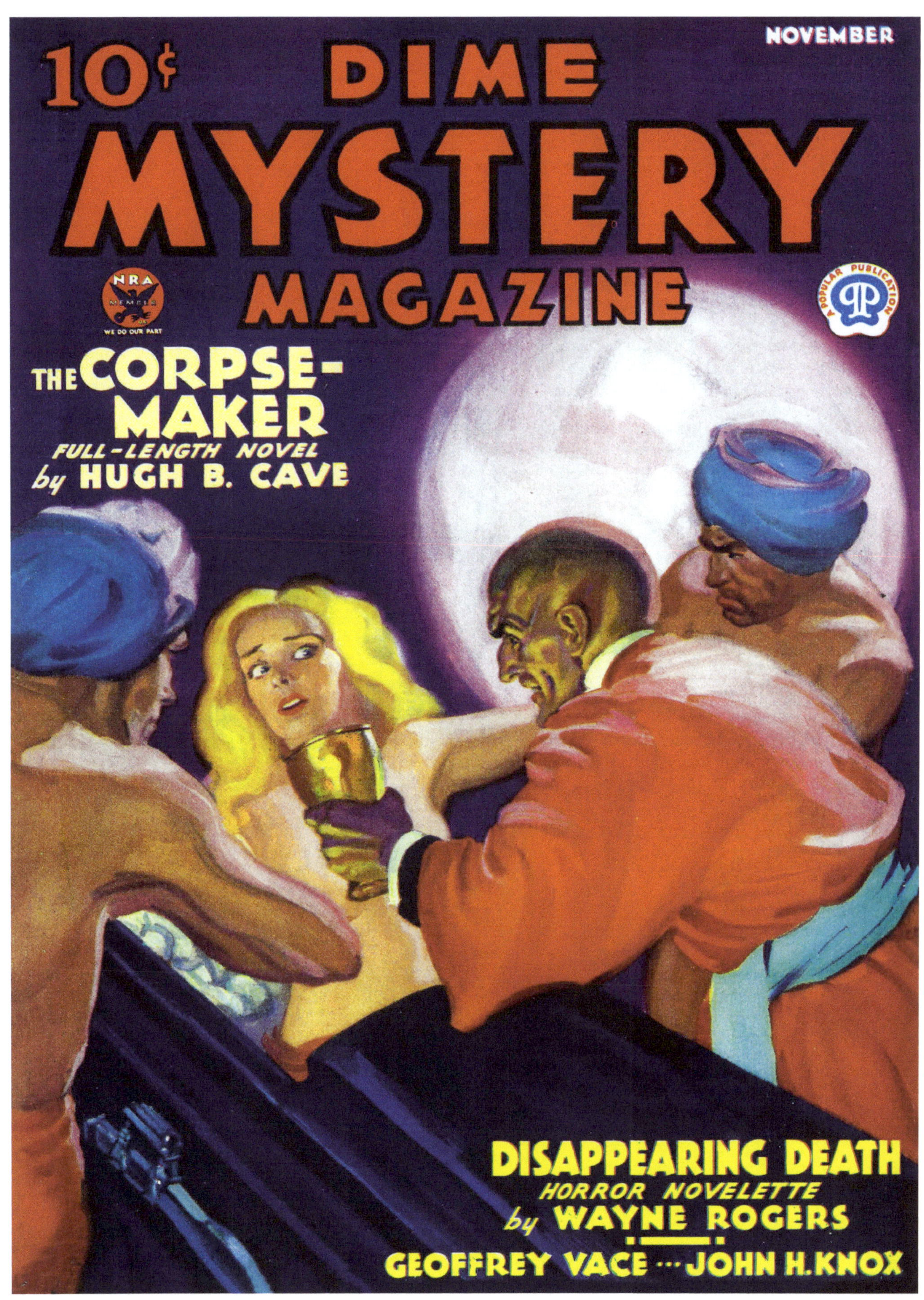

NOVEMBER
10¢
DIME
MYSTERY
MAGAZINE
THE CORPSE-MAKER
FULL-LENGTH NOVEL
by HUGH B. CAVE
DISAPPEARING DEATH
HORROR NOVELETTE
by WAYNE ROGERS
GEOFFREY VACE ···· JOHN H. KNOX

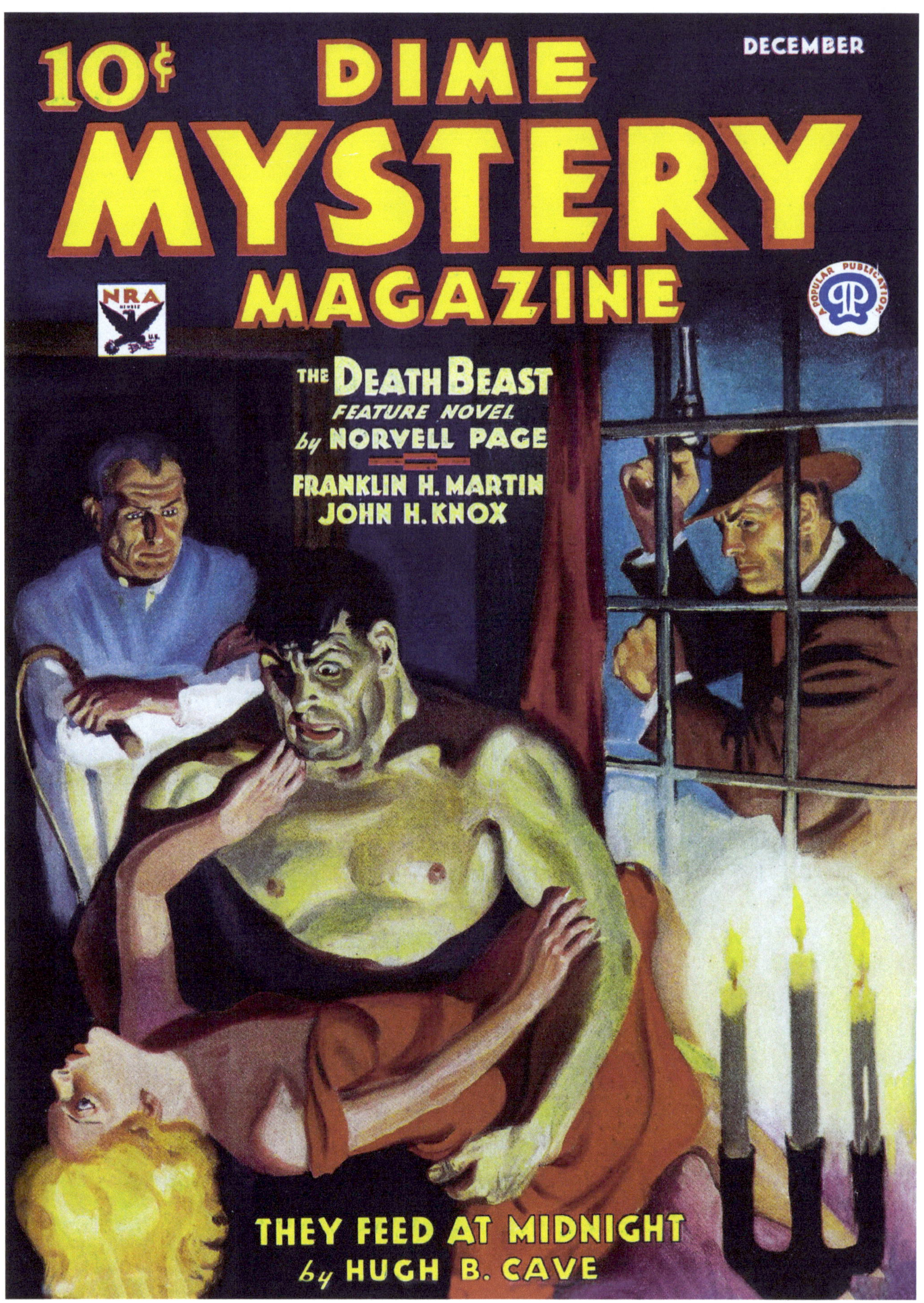

DIME MYSTERY
DECEMBER 1933

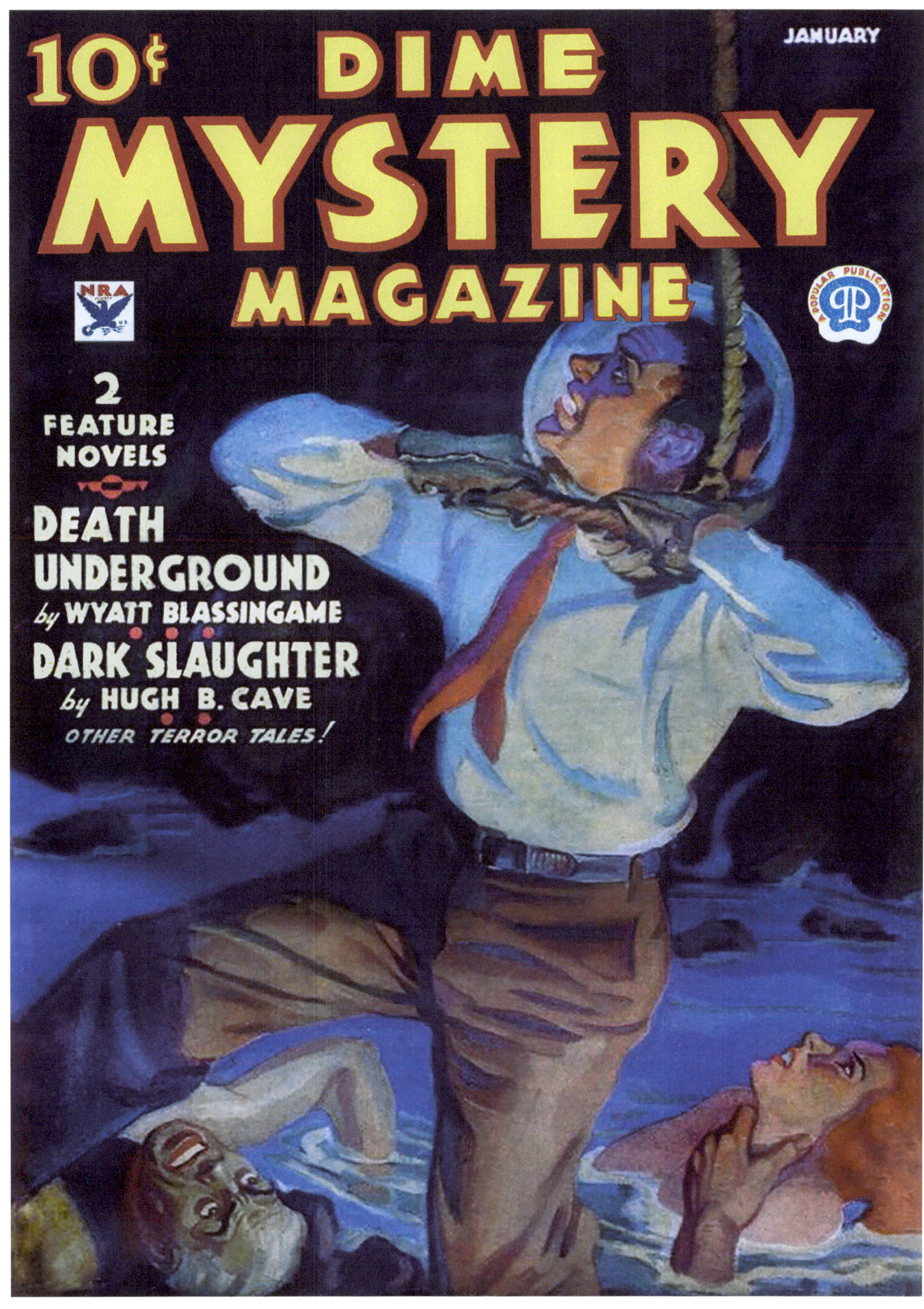

JANUARY
10¢
DIME MYSTERY MAGAZINE
NRA
A POPULAR PUBLICATION
2 FEATURE NOVELS
DEATH UNDERGROUND
by WYATT BLASSINGAME
DARK SLAUGHTER
by HUGH B. CAVE
OTHER TERROR TALES!

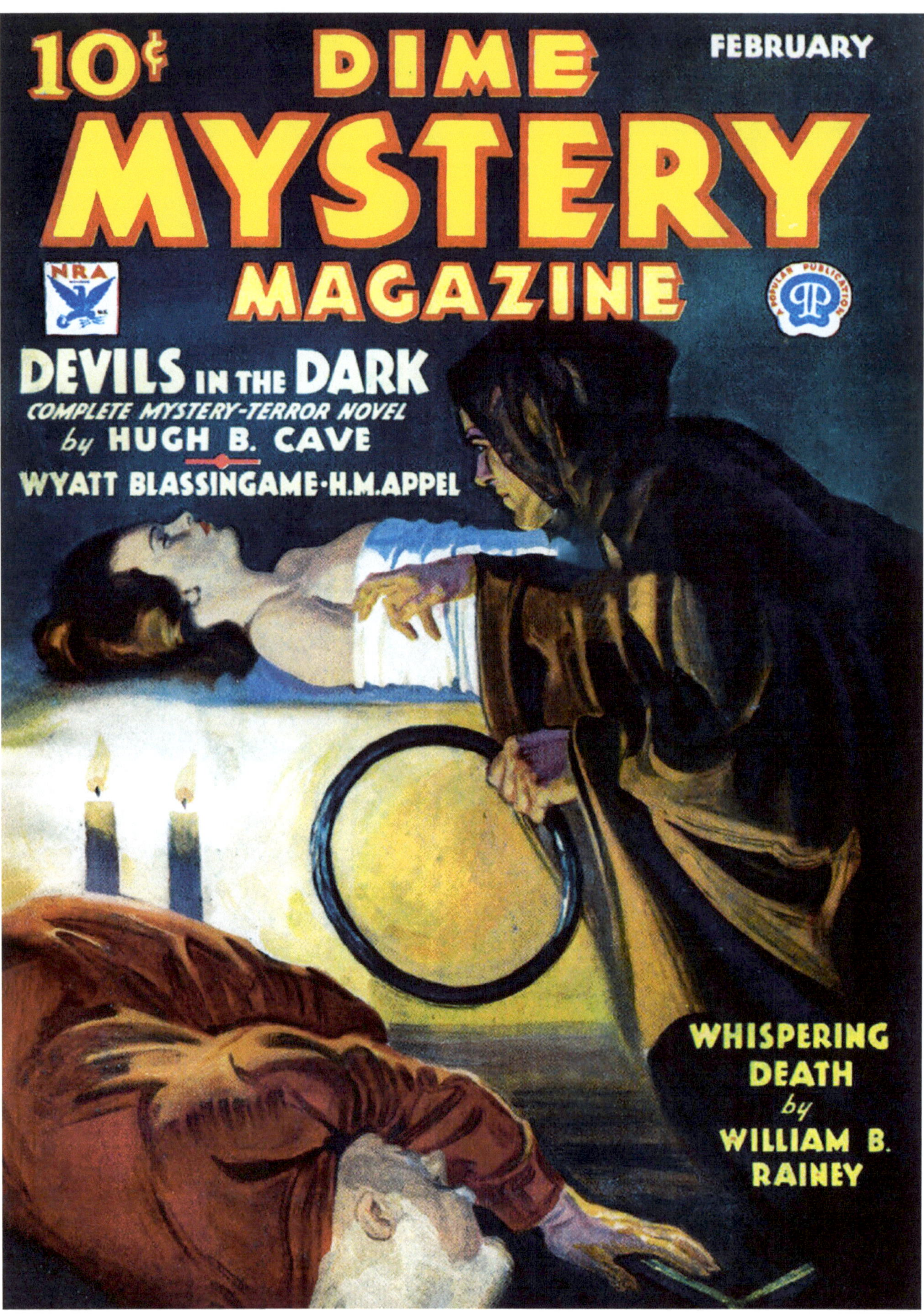

FEBRUARY
10¢
DIME MYSTERY MAGAZINE
NRA
DEVILS IN THE DARK
COMPLETE MYSTERY-TERROR NOVEL
by HUGH B. CAVE
WYATT BLASSINGAME · H.M.APPEL
WHISPERING DEATH
by WILLIAM B. RAINEY

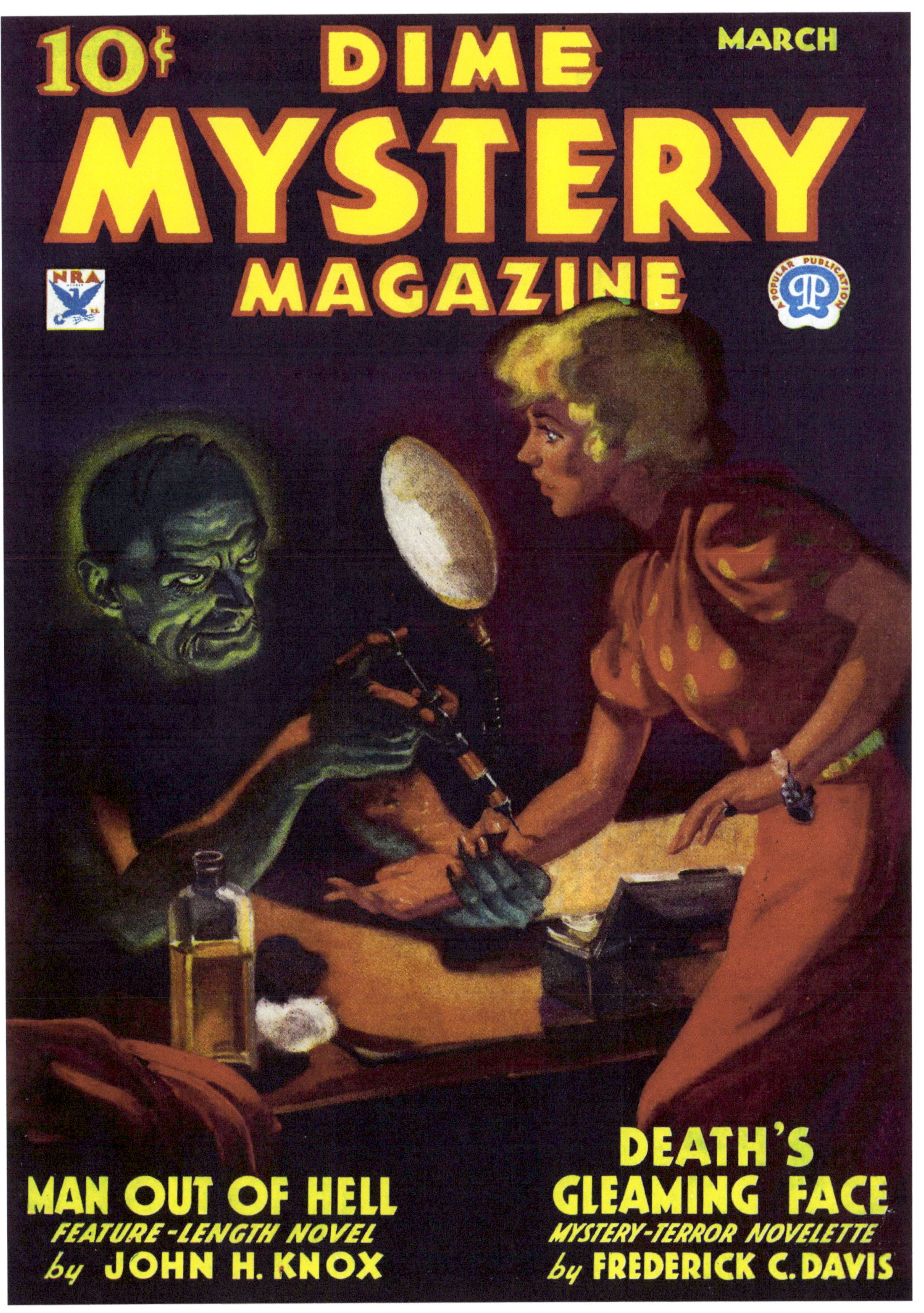

10¢
MARCH
DIME
MYSTERY
MAGAZINE
NRA
A POPULAR PUBLICATION
MAN OUT OF HELL
FEATURE-LENGTH NOVEL
by JOHN H. KNOX
DEATH'S GLEAMING FACE
MYSTERY-TERROR NOVELETTE
by FREDERICK C. DAVIS

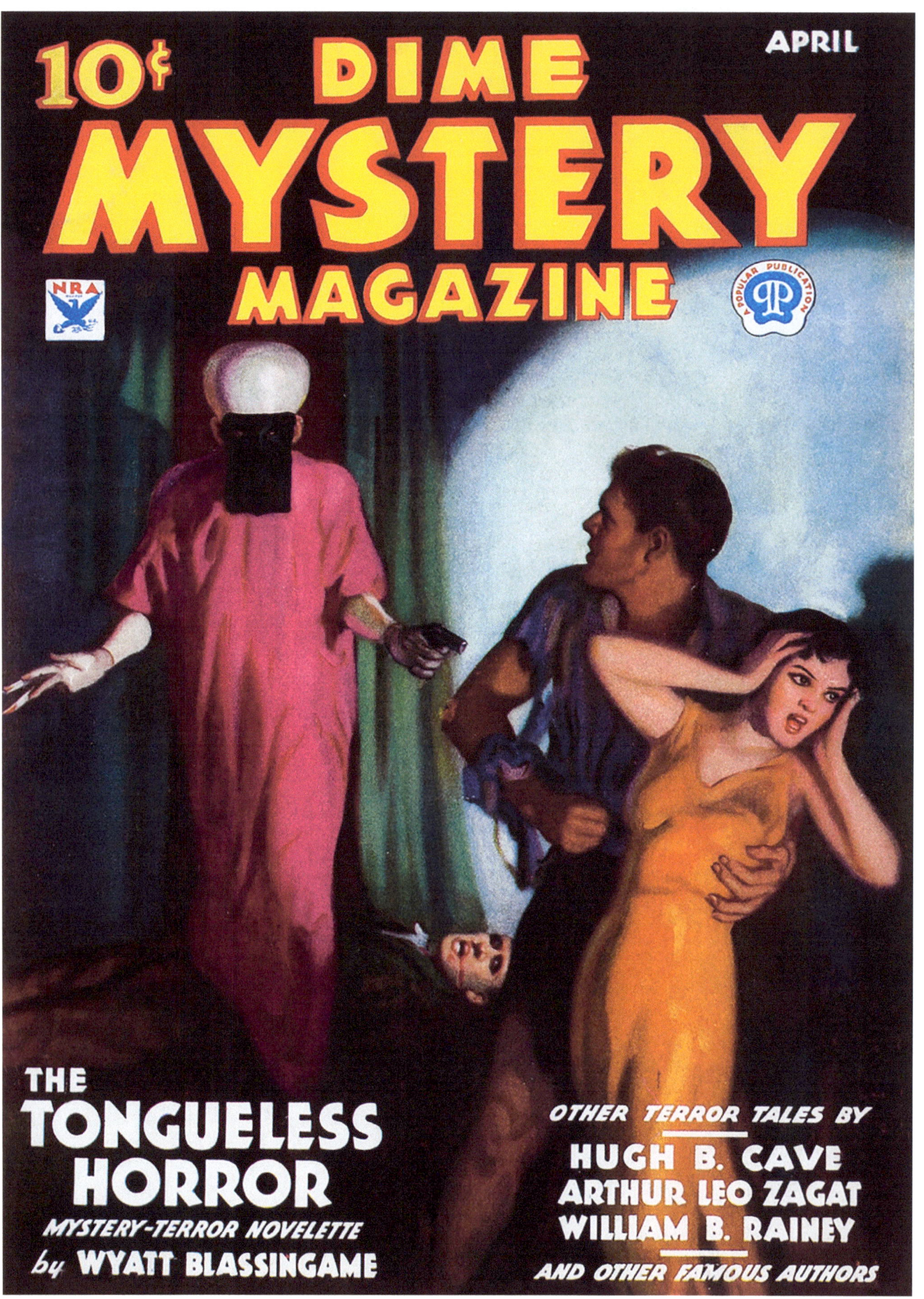
APRIL
10¢
DIME MYSTERY MAGAZINE
NRA
A POPULAR PUBLICATION
THE TONGUELESS HORROR
MYSTERY-TERROR NOVELETTE
by WYATT BLASSINGAME
OTHER TERROR TALES BY
HUGH B. CAVE
ARTHUR LEO ZAGAT
WILLIAM B. RAINEY
AND OTHER FAMOUS AUTHORS

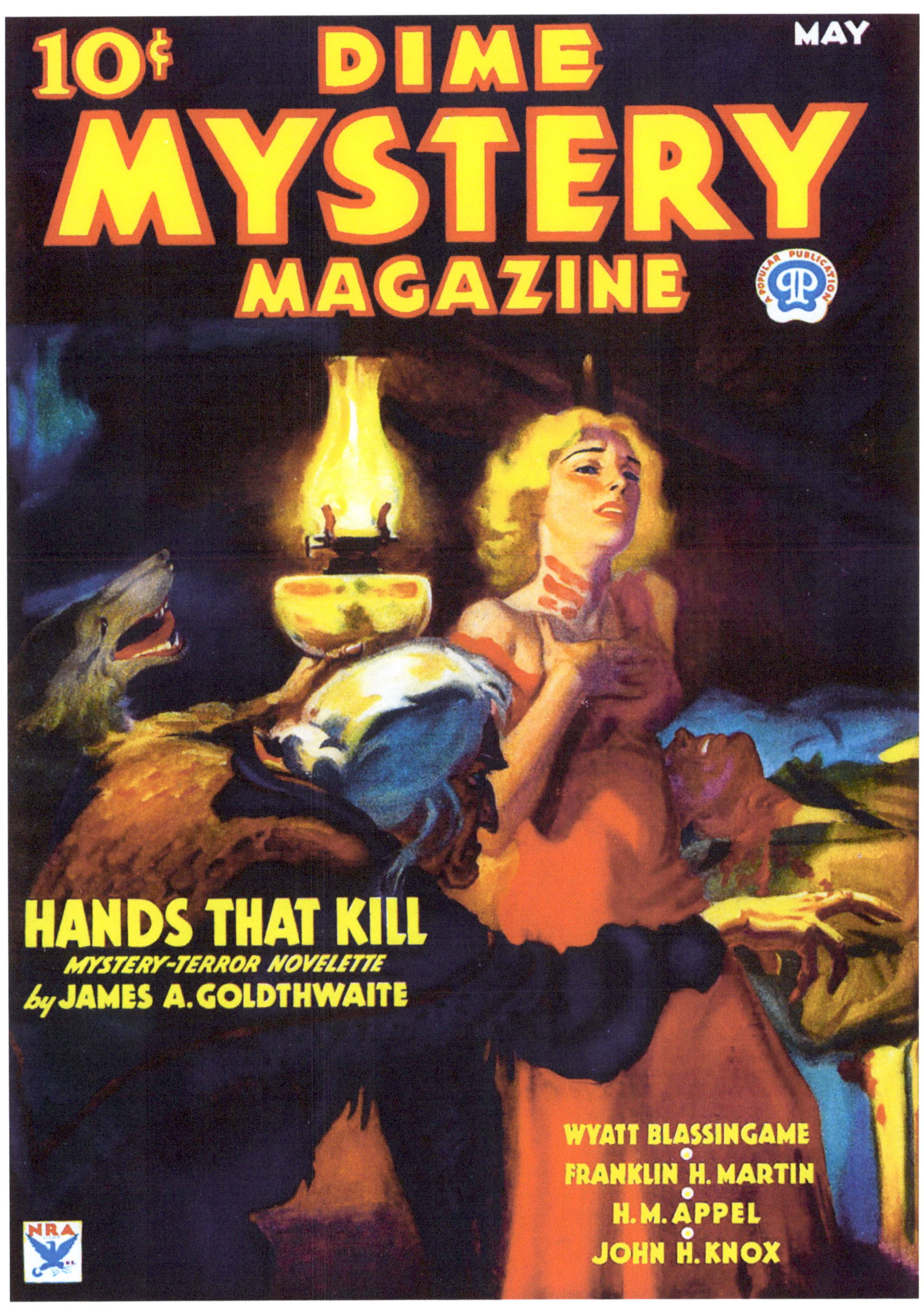

MAY
10¢
DIME MYSTERY MAGAZINE
A POPULAR PUBLICATION
HANDS THAT KILL
MYSTERY-TERROR NOVELETTE
by JAMES A. GOLDTHWAITE
WYATT BLASSINGAME
FRANKLIN H. MARTIN
H. M. APPEL
JOHN H. KNOX
NRA

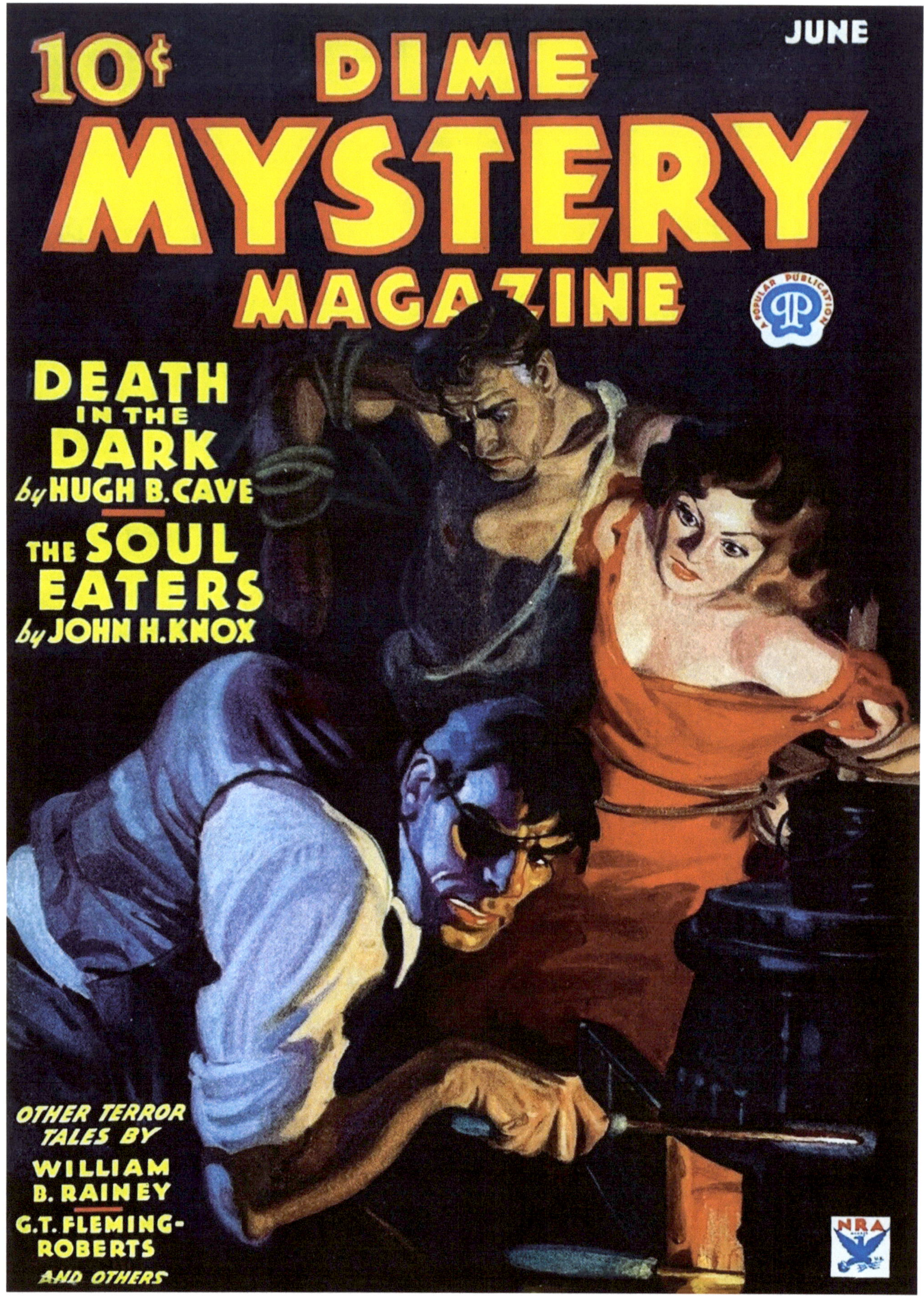
JUNE
10¢
DIME
MYSTERY
MAGAZINE
A POPULAR PUBLICATION
DEATH
IN THE
DARK
by HUGH B. CAVE
THE SOUL
EATERS
by JOHN H. KNOX
OTHER TERROR
TALES BY
WILLIAM
B. RAINEY
G.T. FLEMING-
ROBERTS
AND OTHERS
NRA

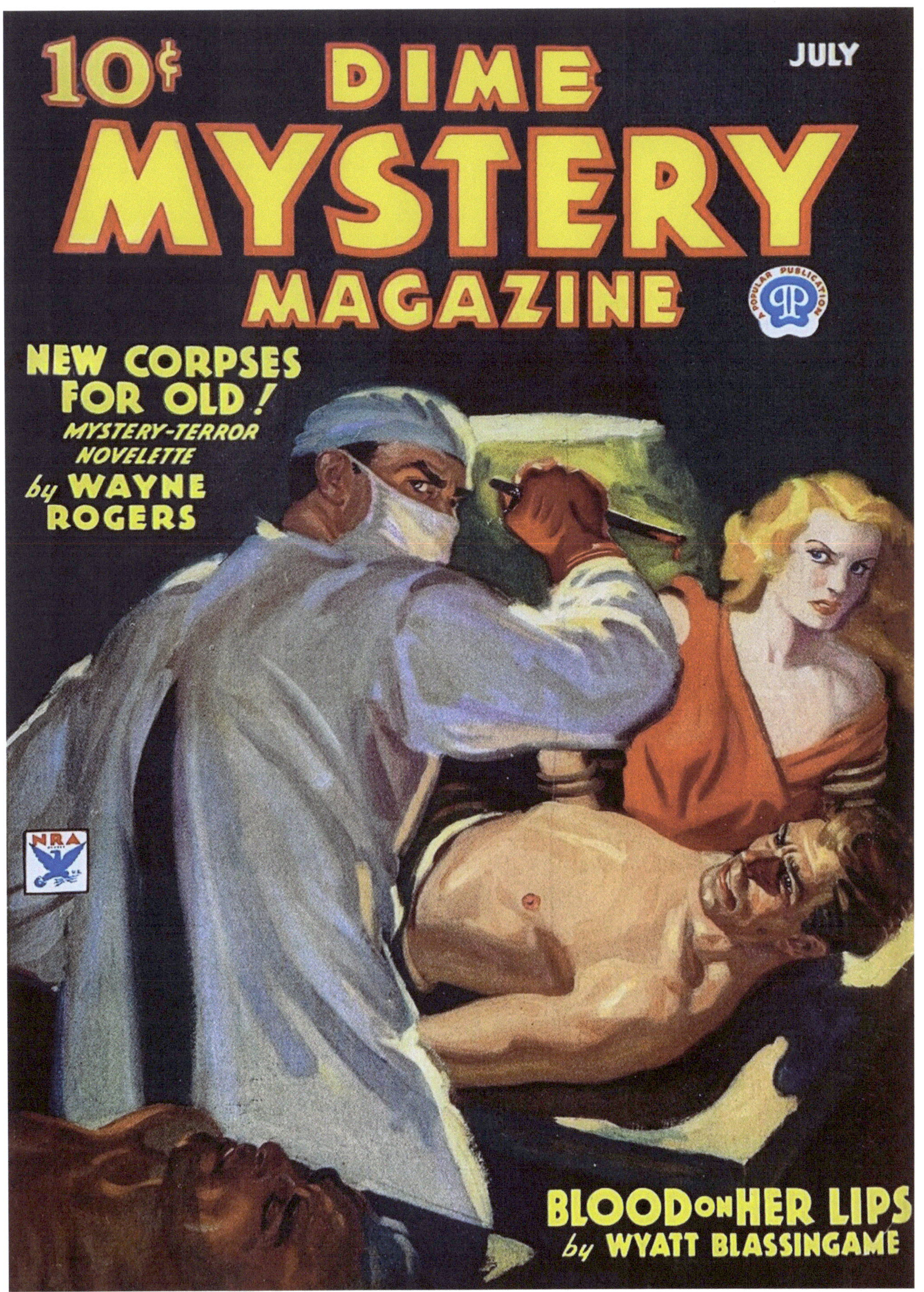

10¢
JULY
DIME MYSTERY MAGAZINE
A POPULAR PUBLICATION
NEW CORPSES FOR OLD !
MYSTERY-TERROR NOVELETTE
by WAYNE ROGERS
NRA
BLOOD on HER LIPS
by WYATT BLASSINGAME

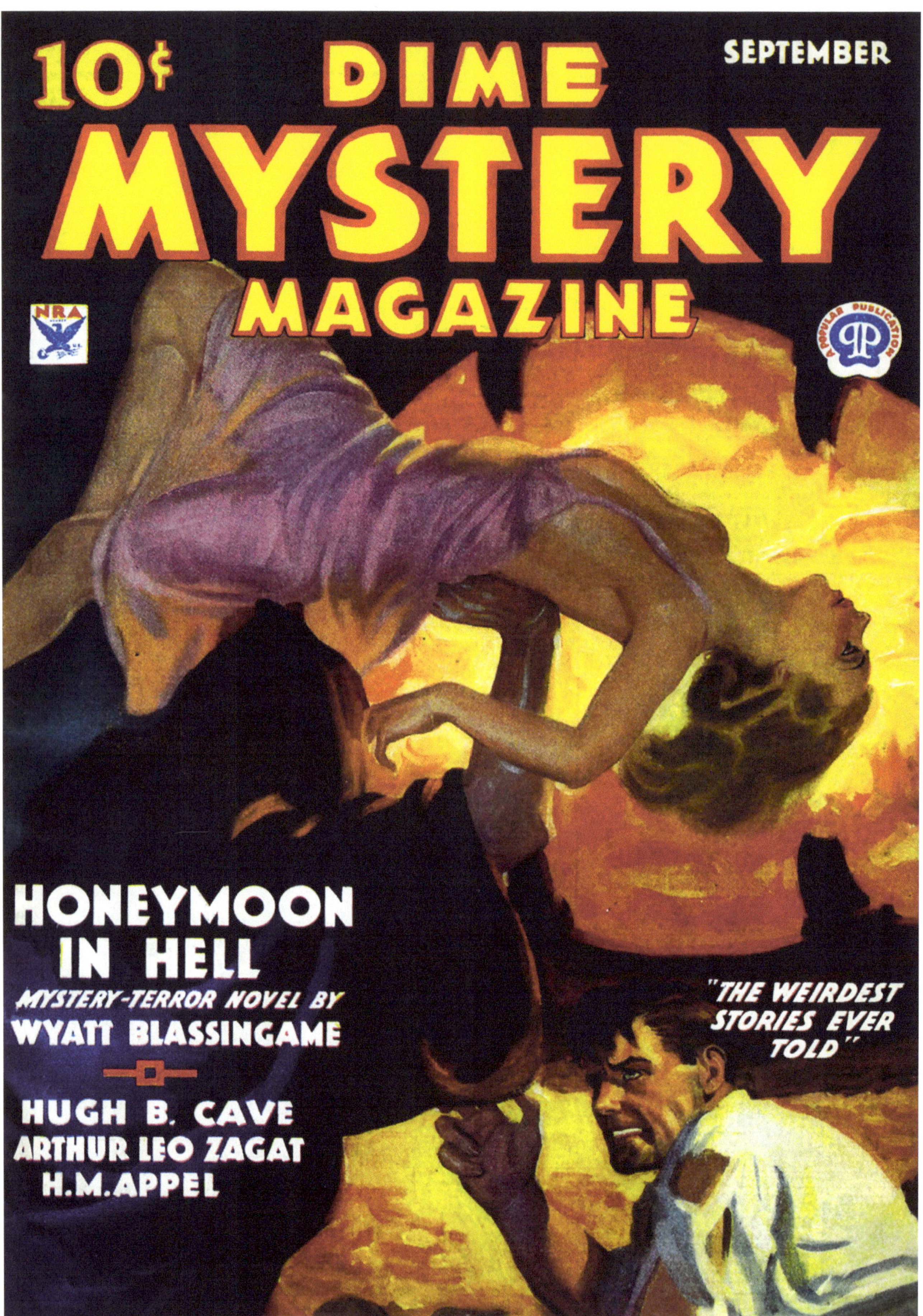

SEPTEMBER
10¢
DIME
MYSTERY
MAGAZINE
NRA
A POPULAR PUBLICATION
HONEYMOON
IN HELL
MYSTERY-TERROR NOVEL BY
WYATT BLASSINGAME
HUGH B. CAVE
ARTHUR LEO ZAGAT
H. M. APPEL
"THE WEIRDEST STORIES EVER TOLD"

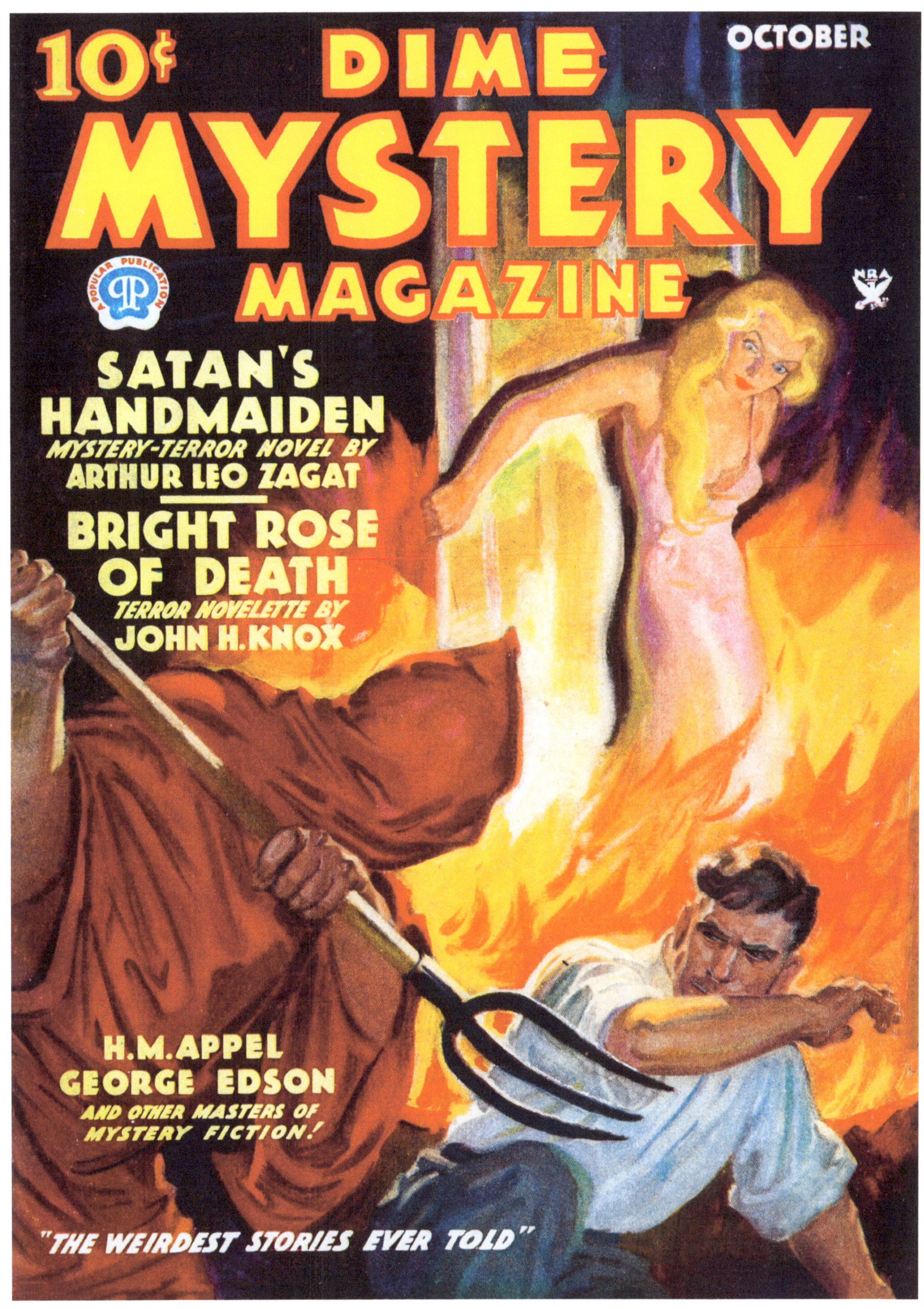

OCTOBER
10¢
DIME
MYSTERY
MAGAZINE
A POPULAR PUBLICATION
SATAN'S HANDMAIDEN
MYSTERY-TERROR NOVEL BY
ARTHUR LEO ZAGAT
BRIGHT ROSE OF DEATH
TERROR NOVELETTE BY
JOHN H. KNOX
H.M. APPEL
GEORGE EDSON
AND OTHER MASTERS OF
MYSTERY FICTION!
"THE WEIRDEST STORIES EVER TOLD"

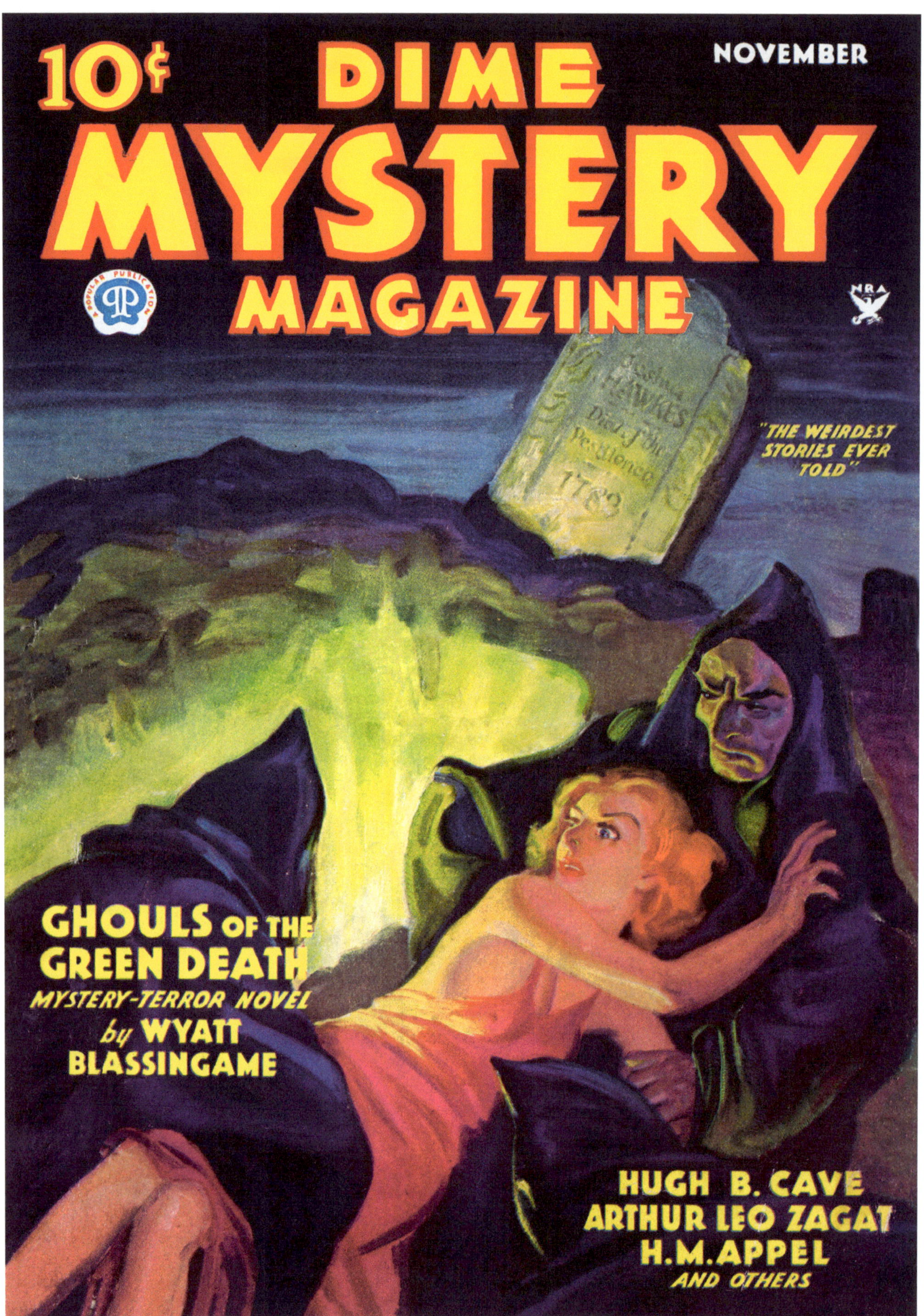

DIME MYSTERY

NOVEMBER 1934

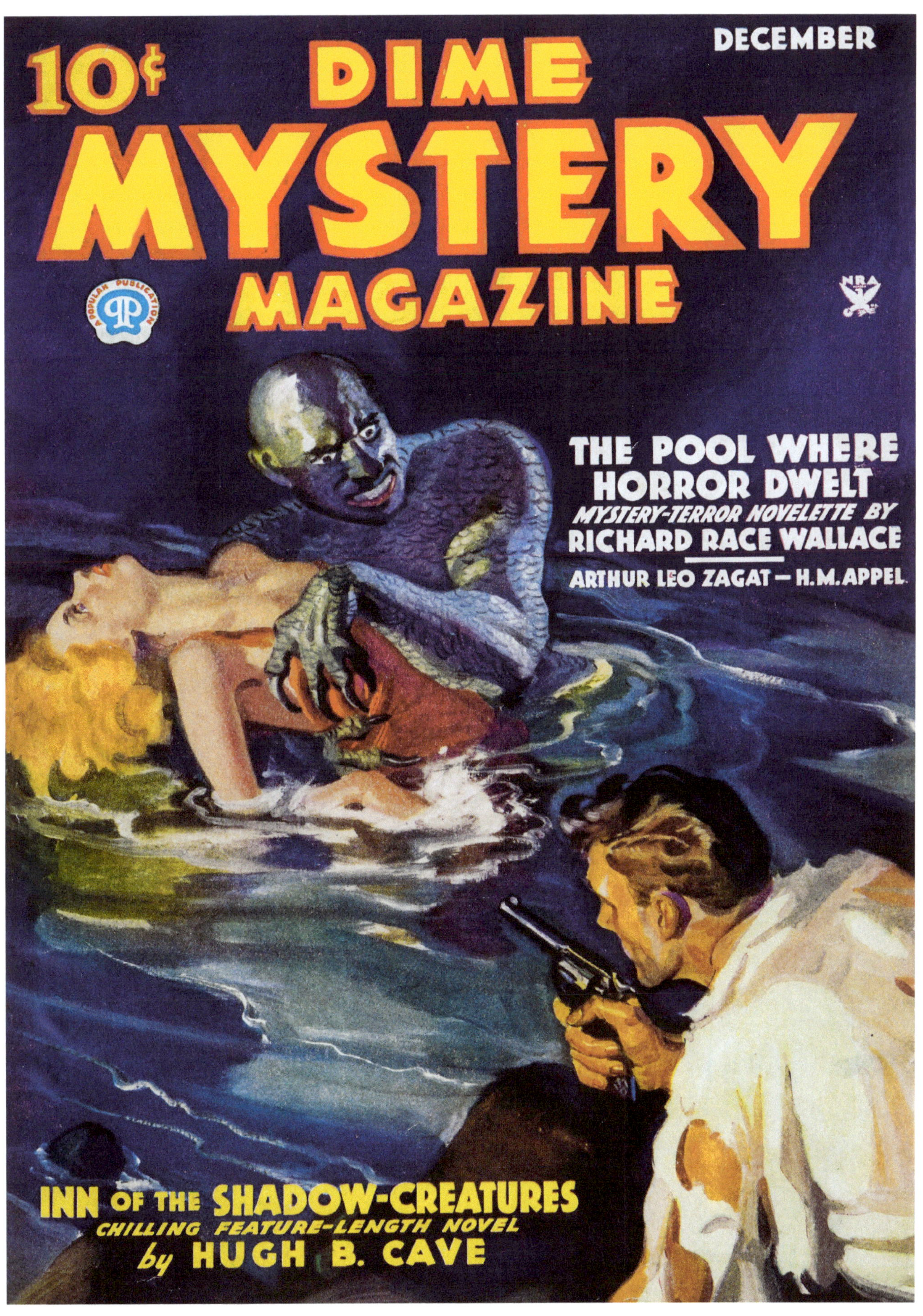
DECEMBER
10¢
DIME
MYSTERY
MAGAZINE
THE POOL WHERE
HORROR DWELT
MYSTERY-TERROR NOVELETTE BY
RICHARD RACE WALLACE
ARTHUR LEO ZAGAT — H. M. APPEL
INN OF THE SHADOW-CREATURES
CHILLING FEATURE-LENGTH NOVEL
by HUGH B. CAVE

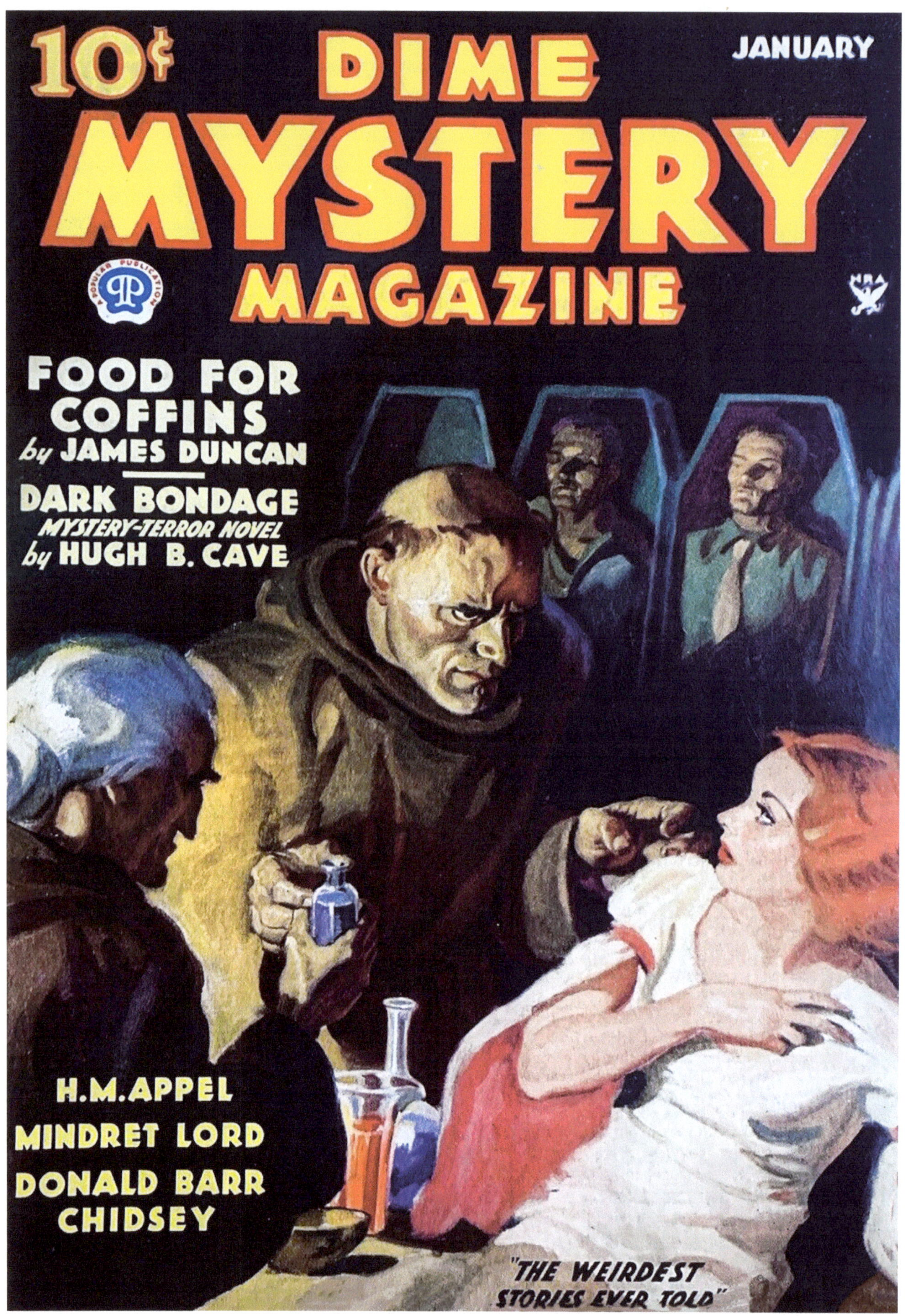

DIME MYSTERY

JANUARY 1935

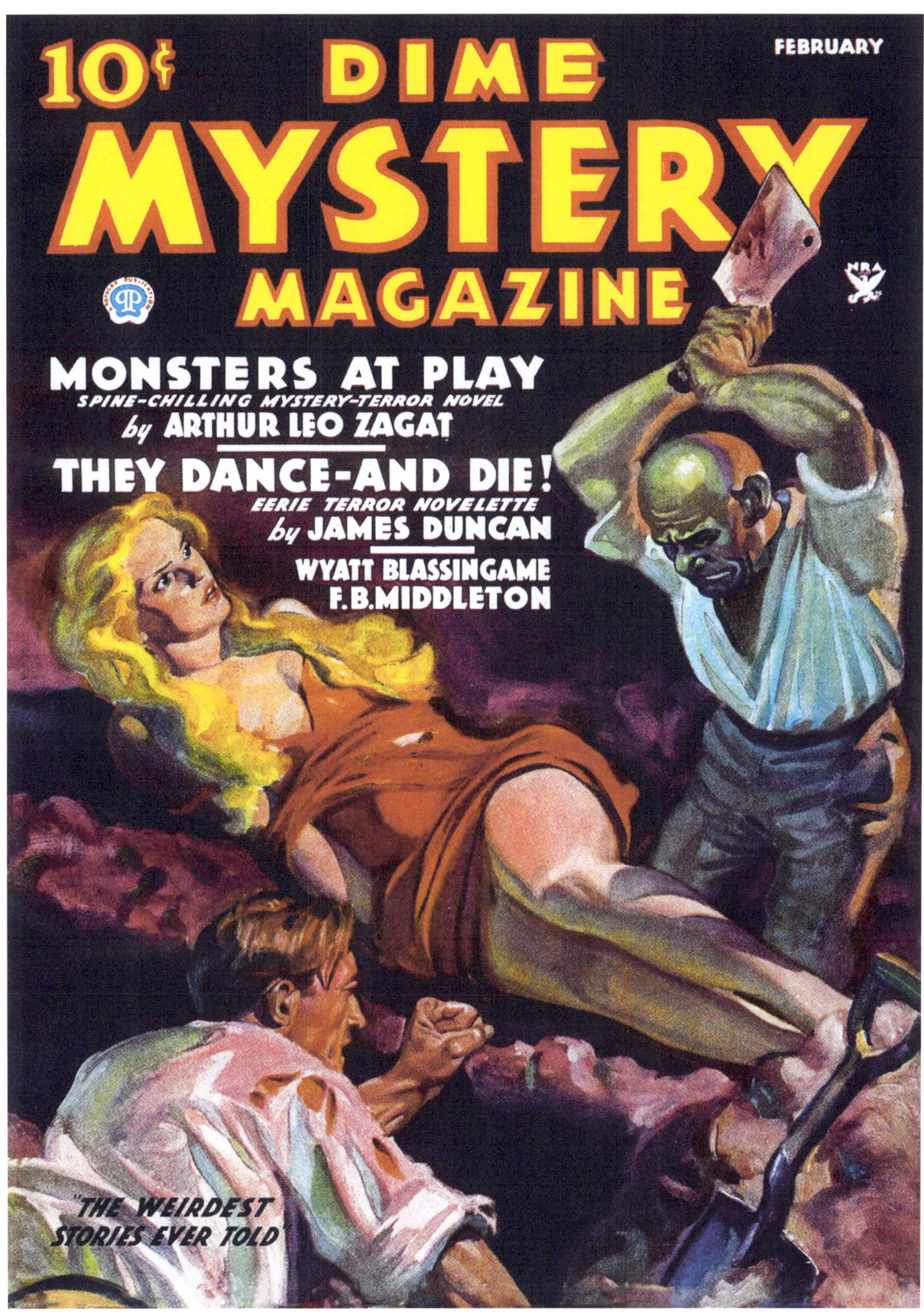
FEBRUARY
10¢
DIME MYSTERY MAGAZINE
MONSTERS AT PLAY
SPINE-CHILLING MYSTERY-TERROR NOVEL
by ARTHUR LEO ZAGAT
THEY DANCE—AND DIE!
EERIE TERROR NOVELETTE
by JAMES DUNCAN
WYATT BLASSINGAME
F. B. MIDDLETON
"THE WEIRDEST STORIES EVER TOLD"

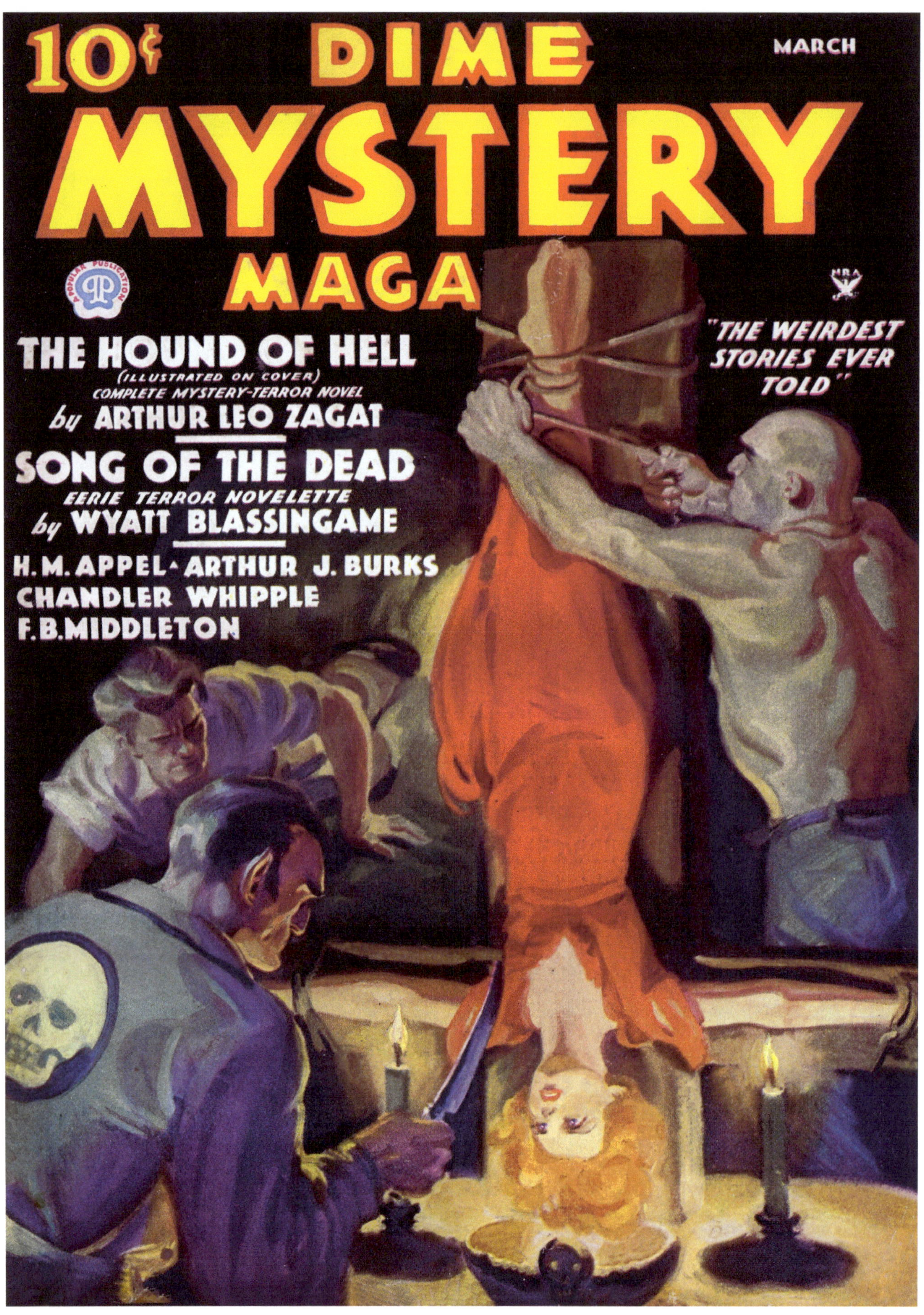

DIME MYSTERY

MARCH 1935

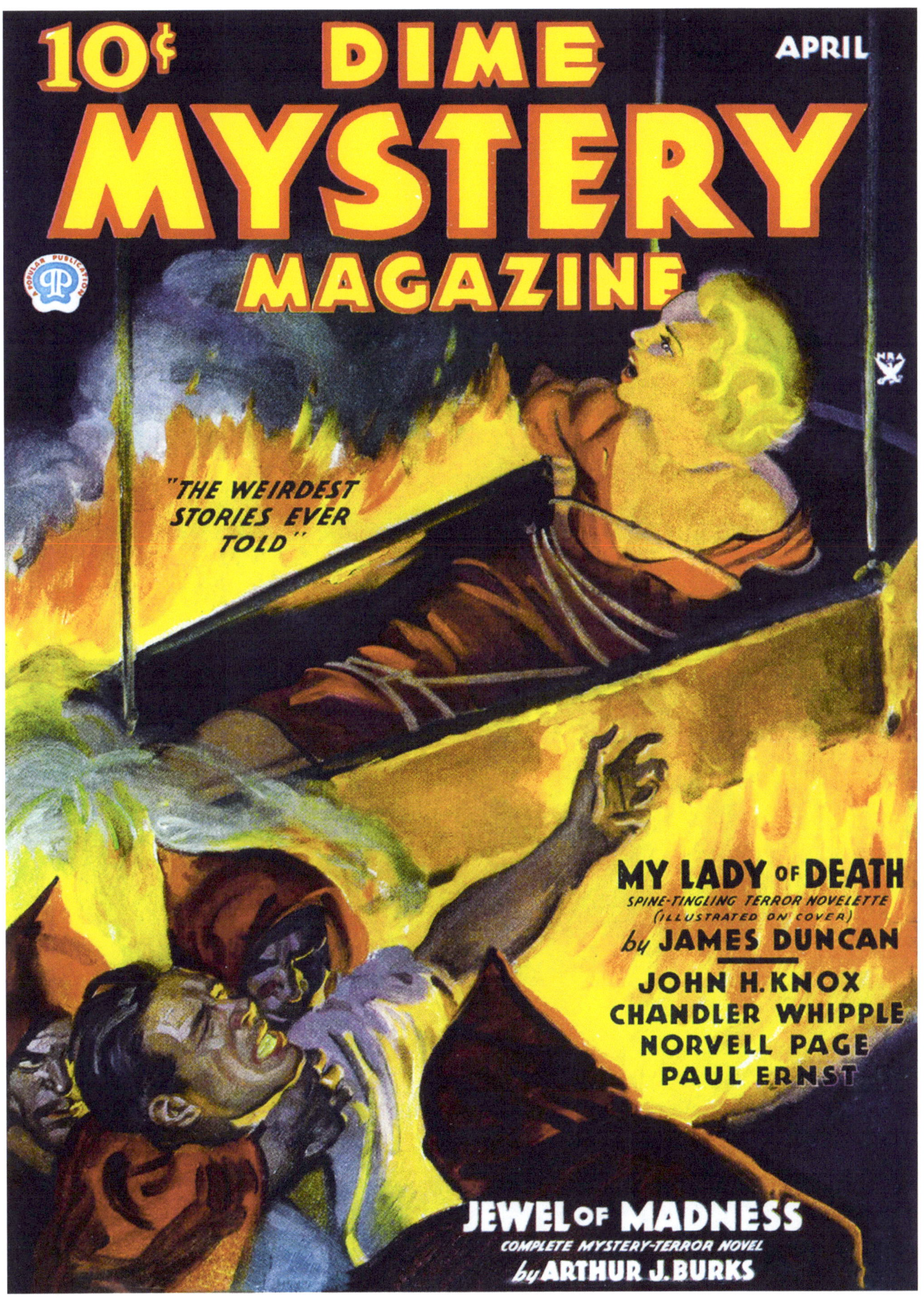

10¢
APRIL
DIME MYSTERY MAGAZINE
A POPULAR PUBLICATION
"THE WEIRDEST STORIES EVER TOLD"
MY LADY OF DEATH
SPINE-TINGLING TERROR NOVELETTE
(ILLUSTRATED ON COVER)
by JAMES DUNCAN
JOHN H. KNOX
CHANDLER WHIPPLE
NORVELL PAGE
PAUL ERNST
JEWEL OF MADNESS
COMPLETE MYSTERY-TERROR NOVEL
by ARTHUR J. BURKS

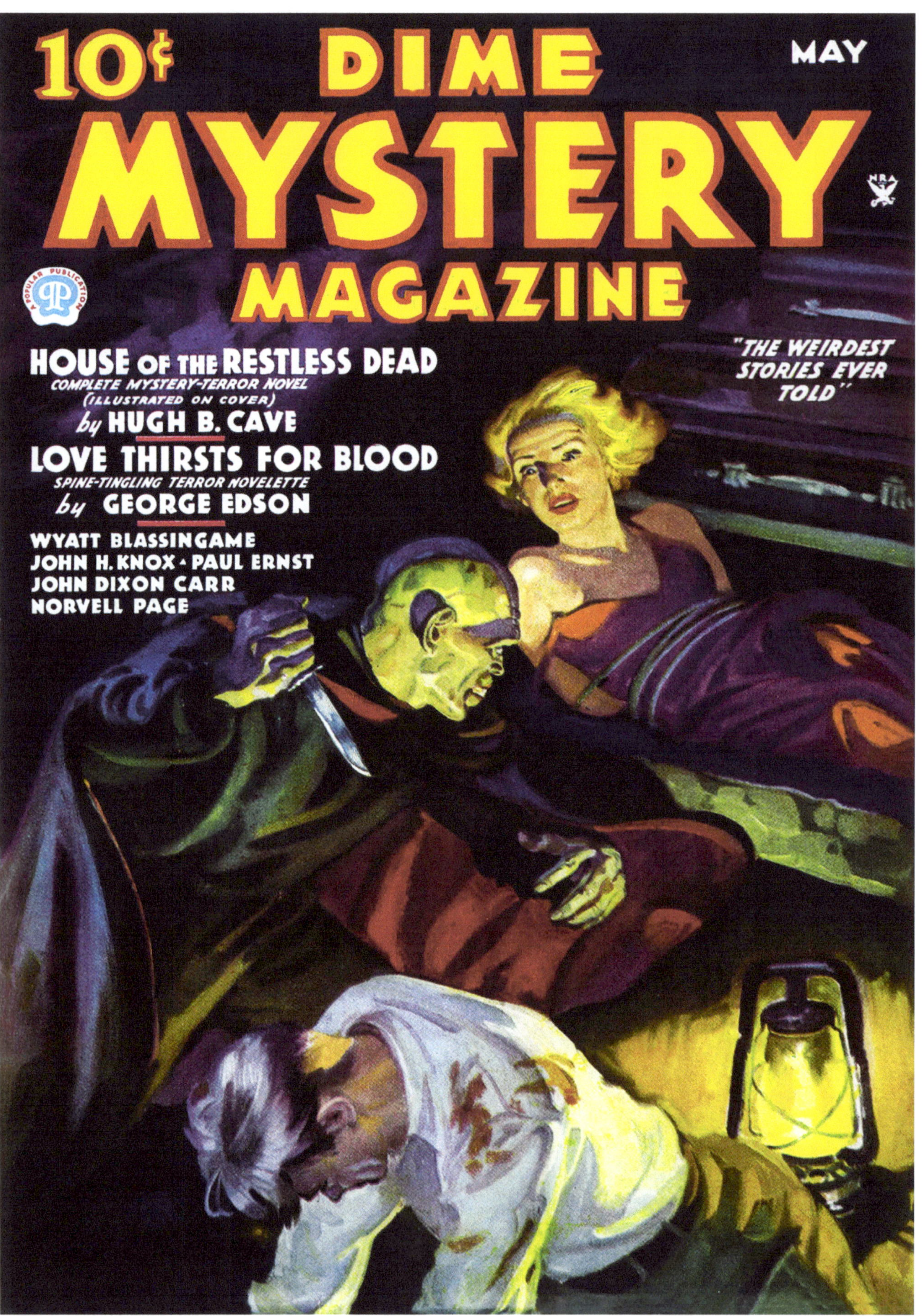

10¢
MAY
DIME MYSTERY MAGAZINE
"THE WEIRDEST STORIES EVER TOLD"
HOUSE of the RESTLESS DEAD
COMPLETE MYSTERY-TERROR NOVEL
(ILLUSTRATED ON COVER)
by HUGH B. CAVE
LOVE THIRSTS FOR BLOOD
SPINE-TINGLING TERROR NOVELETTE
by GEORGE EDSON
WYATT BLASSINGAME
JOHN H. KNOX · PAUL ERNST
JOHN DIXON CARR
NORVELL PAGE
A POPULAR PUBLICATION

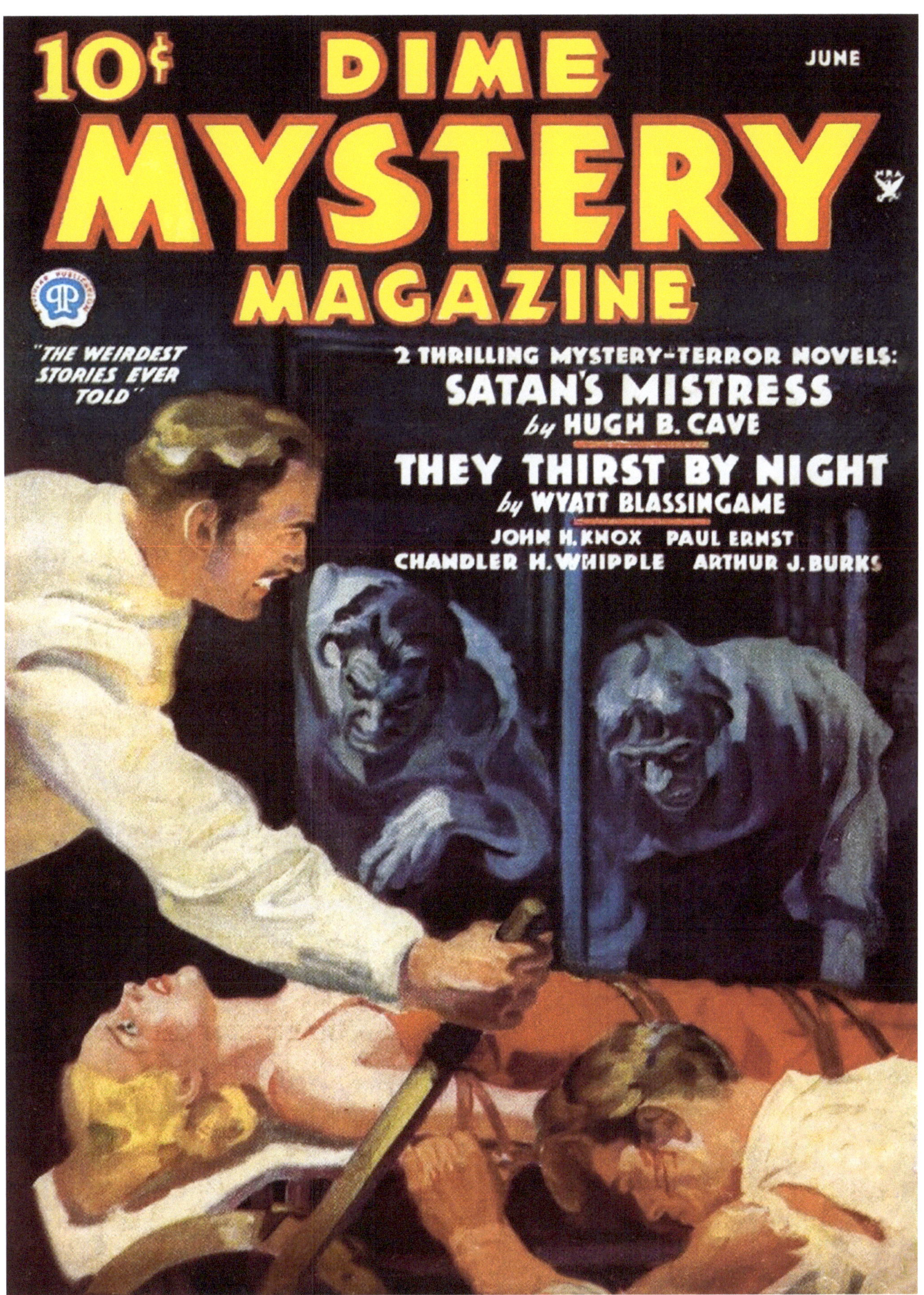

10¢
JUNE
DIME MYSTERY MAGAZINE
"THE WEIRDEST STORIES EVER TOLD"
2 THRILLING MYSTERY-TERROR NOVELS:
SATAN'S MISTRESS
by HUGH B. CAVE
THEY THIRST BY NIGHT
by WYATT BLASSINGAME
JOHN H. KNOX   PAUL ERNST
CHANDLER H. WHIPPLE   ARTHUR J. BURKS

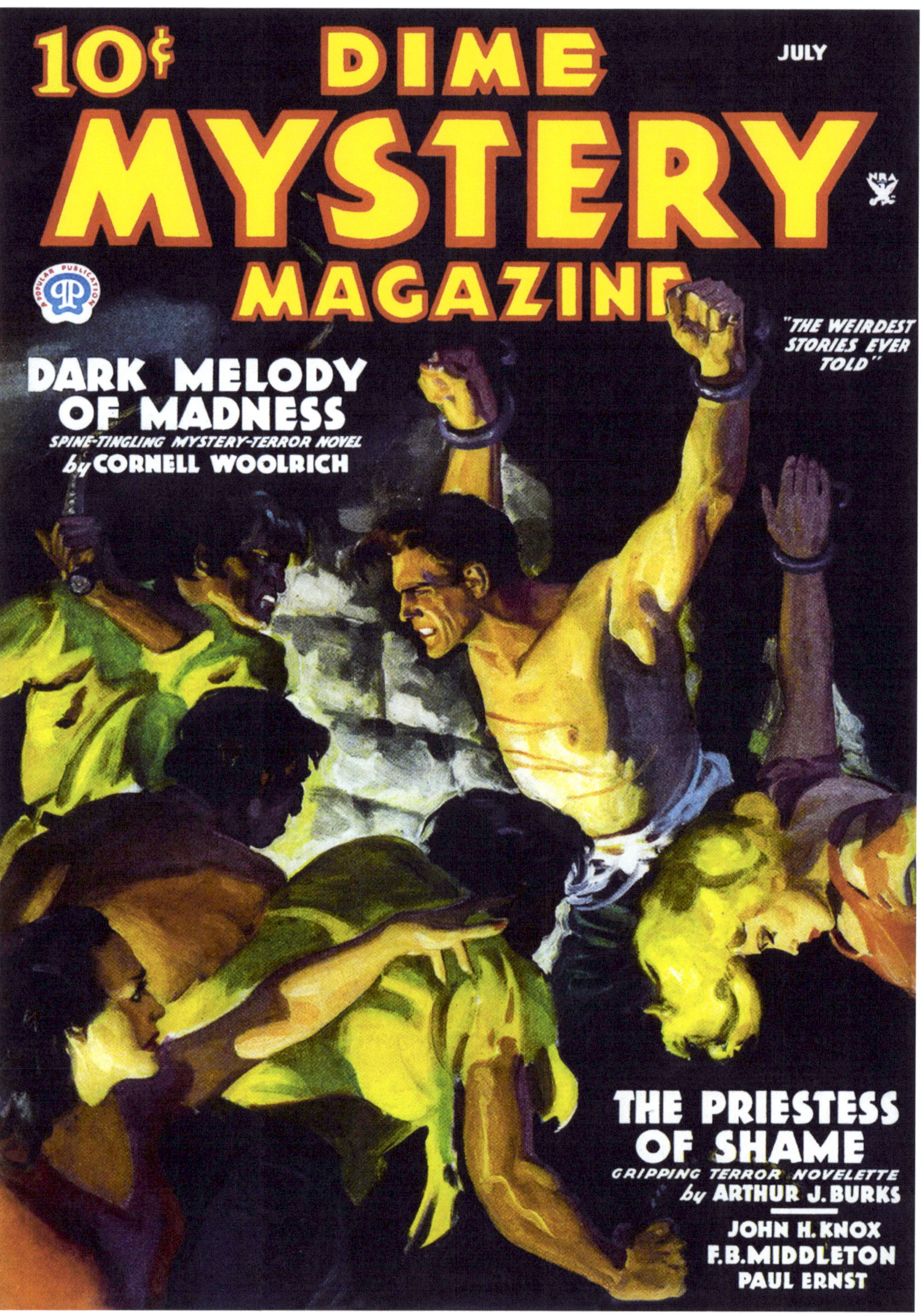
10¢
JULY
DIME MYSTERY MAGAZINE
"THE WEIRDEST STORIES EVER TOLD"
DARK MELODY OF MADNESS
SPINE-TINGLING MYSTERY-TERROR NOVEL
by CORNELL WOOLRICH
THE PRIESTESS OF SHAME
GRIPPING TERROR NOVELETTE
by ARTHUR J. BURKS
JOHN H. KNOX
F. B. MIDDLETON
PAUL ERNST

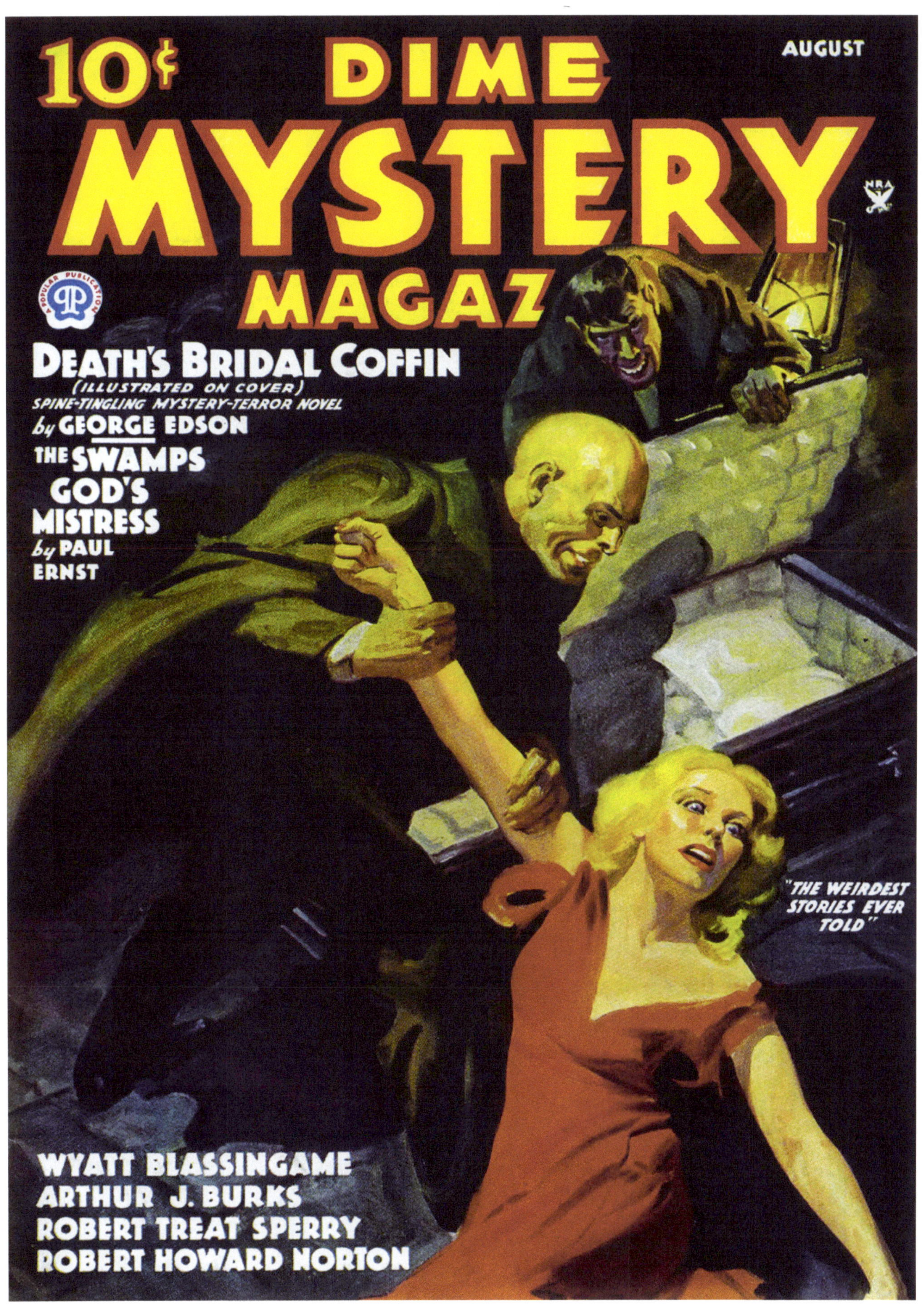

AUGUST
10¢
DIME
MYSTERY
MAGAZ
A POPULAR PUBLICATION
DEATH'S BRIDAL COFFIN
(ILLUSTRATED ON COVER)
SPINE-TINGLING MYSTERY-TERROR NOVEL
by GEORGE EDSON
THE SWAMPS GOD'S MISTRESS
by PAUL ERNST
"THE WEIRDEST STORIES EVER TOLD"
WYATT BLASSINGAME
ARTHUR J. BURKS
ROBERT TREAT SPERRY
ROBERT HOWARD NORTON

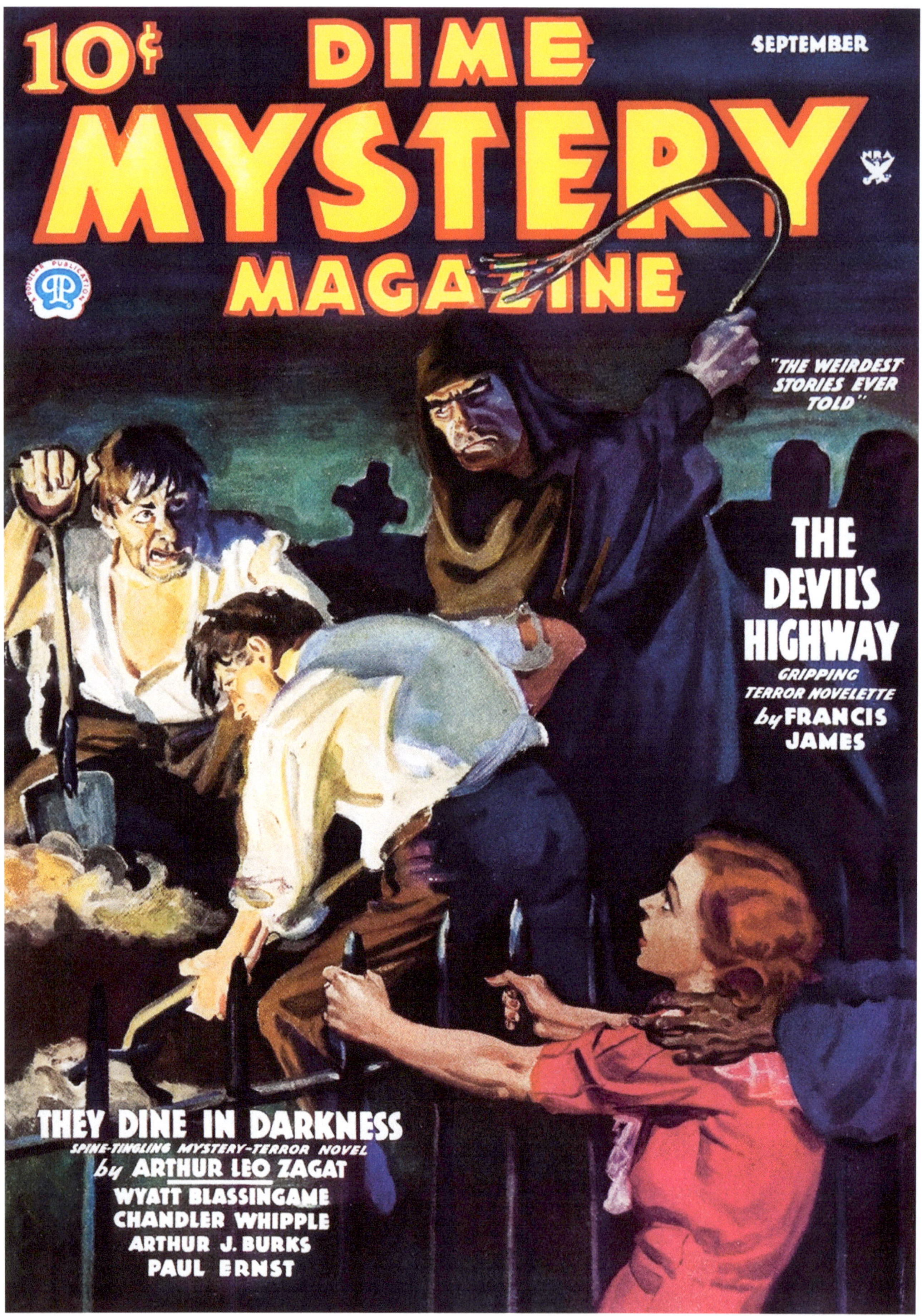

DIME MYSTERY

SEPTEMBER 1935

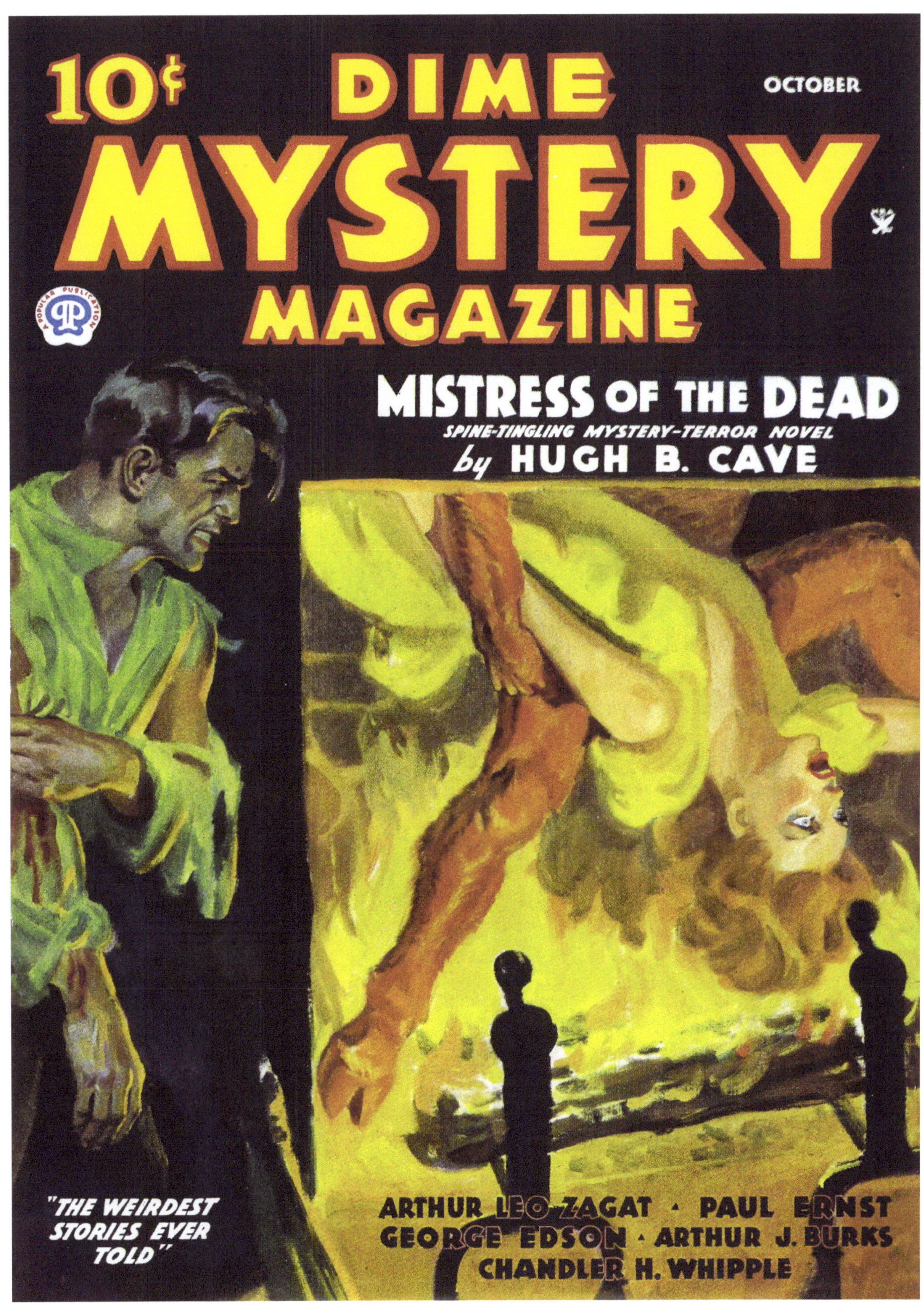

10¢
OCTOBER
DIME MYSTERY MAGAZINE
A POPULAR PUBLICATION
MISTRESS OF THE DEAD
SPINE-TINGLING MYSTERY-TERROR NOVEL
by HUGH B. CAVE
"THE WEIRDEST STORIES EVER TOLD"
ARTHUR LEO ZAGAT • PAUL ERNST
GEORGE EDSON • ARTHUR J. BURKS
CHANDLER H. WHIPPLE

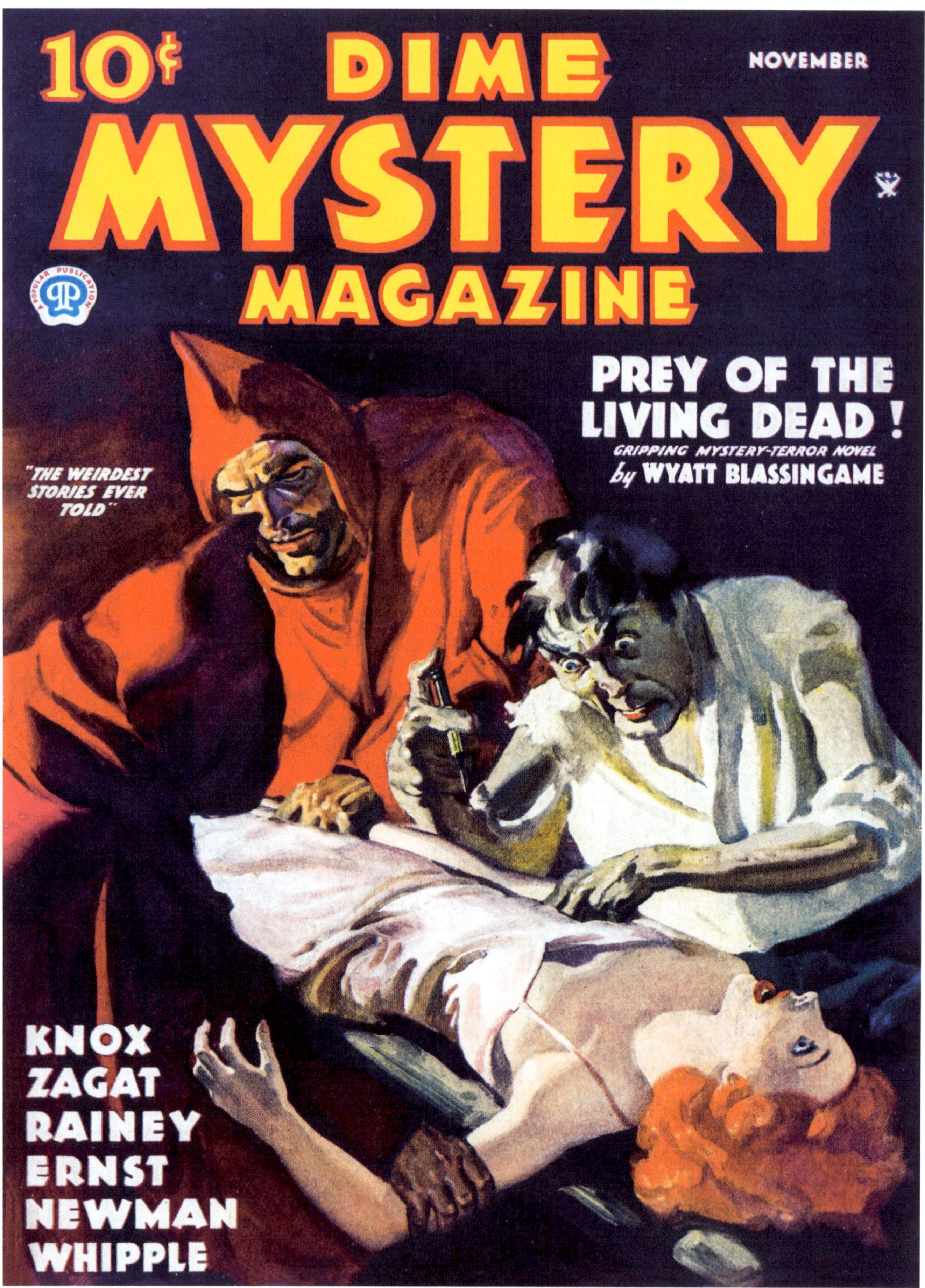

DIME MYSTERY

NOVEMBER 1935

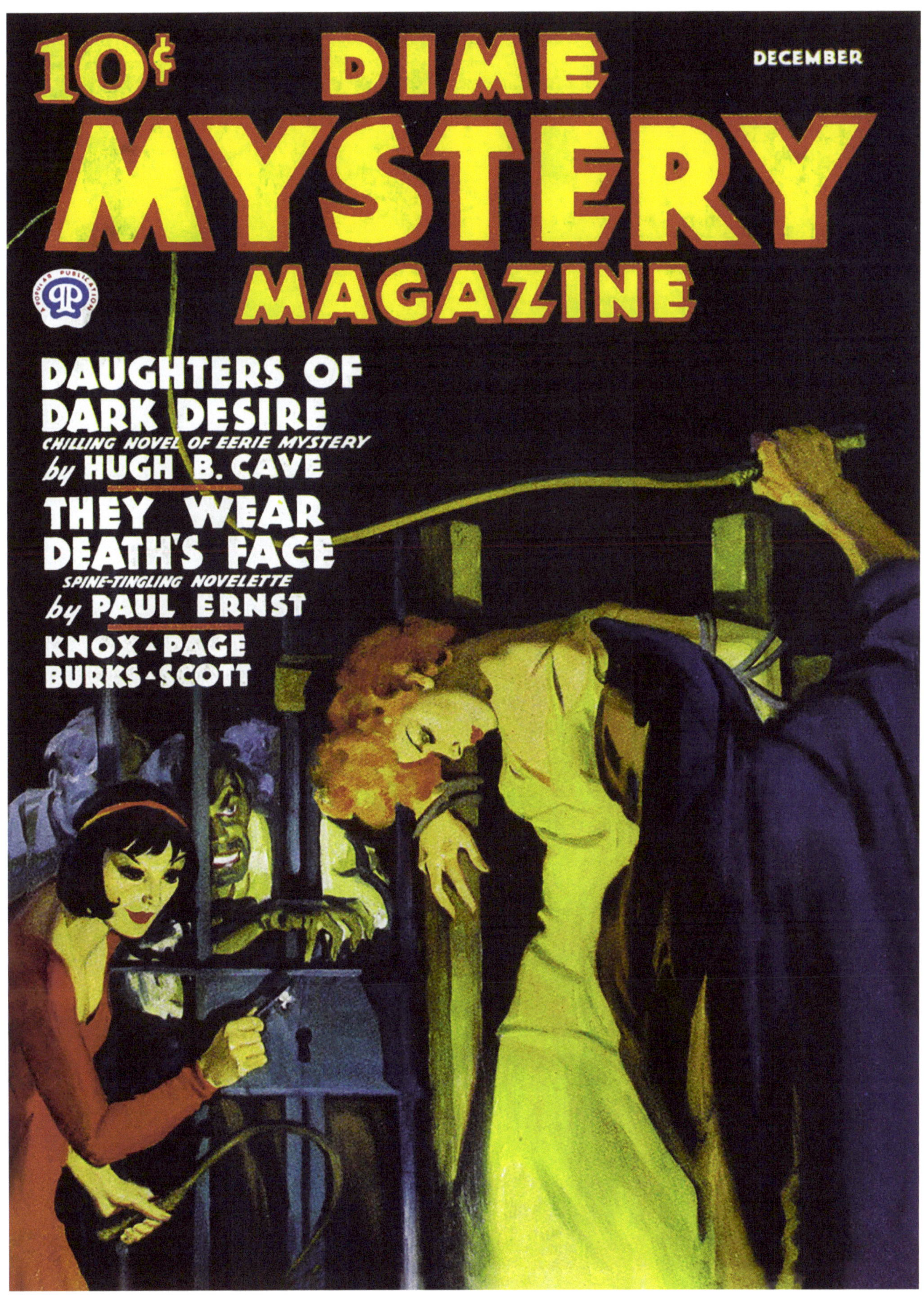

10¢
DECEMBER
DIME MYSTERY MAGAZINE
A POPULAR PUBLICATION
DAUGHTERS OF DARK DESIRE
CHILLING NOVEL OF EERIE MYSTERY
by HUGH B. CAVE
THEY WEAR DEATH'S FACE
SPINE-TINGLING NOVELETTE
by PAUL ERNST
KNOX • PAGE
BURKS • SCOTT

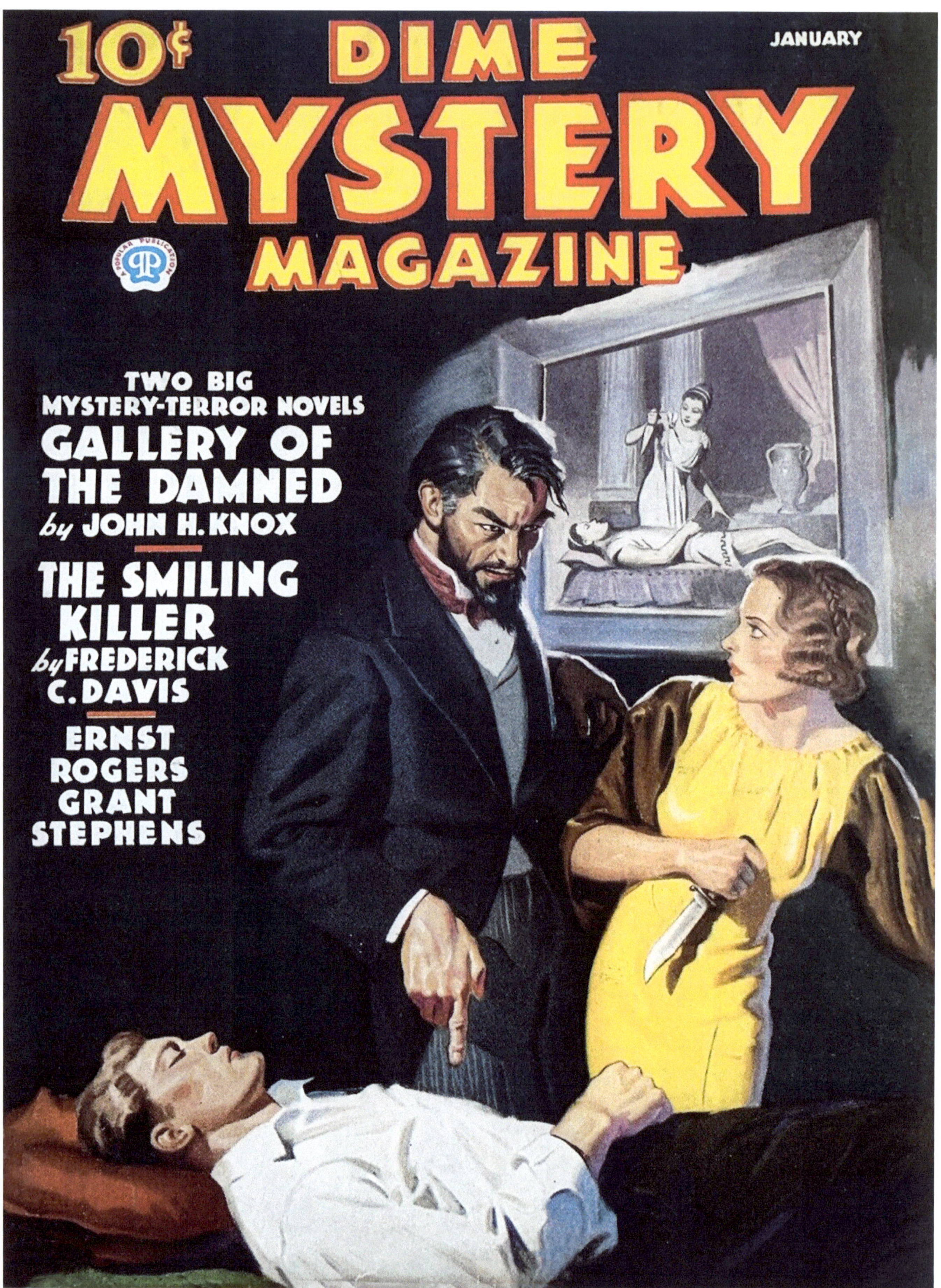
10¢
JANUARY
DIME
MYSTERY
MAGAZINE
POPULAR PUBLICATION
PP
TWO BIG
MYSTERY-TERROR NOVELS
GALLERY OF
THE DAMNED
by JOHN H. KNOX
THE SMILING
KILLER
by FREDERICK
C. DAVIS
ERNST
ROGERS
GRANT
STEPHENS

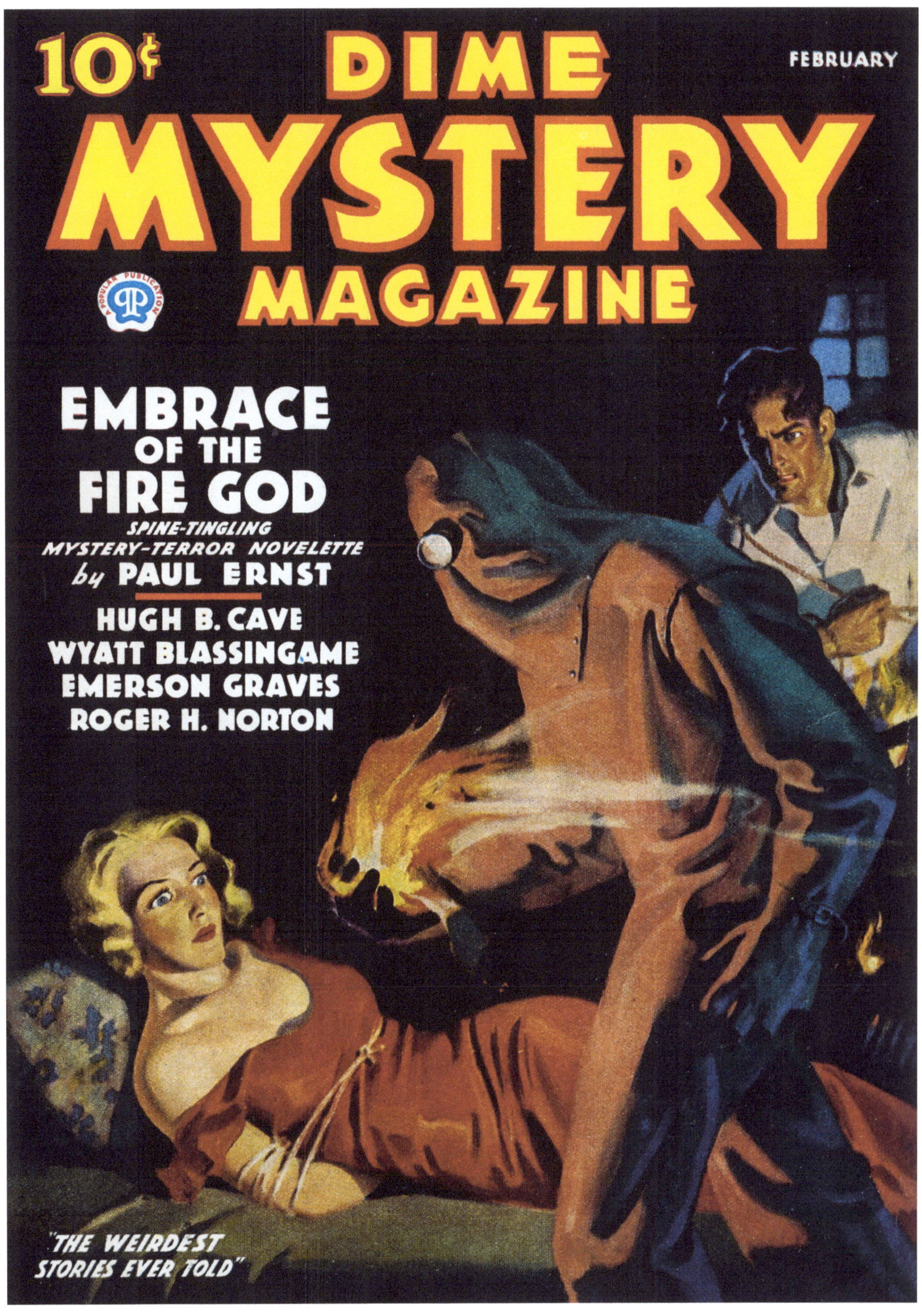

10¢
FEBRUARY
DIME MYSTERY MAGAZINE
A POPULAR PUBLICATION
EMBRACE OF THE FIRE GOD
SPINE-TINGLING MYSTERY-TERROR NOVELETTE
by PAUL ERNST
HUGH B. CAVE
WYATT BLASSINGAME
EMERSON GRAVES
ROGER H. NORTON
"THE WEIRDEST STORIES EVER TOLD"

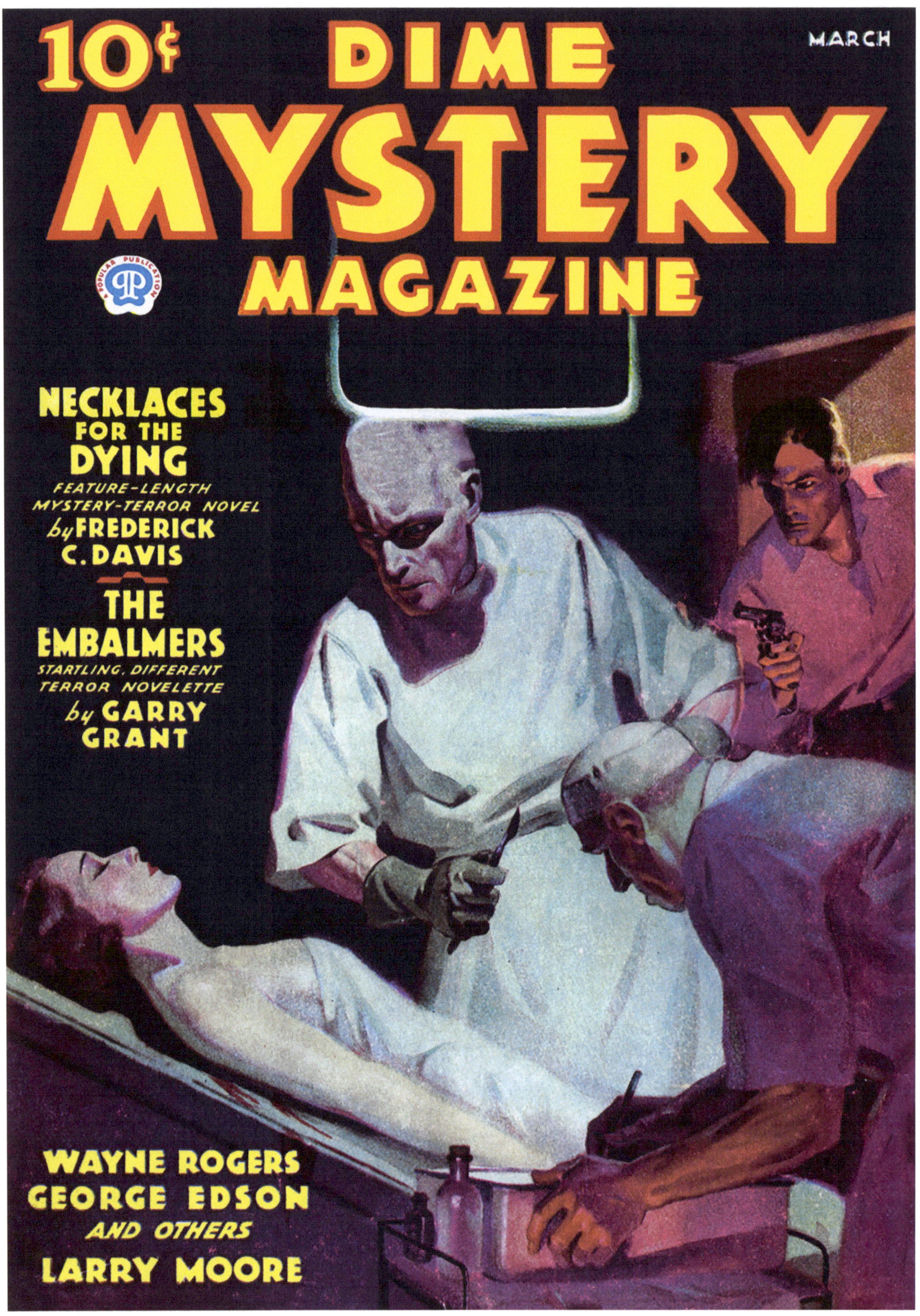

DIME MYSTERY

MARCH 1936

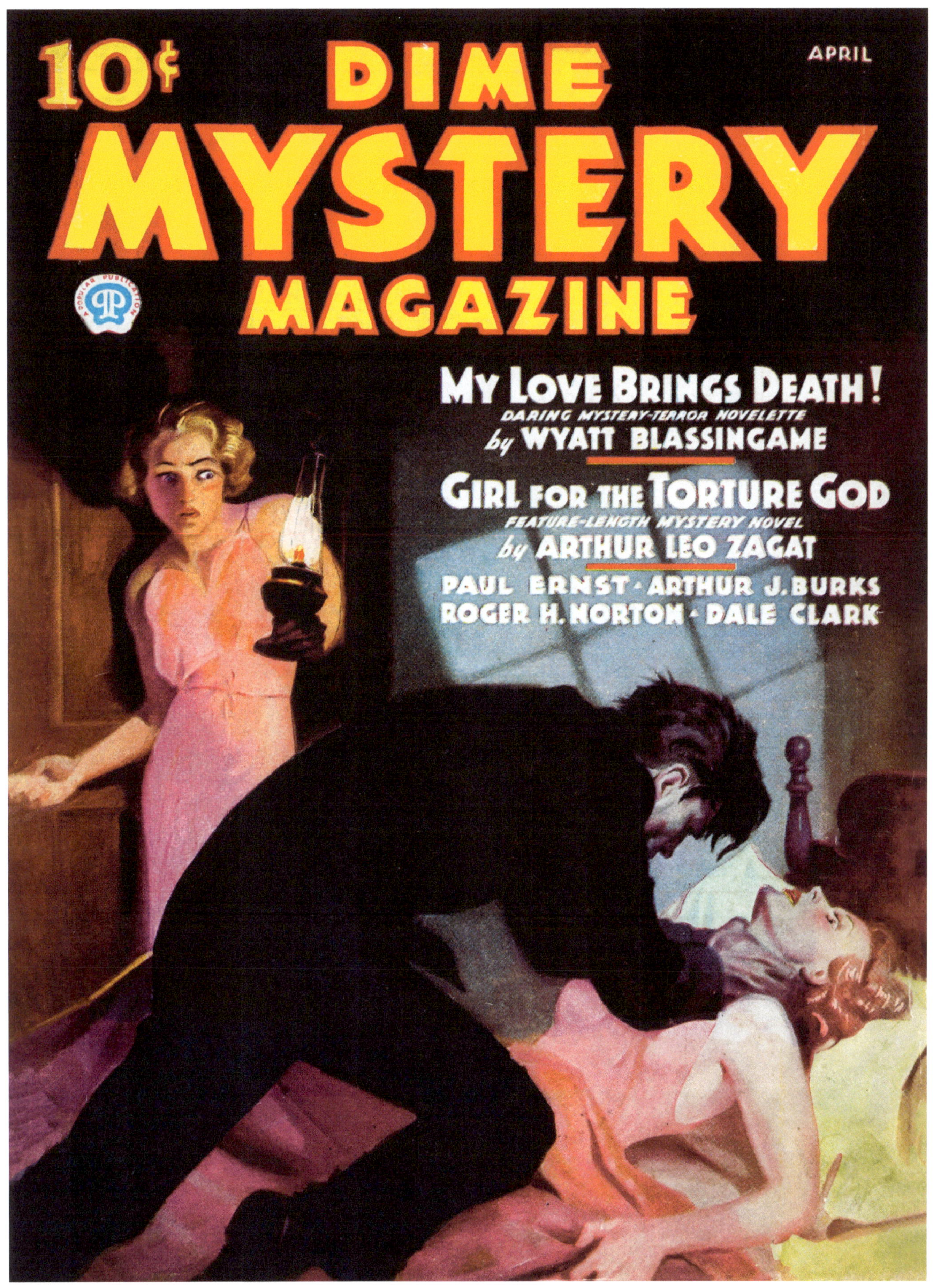

10¢
APRIL
DIME MYSTERY MAGAZINE
A POPULAR PUBLICATION
MY LOVE BRINGS DEATH!
DARING MYSTERY-TERROR NOVELETTE
by WYATT BLASSINGAME
GIRL FOR THE TORTURE GOD
FEATURE-LENGTH MYSTERY NOVEL
by ARTHUR LEO ZAGAT
PAUL ERNST · ARTHUR J. BURKS
ROGER H. NORTON · DALE CLARK

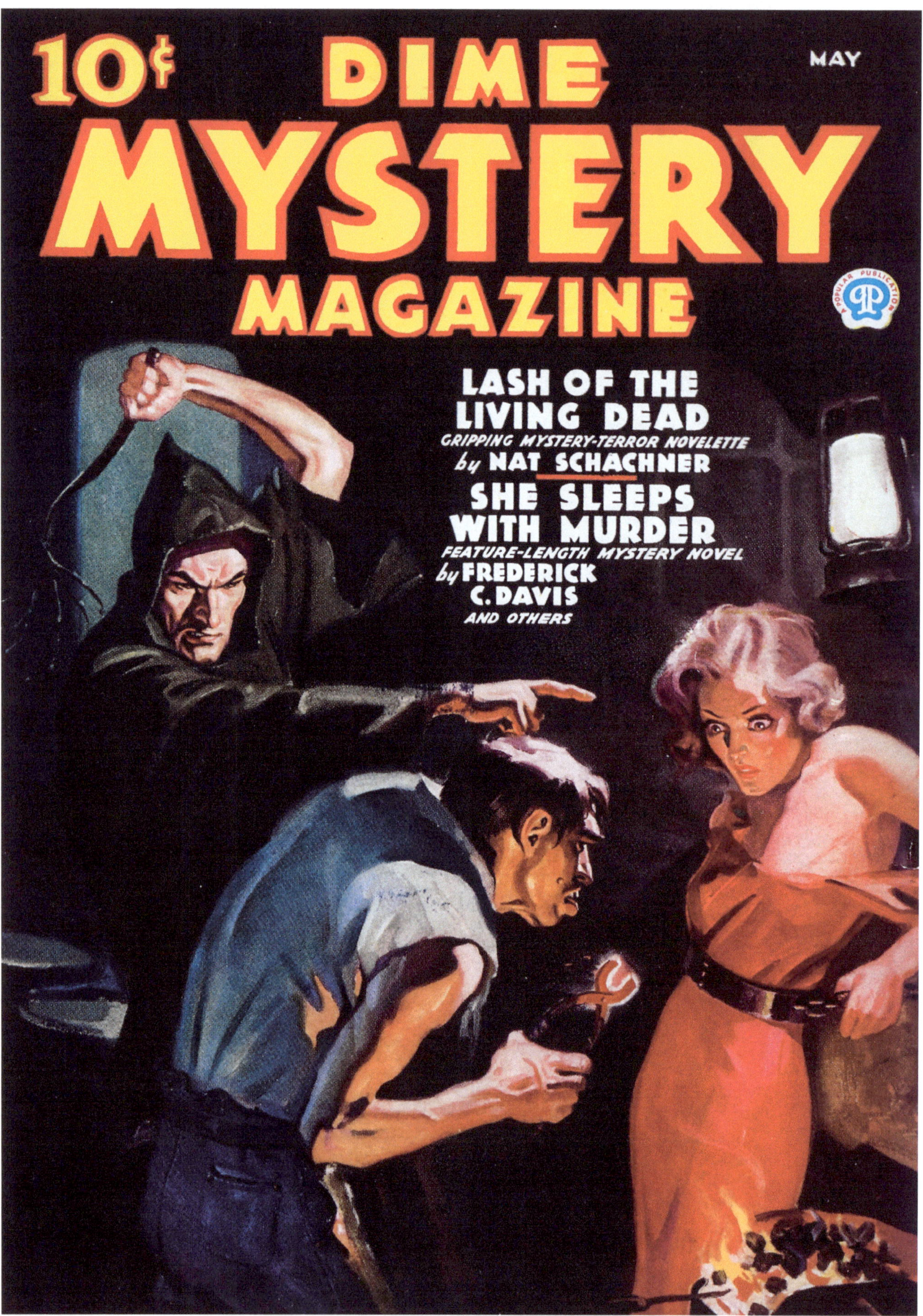

10¢
MAY
DIME MYSTERY MAGAZINE
A POPULAR PUBLICATION
LASH OF THE LIVING DEAD
GRIPPING MYSTERY-TERROR NOVELETTE
by NAT SCHACHNER
SHE SLEEPS WITH MURDER
FEATURE-LENGTH MYSTERY NOVEL
by FREDERICK C. DAVIS
AND OTHERS

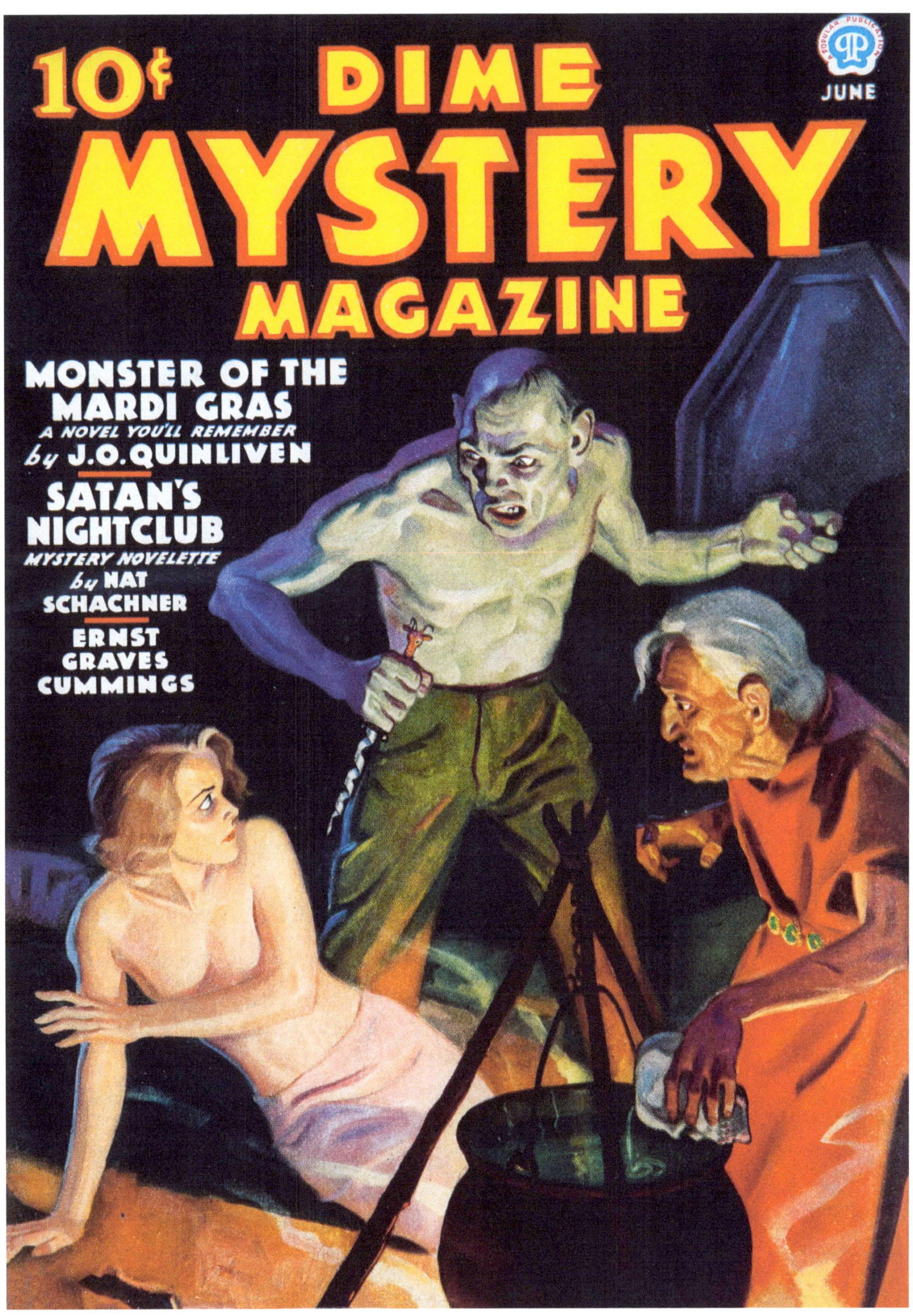

10¢
DIME
MYSTERY
MAGAZINE
JUNE
MONSTER OF THE MARDI GRAS
A NOVEL YOU'LL REMEMBER
by J.O. QUINLIVEN
SATAN'S NIGHTCLUB
MYSTERY NOVELETTE
by NAT SCHACHNER
ERNST GRAVES CUMMINGS

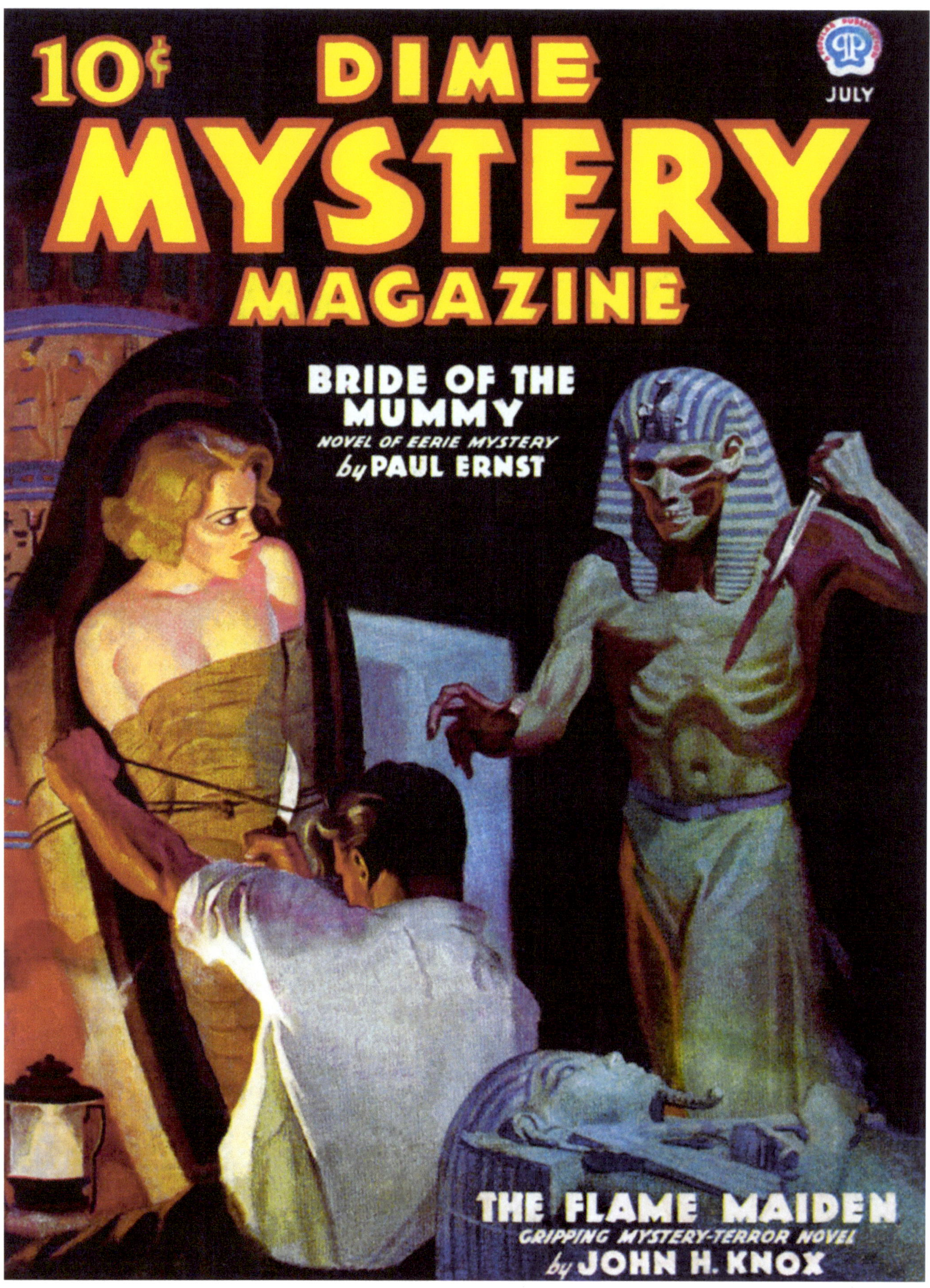

10¢
JULY
DIME
MYSTERY
MAGAZINE
BRIDE OF THE MUMMY
NOVEL OF EERIE MYSTERY
by PAUL ERNST
THE FLAME MAIDEN
GRIPPING MYSTERY-TERROR NOVEL
by JOHN H. KNOX

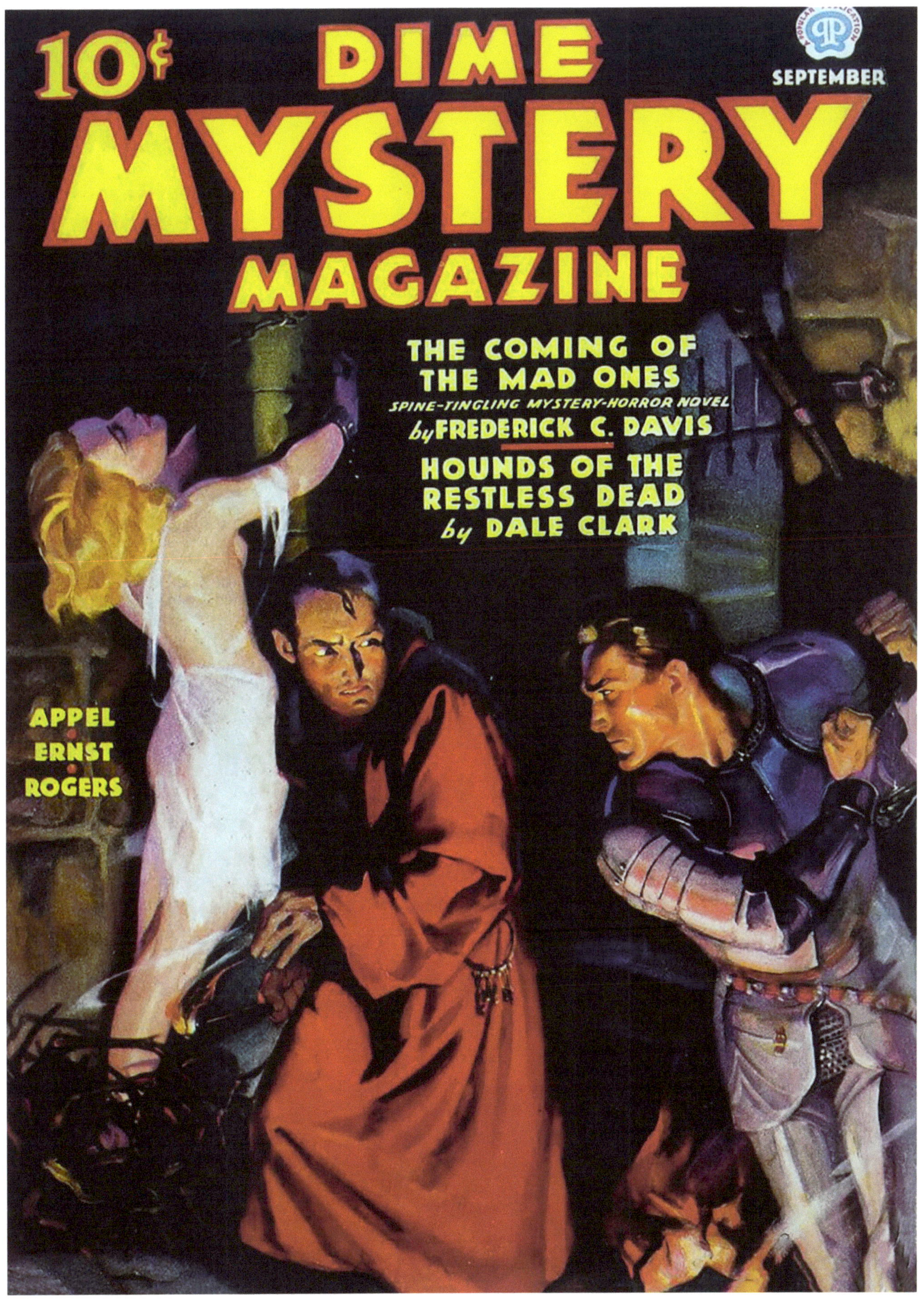

10¢
SEPTEMBER
DIME MYSTERY MAGAZINE
THE COMING OF THE MAD ONES
SPINE-TINGLING MYSTERY-HORROR NOVEL
by FREDERICK C. DAVIS
HOUNDS OF THE RESTLESS DEAD
by DALE CLARK
APPEL
ERNST
ROGERS

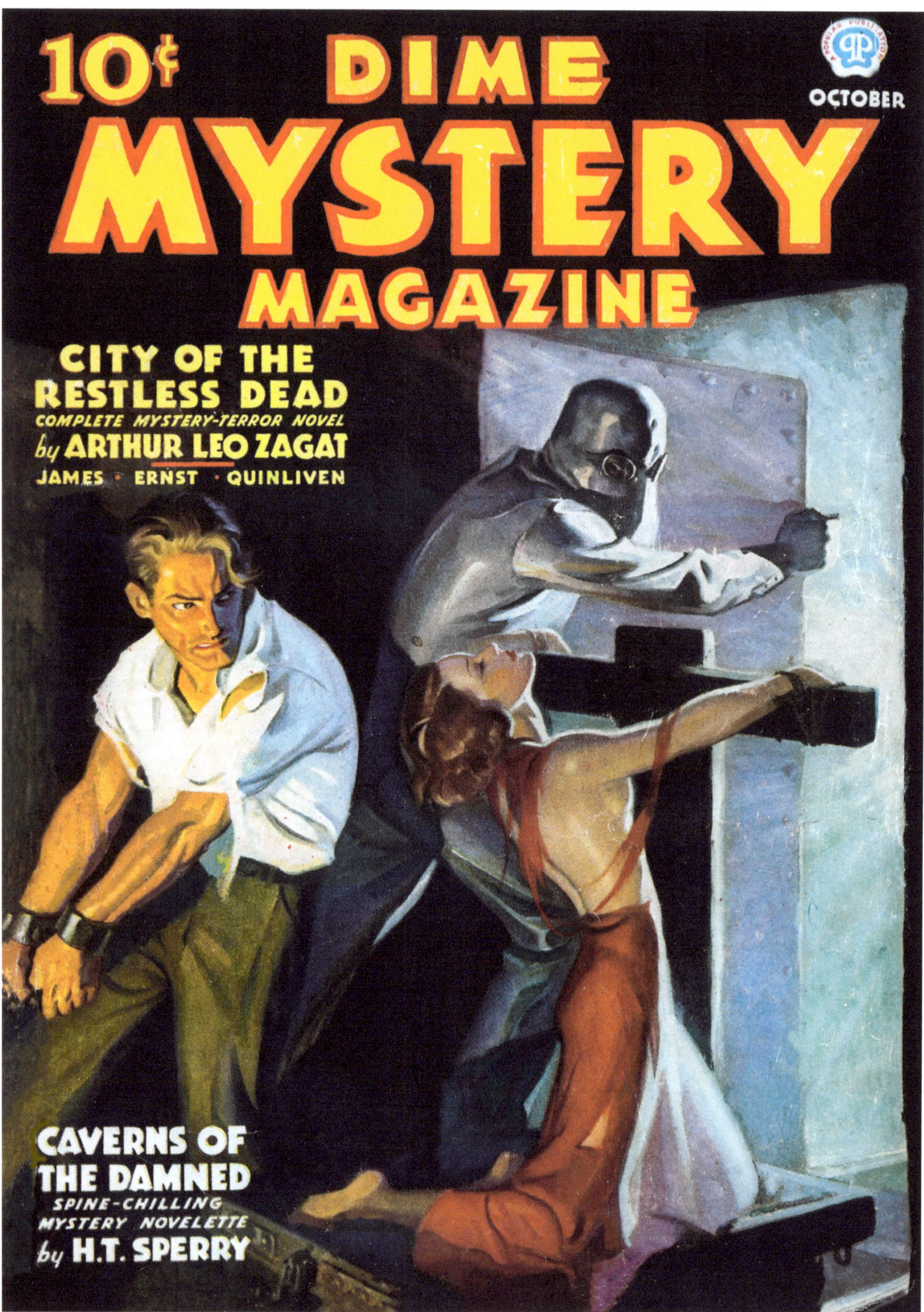

DIME MYSTERY

OCTOBER 1936

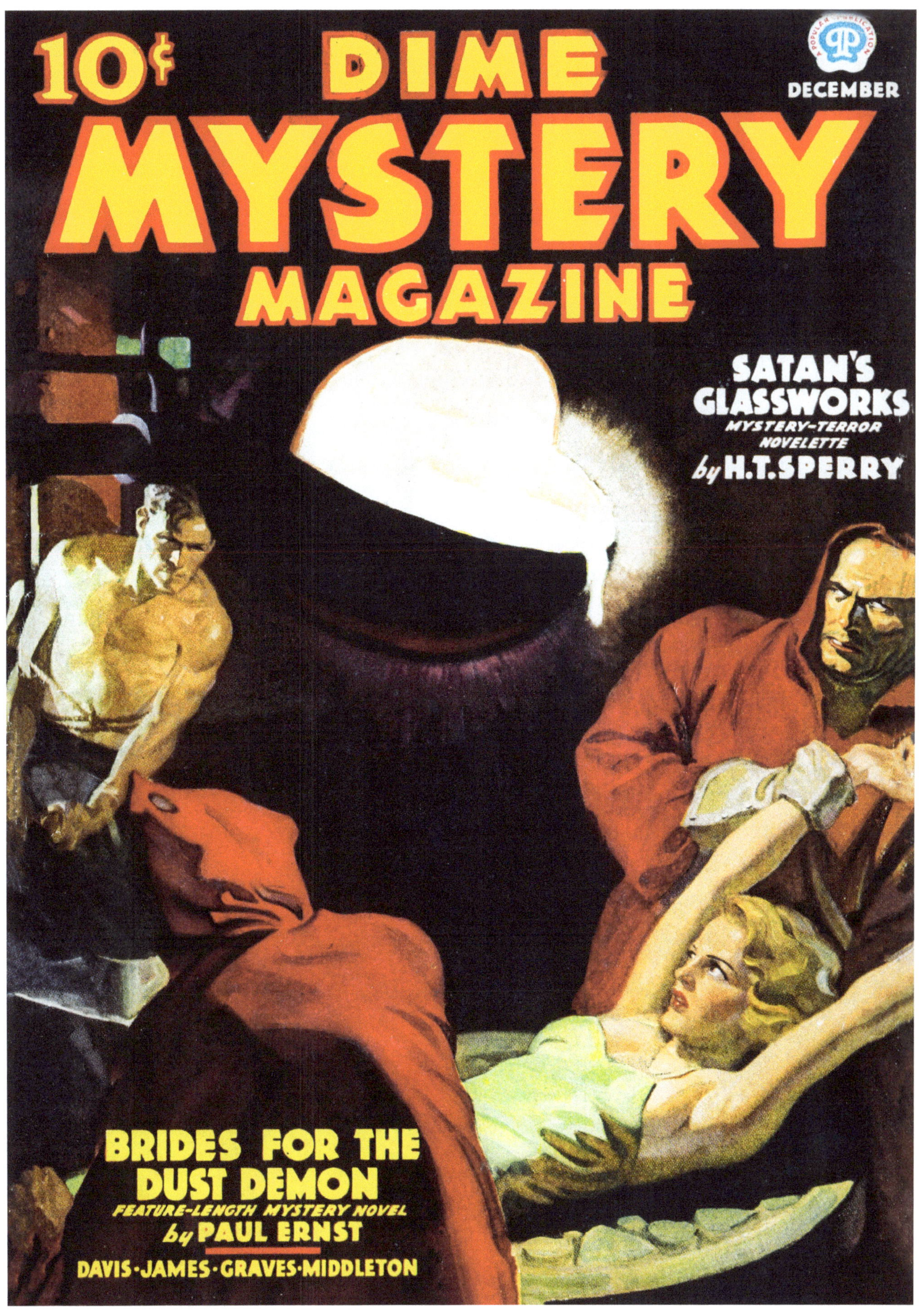

10¢
DECEMBER
DIME MYSTERY MAGAZINE
SATAN'S GLASSWORKS
MYSTERY-TERROR NOVELETTE
by H.T. SPERRY
BRIDES FOR THE DUST DEMON
FEATURE-LENGTH MYSTERY NOVEL
by PAUL ERNST
DAVIS·JAMES·GRAVES·MIDDLETON

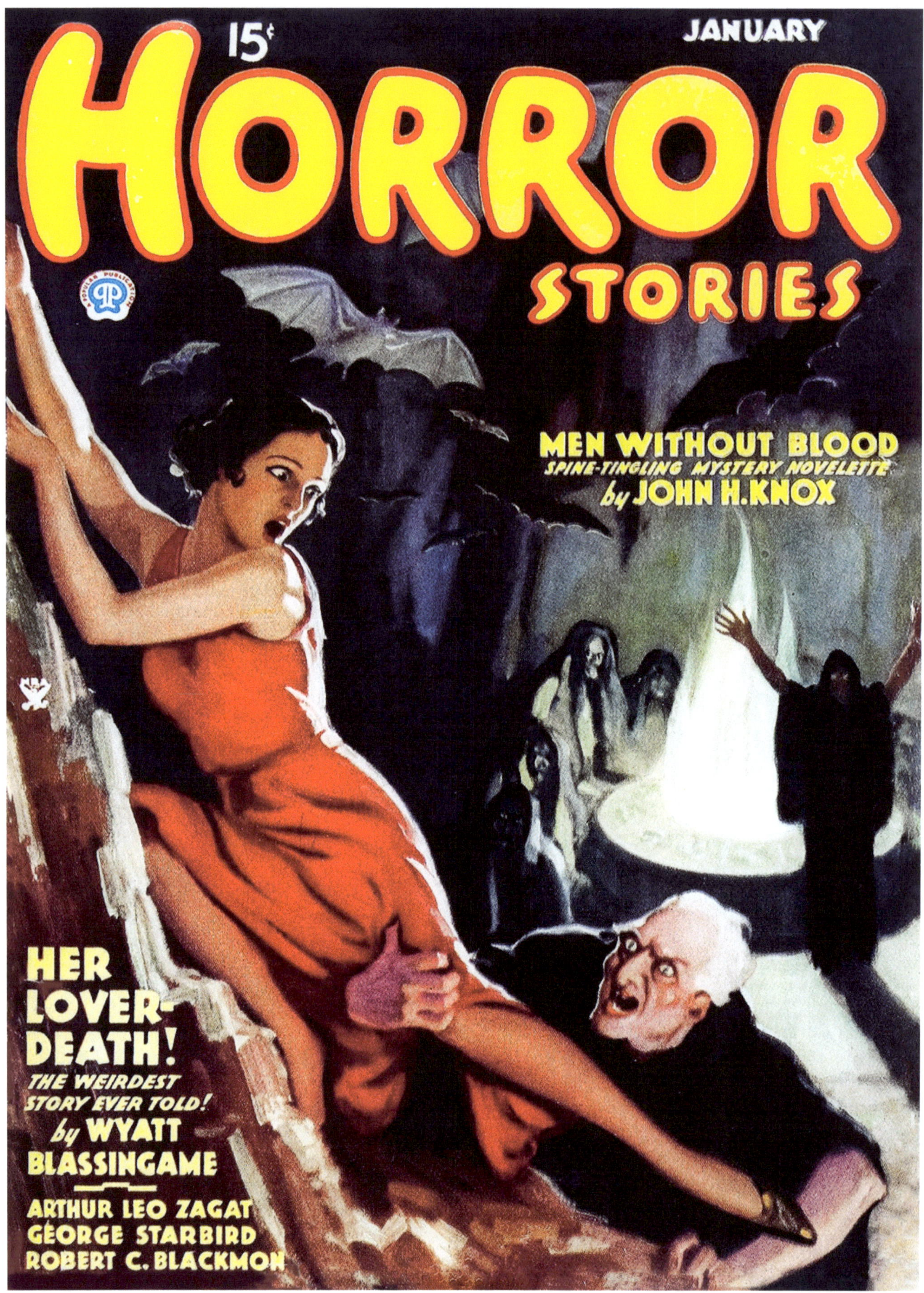

JANUARY
15¢
HORROR STORIES
MEN WITHOUT BLOOD
SPINE-TINGLING MYSTERY NOVELETTE
by JOHN H. KNOX
HER LOVER-DEATH!
THE WEIRDEST STORY EVER TOLD!
by WYATT BLASSINGAME
ARTHUR LEO ZAGAT
GEORGE STARBIRD
ROBERT C. BLACKMON

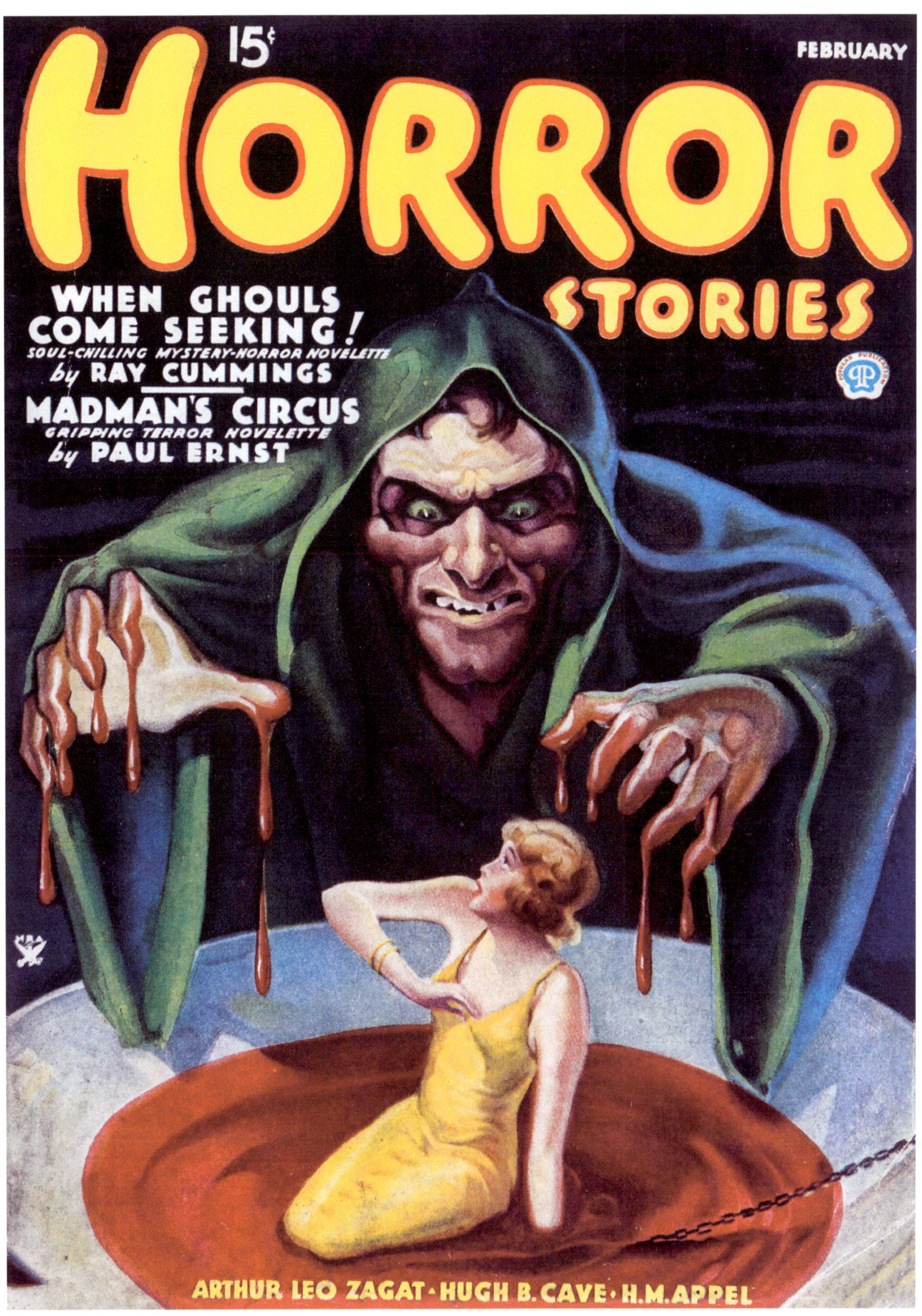

15¢
FEBRUARY
HORROR STORIES
WHEN GHOULS COME SEEKING!
SOUL-CHILLING MYSTERY-HORROR NOVELETTE
by RAY CUMMINGS
MADMAN'S CIRCUS
GRIPPING TERROR NOVELETTE
by PAUL ERNST
ARTHUR LEO ZAGAT · HUGH B. CAVE · H.M. APPEL

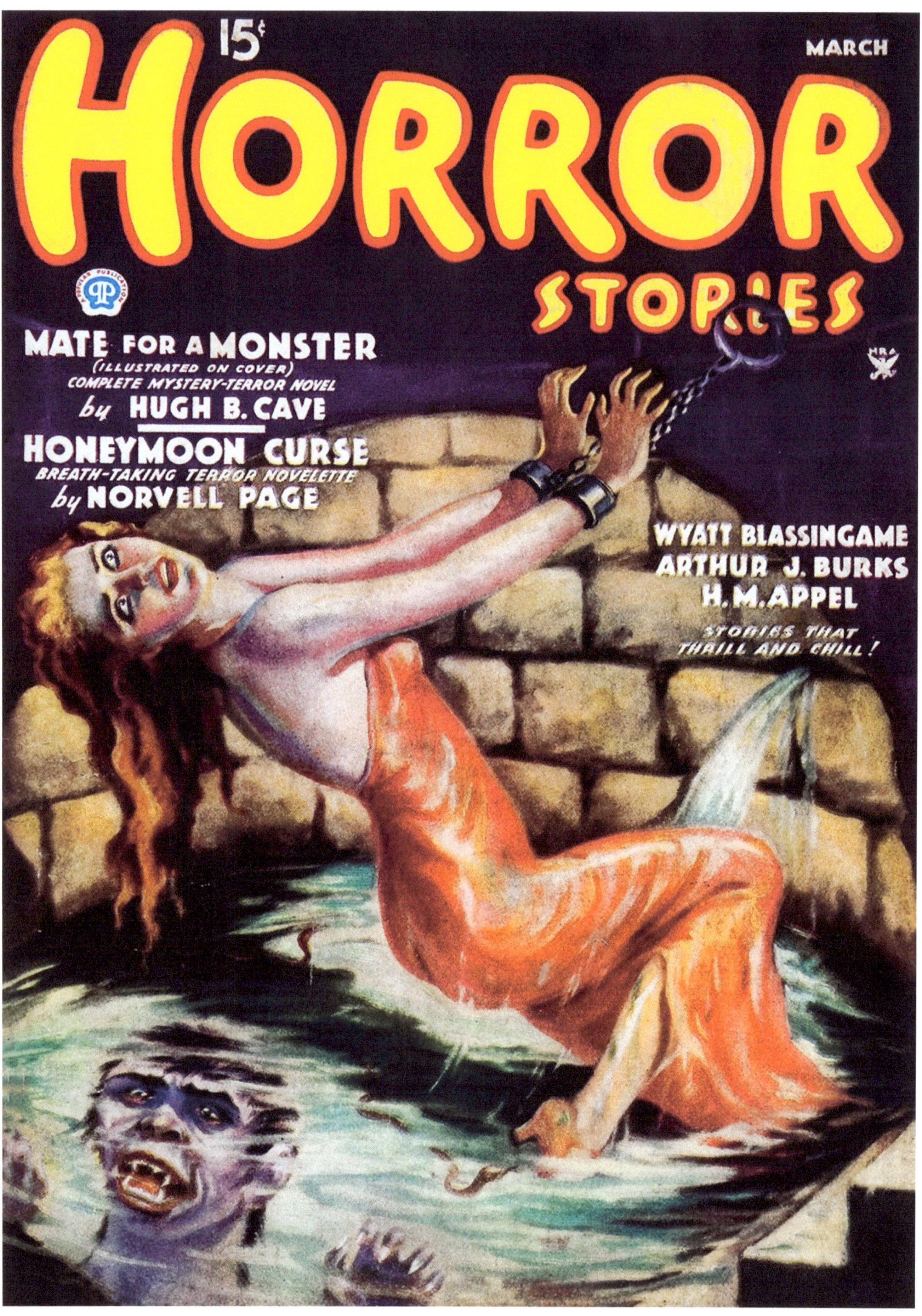

15¢
MARCH
HORROR STORIES
MATE FOR A MONSTER
(ILLUSTRATED ON COVER)
COMPLETE MYSTERY-TERROR NOVEL
by HUGH B. CAVE
HONEYMOON CURSE
BREATH-TAKING TERROR NOVELETTE
by NORVELL PAGE
WYATT BLASSINGAME
ARTHUR J. BURKS
H. M. APPEL
STORIES THAT THRILL AND CHILL!

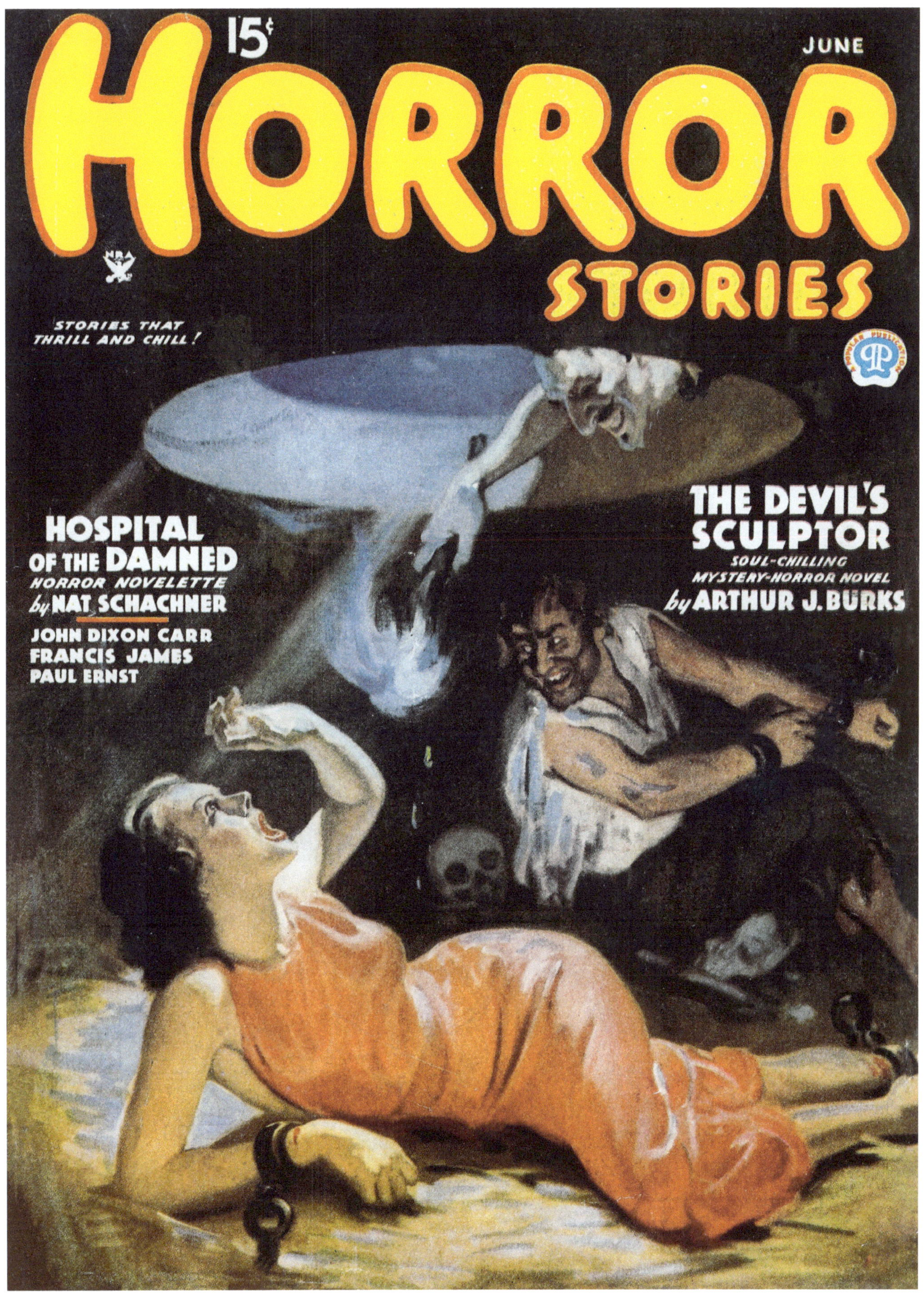

15¢
JUNE
Horror
STORIES
STORIES THAT THRILL AND CHILL!
HOSPITAL OF THE DAMNED
HORROR NOVELETTE
by NAT SCHACHNER
JOHN DIXON CARR
FRANCIS JAMES
PAUL ERNST
THE DEVIL'S SCULPTOR
SOUL-CHILLING
MYSTERY-HORROR NOVEL
by ARTHUR J. BURKS

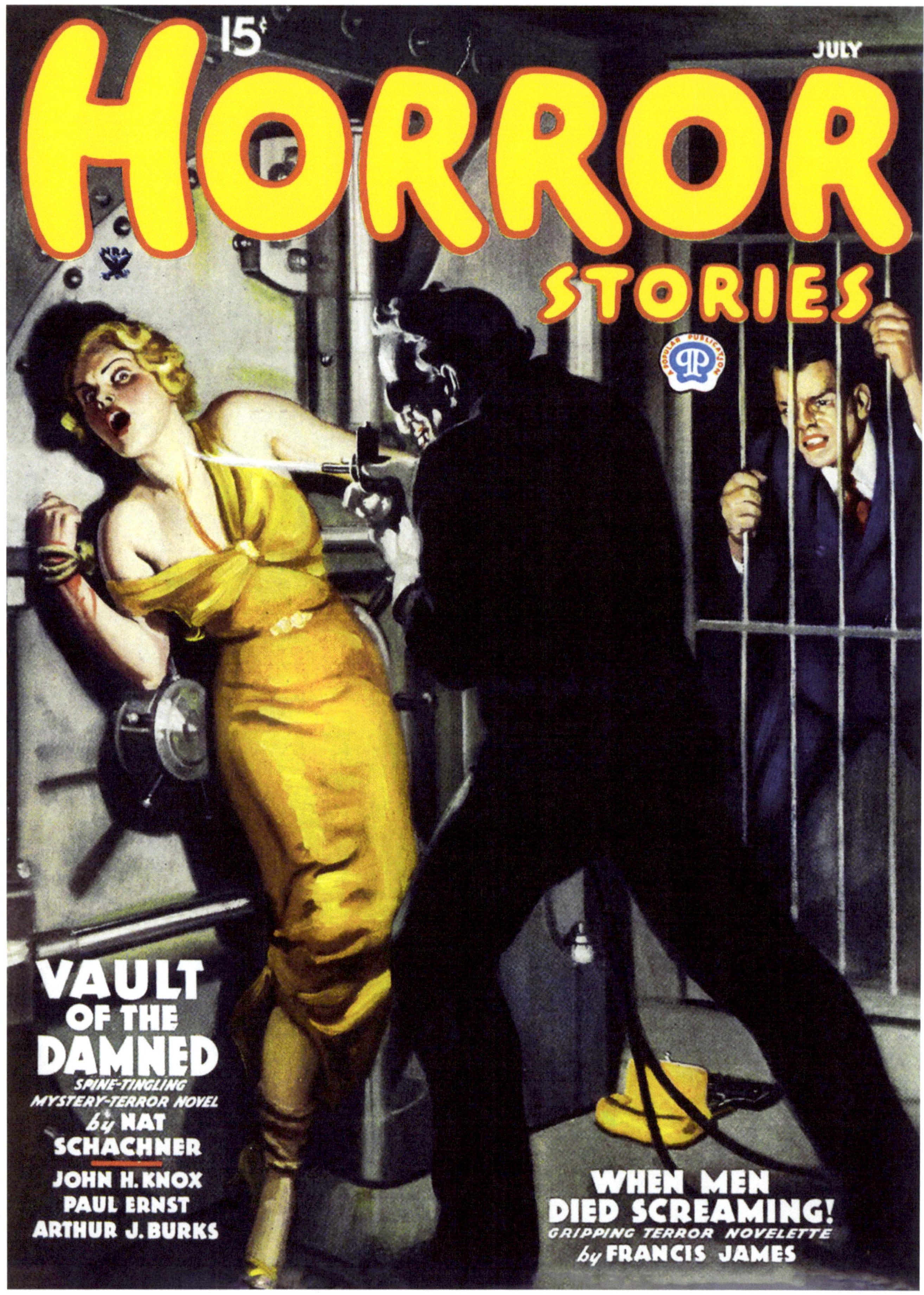

15¢
JULY
HORROR
STORIES
A POPULAR PUBLICATION
VAULT
OF THE
DAMNED
SPINE-TINGLING
MYSTERY-TERROR NOVEL
by NAT
SCHACHNER
JOHN H. KNOX
PAUL ERNST
ARTHUR J. BURKS
WHEN MEN
DIED SCREAMING!
GRIPPING TERROR NOVELETTE
by FRANCIS JAMES

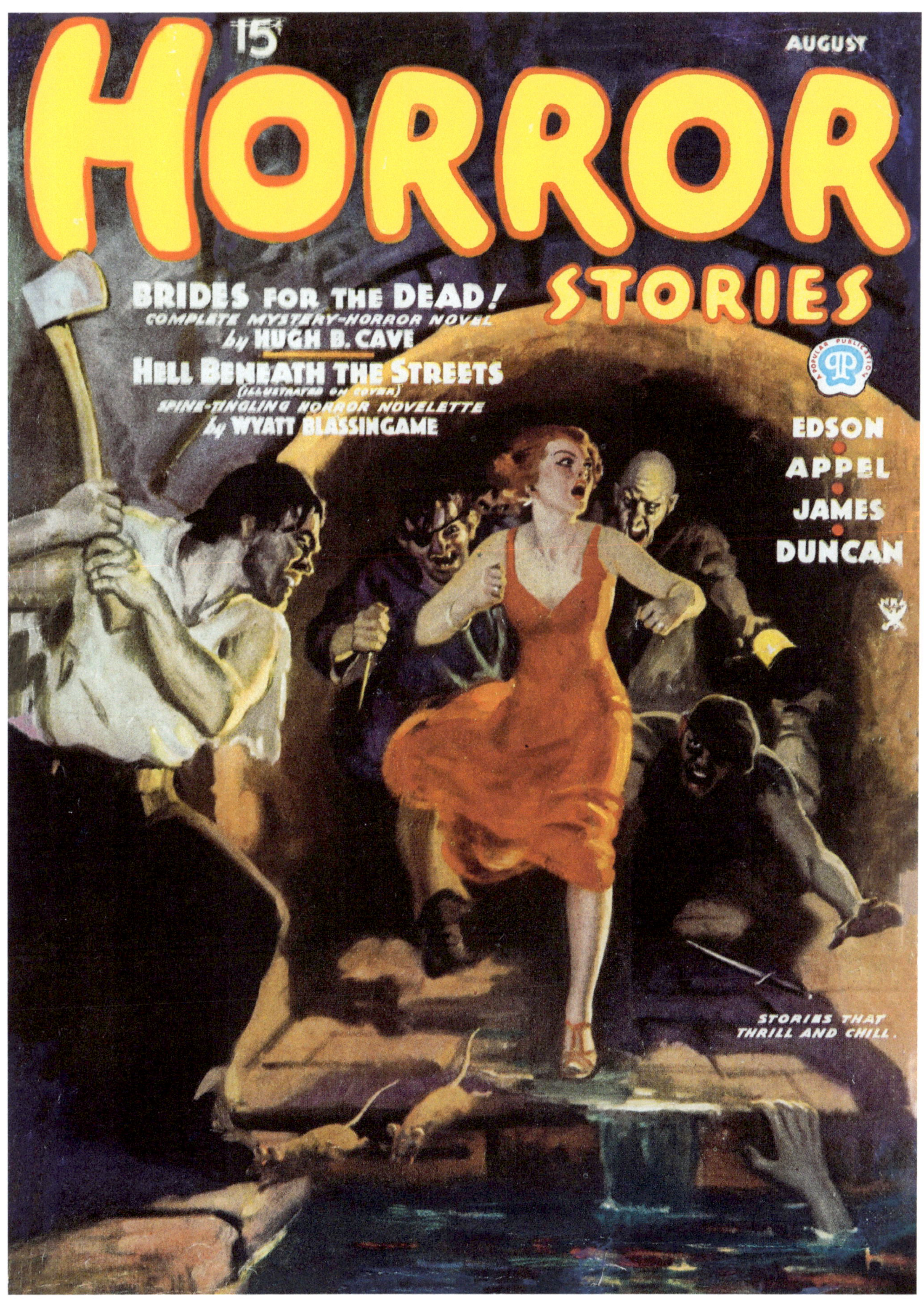

15¢
AUGUST
Horror
STORIES
BRIDES FOR THE DEAD!
COMPLETE MYSTERY-HORROR NOVEL
by HUGH B. CAVE
HELL BENEATH THE STREETS
(ILLUSTRATED ON COVER)
SPINE-TINGLING HORROR NOVELETTE
by WYATT BLASSINGAME
EDSON
APPEL
JAMES
DUNCAN
STORIES THAT
THRILL AND CHILL.

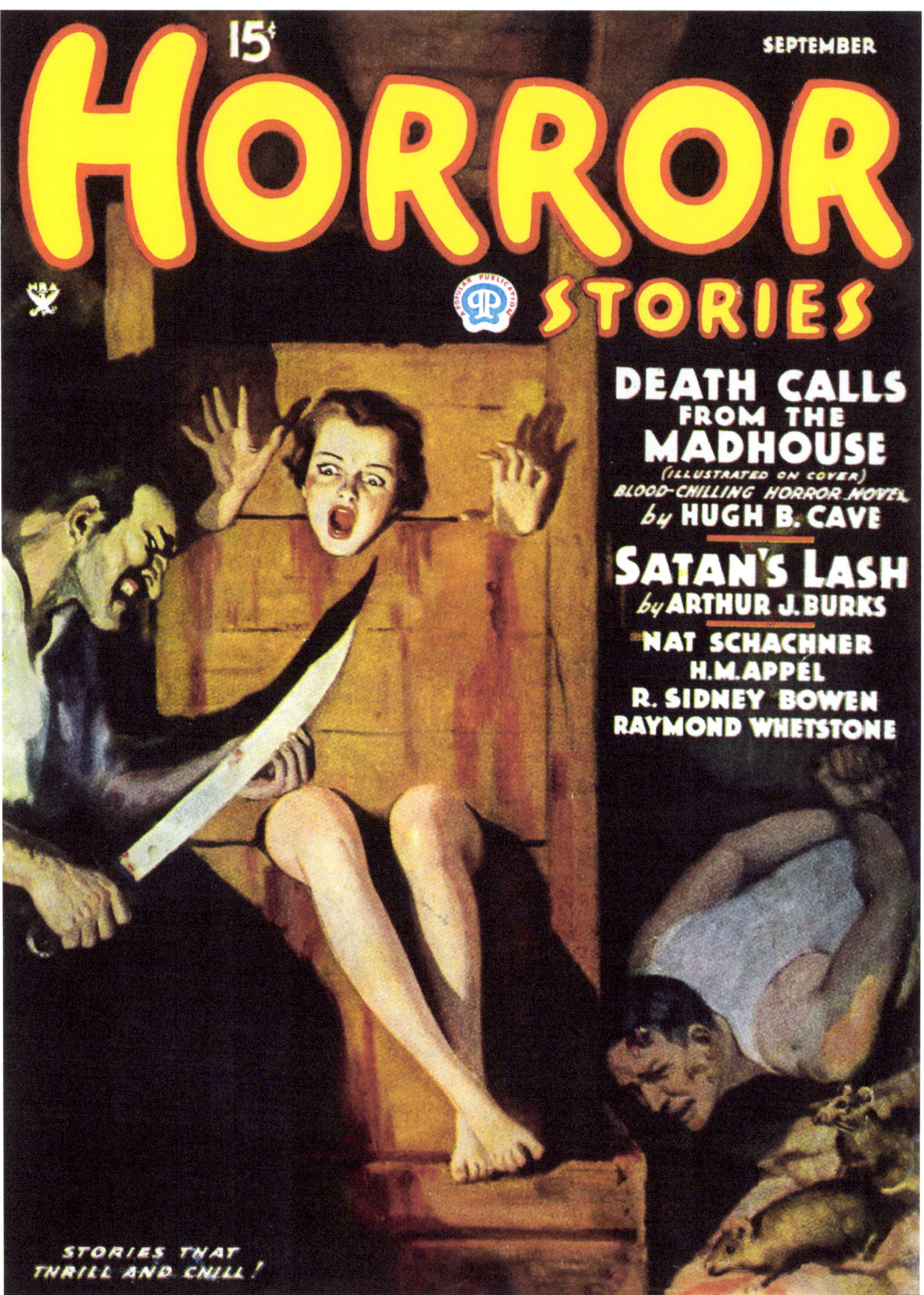

15¢
SEPTEMBER
HORROR STORIES
A POPULAR PUBLICATION
DEATH CALLS FROM THE MADHOUSE
(ILLUSTRATED ON COVER)
BLOOD-CHILLING HORROR NOVEL
by HUGH B. CAVE
SATAN'S LASH
by ARTHUR J. BURKS
NAT SCHACHNER
H. M. APPEL
R. SIDNEY BOWEN
RAYMOND WHETSTONE
STORIES THAT THRILL AND CHILL!

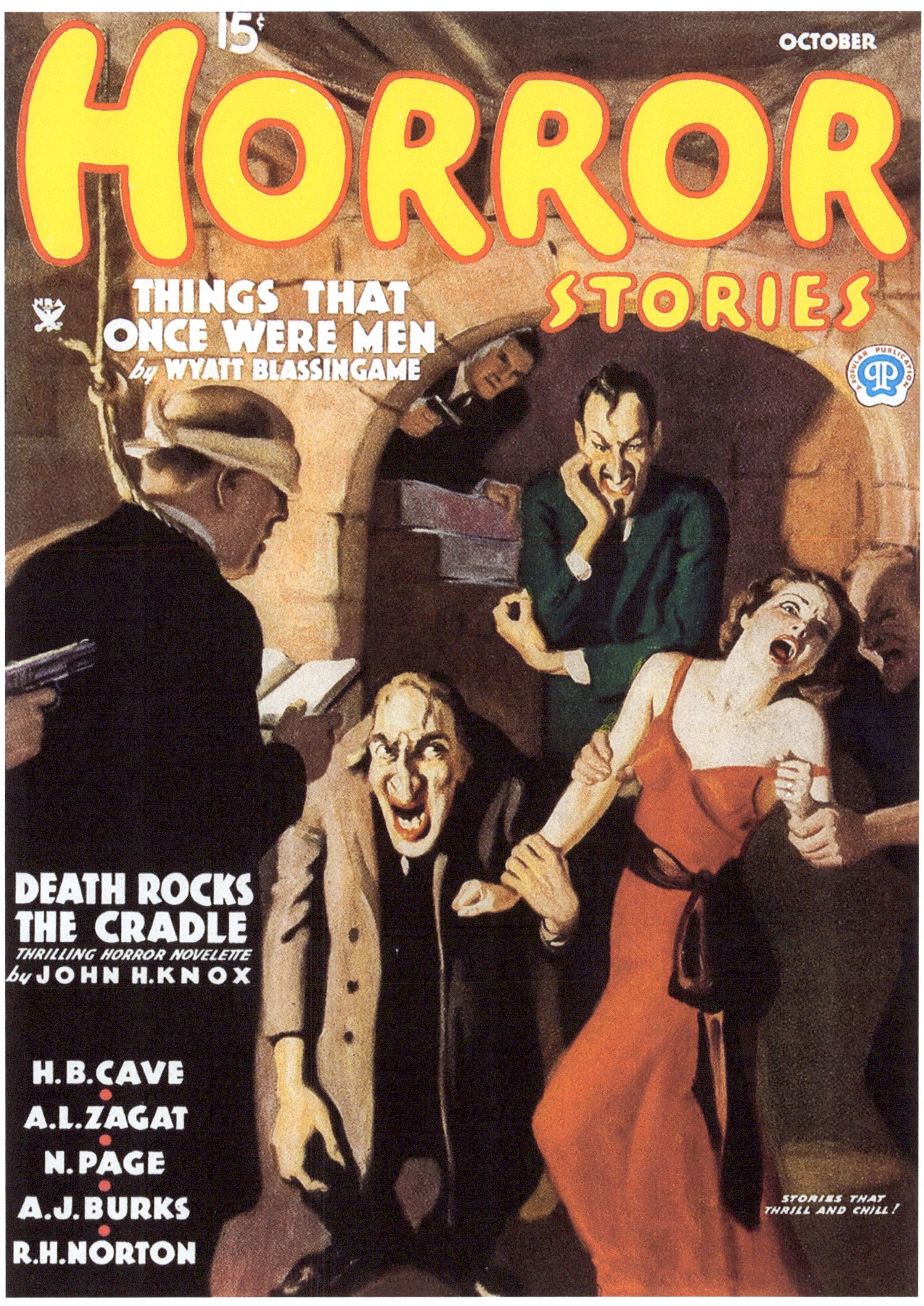

15¢
OCTOBER
HORROR STORIES
THINGS THAT ONCE WERE MEN
by WYATT BLASSINGAME
DEATH ROCKS THE CRADLE
THRILLING HORROR NOVELETTE
by JOHN H. KNOX
H. B. CAVE
A. L. ZAGAT
N. PAGE
A. J. BURKS
R. H. NORTON
STORIES THAT THRILL AND CHILL!

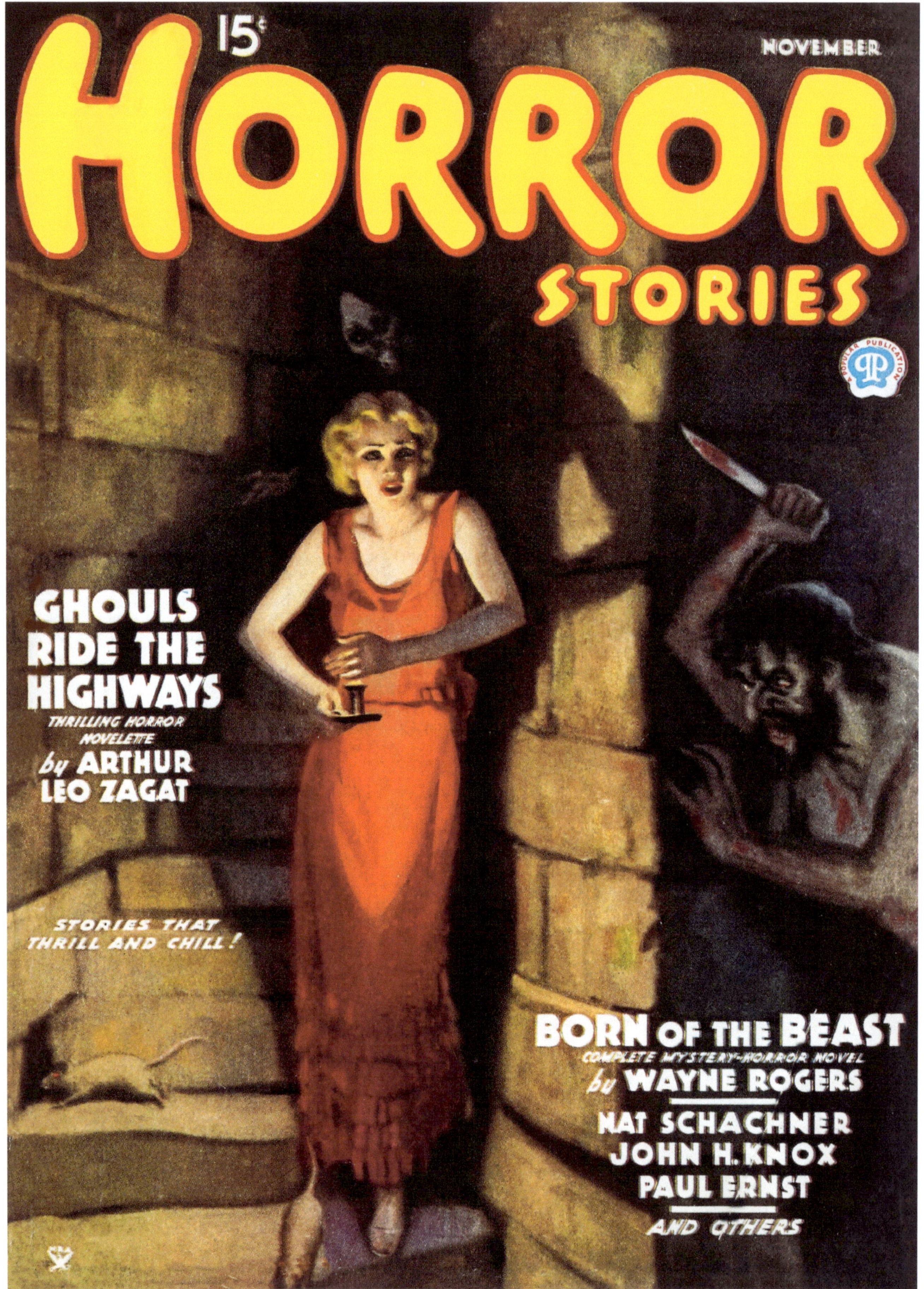

15¢
NOVEMBER
HORROR STORIES
A POPULAR PUBLICATION
GHOULS RIDE THE HIGHWAYS
THRILLING HORROR NOVELETTE
by ARTHUR LEO ZAGAT
STORIES THAT THRILL AND CHILL!
BORN OF THE BEAST
COMPLETE MYSTERY-HORROR NOVEL
by WAYNE ROGERS
NAT SCHACHNER
JOHN H. KNOX
PAUL ERNST
AND OTHERS

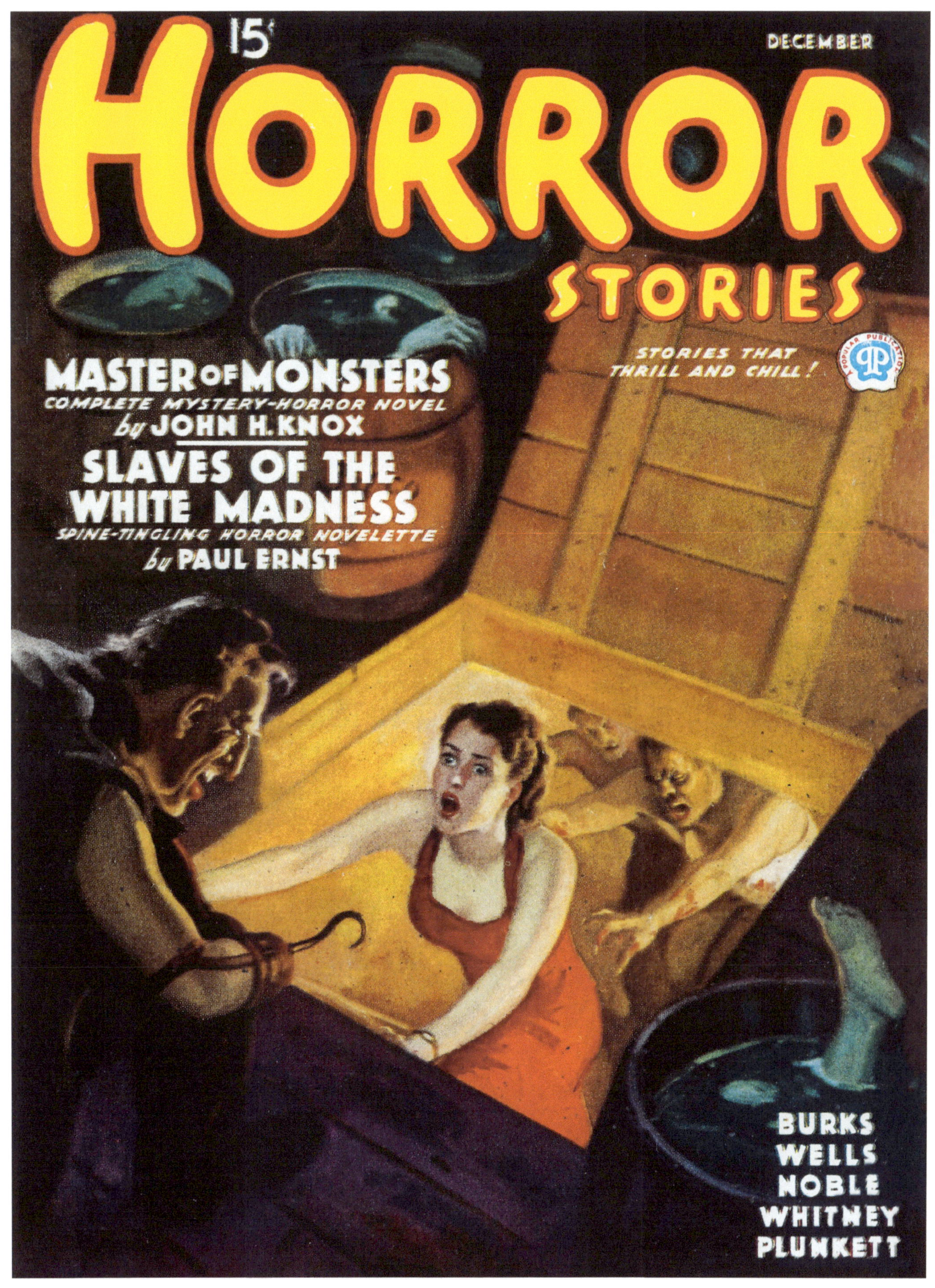

15¢
DECEMBER
HORROR STORIES
STORIES THAT THRILL AND CHILL!
A POPULAR PUBLICATION
PP
MASTER OF MONSTERS
COMPLETE MYSTERY-HORROR NOVEL
by JOHN H. KNOX
SLAVES OF THE WHITE MADNESS
SPINE-TINGLING HORROR NOVELETTE
by PAUL ERNST
BURKS
WELLS
NOBLE
WHITNEY
PLUNKETT

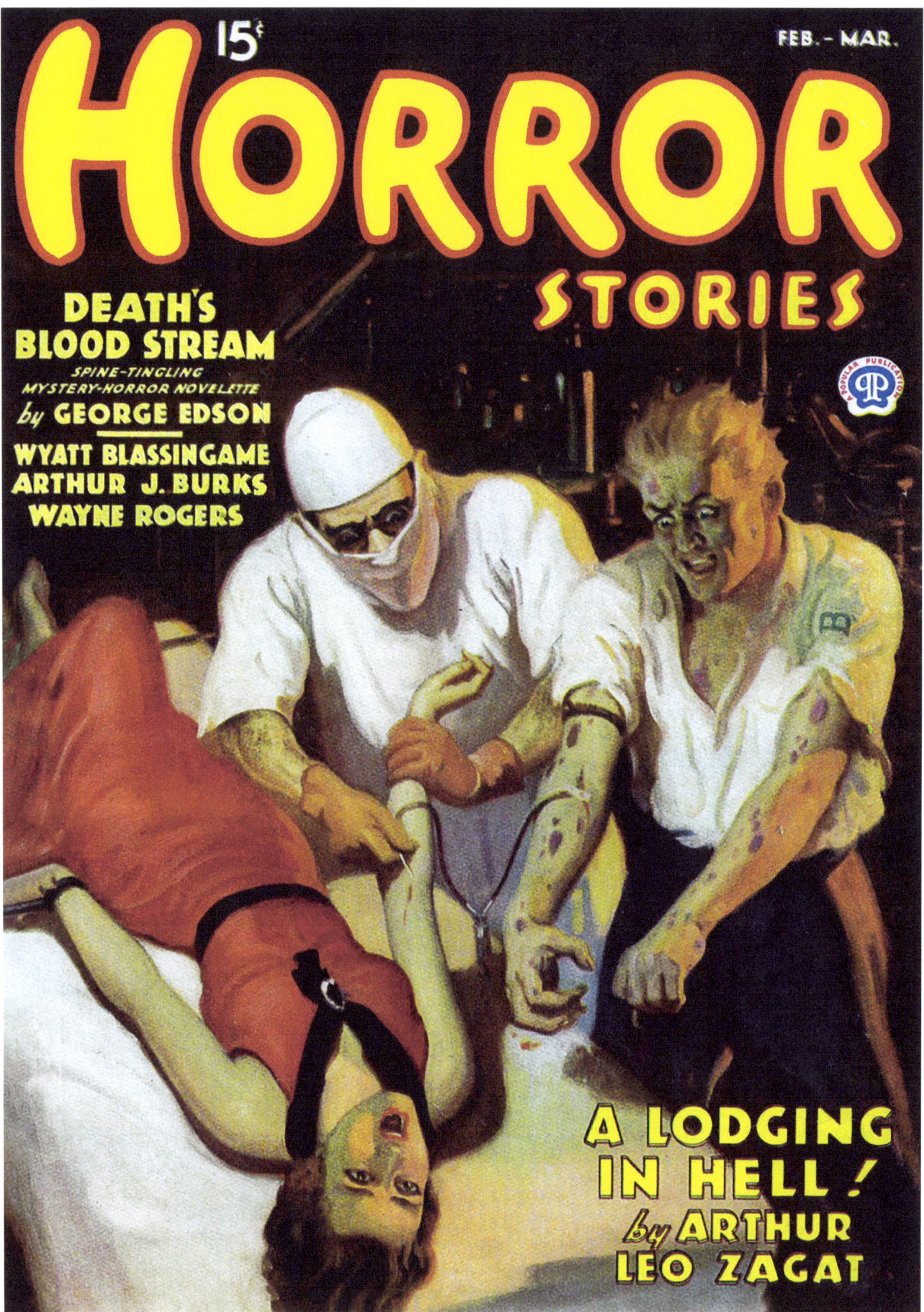

HORROR STORIES
FEBRUARY-MARCH 1936

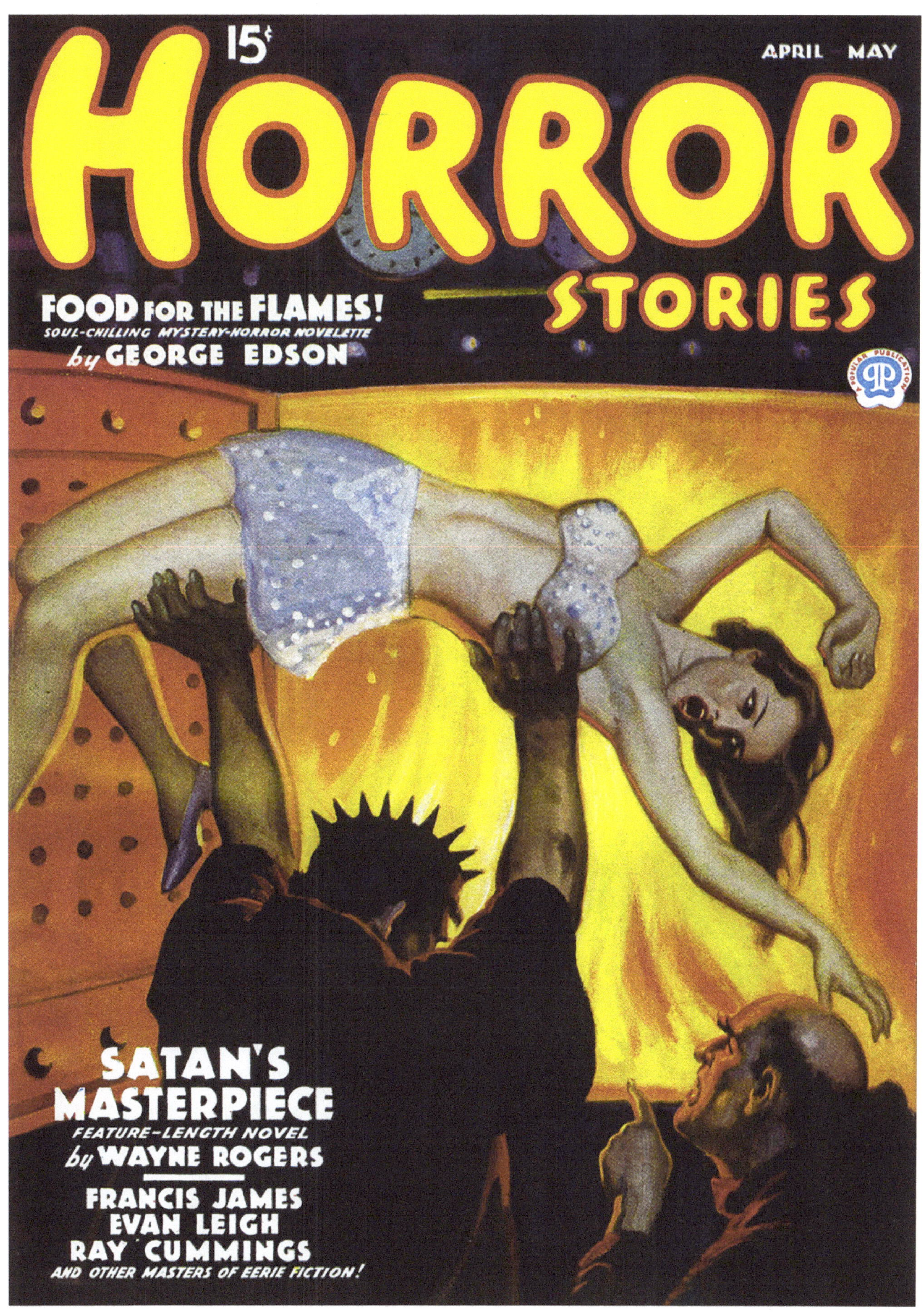
15¢
APRIL MAY
HORROR
STORIES
FOOD for the FLAMES!
SOUL-CHILLING MYSTERY-HORROR NOVELETTE
by GEORGE EDSON
SATAN'S MASTERPIECE
FEATURE-LENGTH NOVEL
by WAYNE ROGERS
FRANCIS JAMES
EVAN LEIGH
RAY CUMMINGS
AND OTHER MASTERS OF EERIE FICTION!

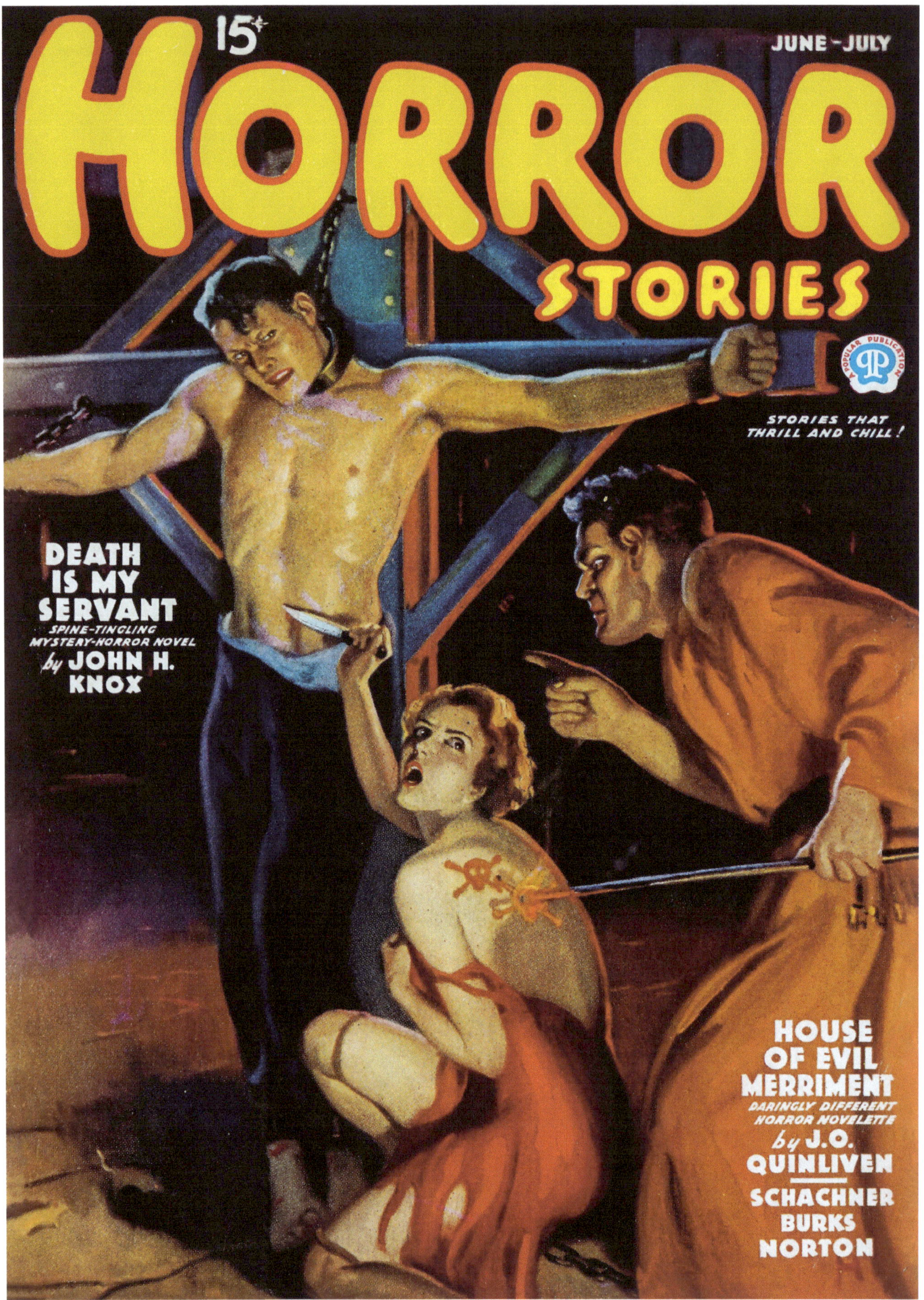

JUNE-JULY 1936

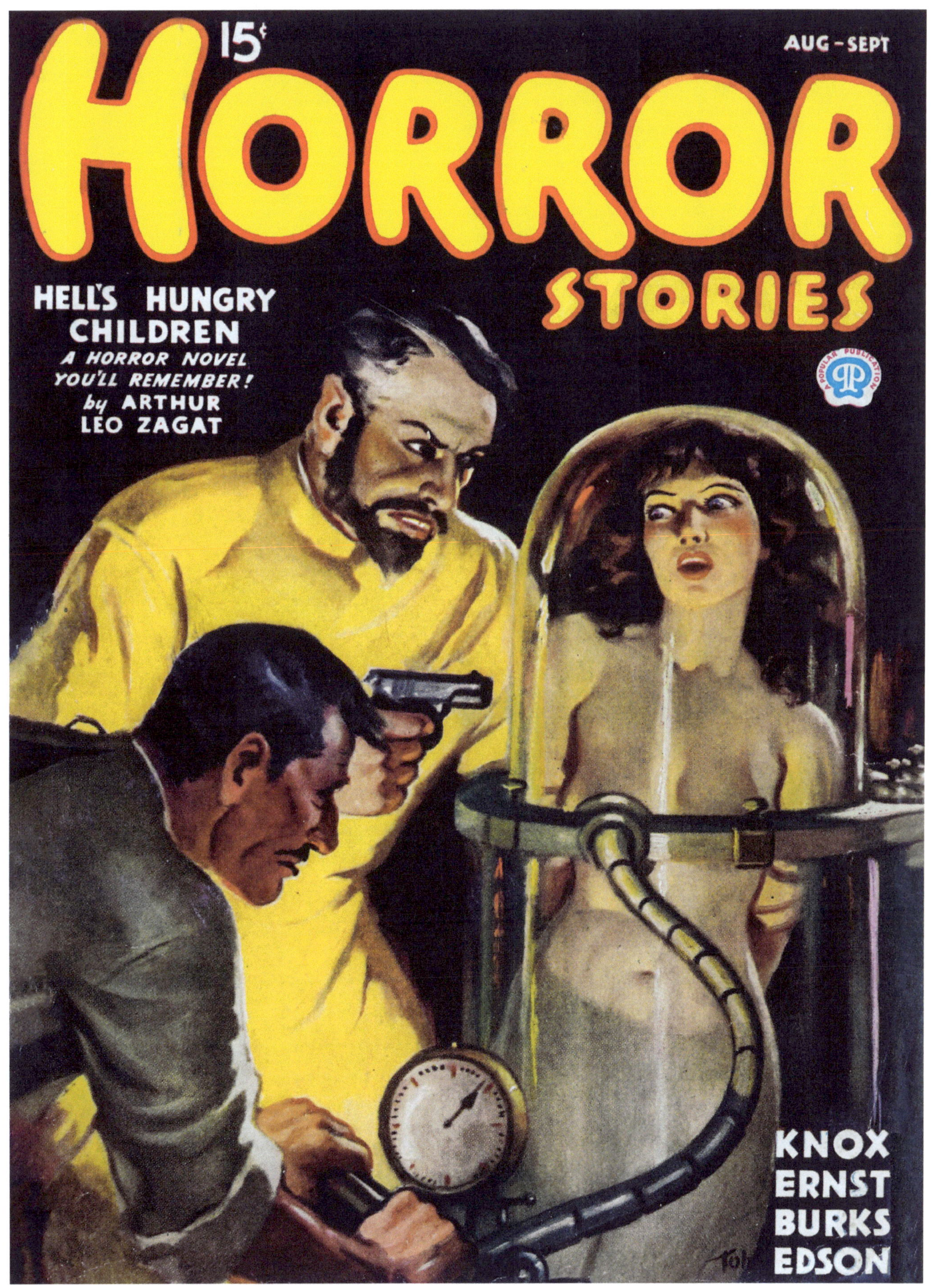

15¢
AUG-SEPT
HORROR STORIES
HELL'S HUNGRY CHILDREN
A HORROR NOVEL YOU'LL REMEMBER!
by ARTHUR LEO ZAGAT
KNOX
ERNST
BURKS
EDSON

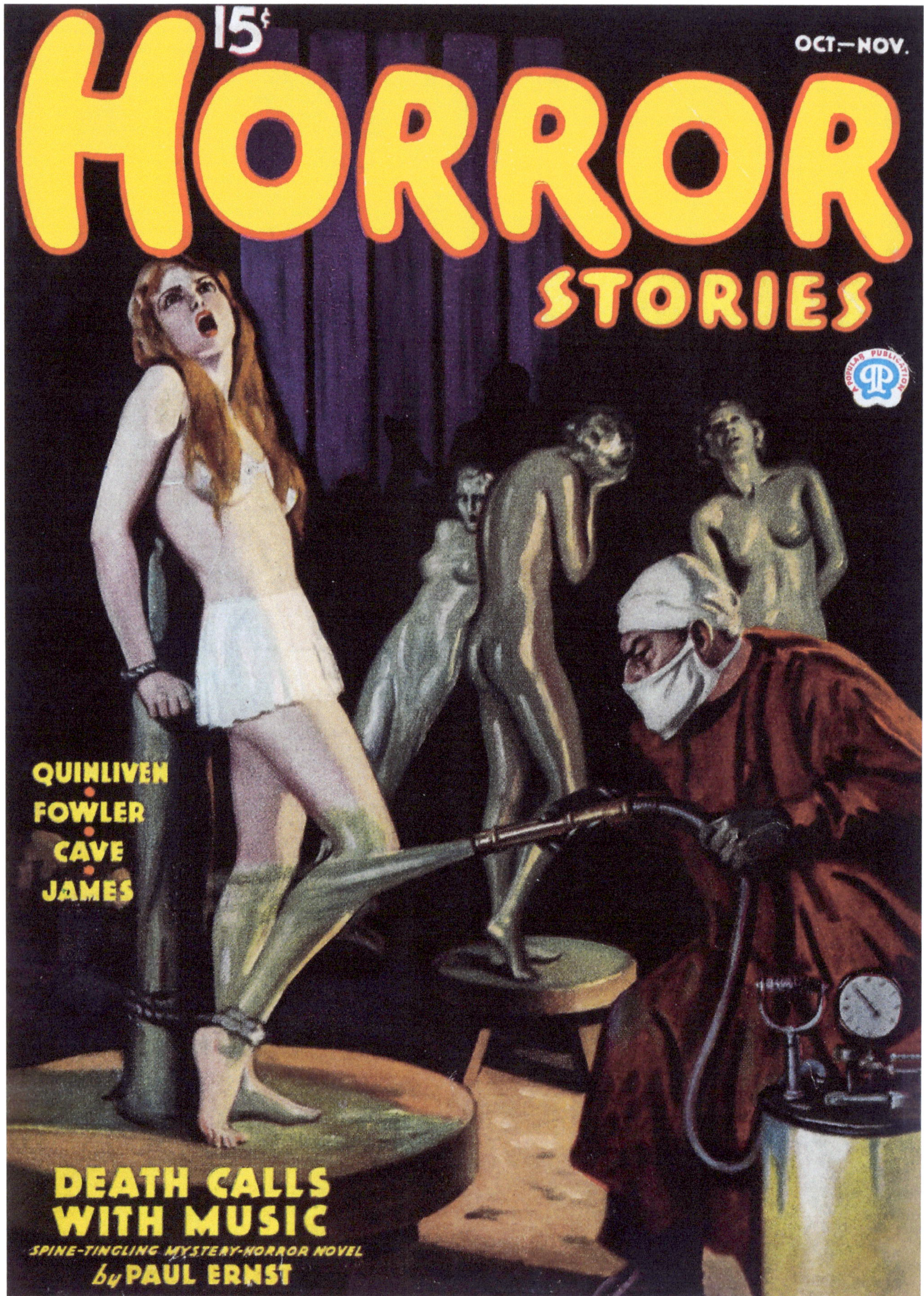

15¢
OCT.—NOV.
Horror
STORIES
A POPULAR PUBLICATION
QUINLIVEN
FOWLER
CAVE
JAMES
DEATH CALLS
WITH MUSIC
SPINE-TINGLING MYSTERY-HORROR NOVEL
by PAUL ERNST

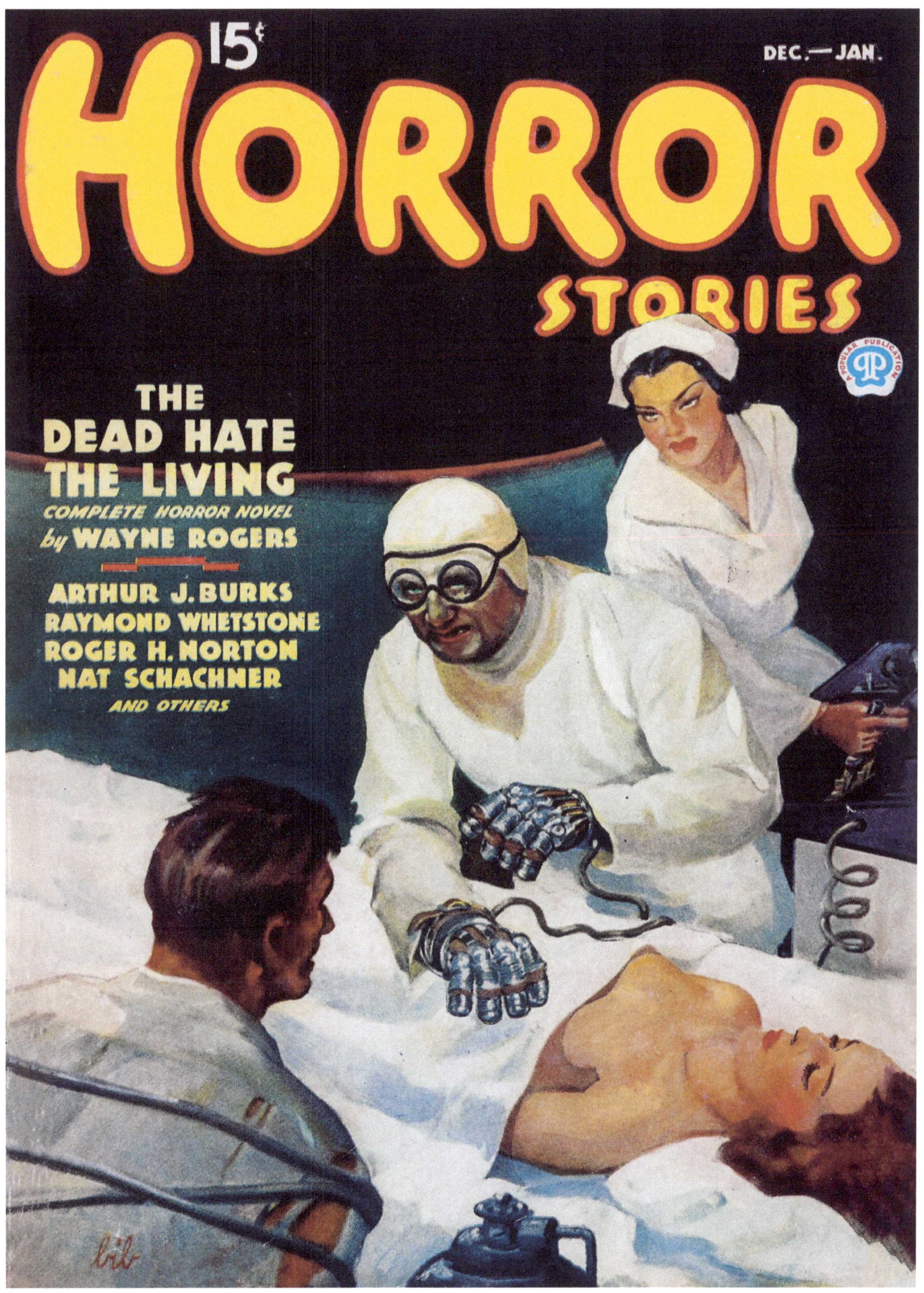

15¢
DEC.—JAN.
Horror
STORIES
A POPULAR PUBLICATION
THE
DEAD HATE
THE LIVING
COMPLETE HORROR NOVEL
by WAYNE ROGERS
ARTHUR J. BURKS
RAYMOND WHETSTONE
ROGER H. NORTON
NAT SCHACHNER
AND OTHERS

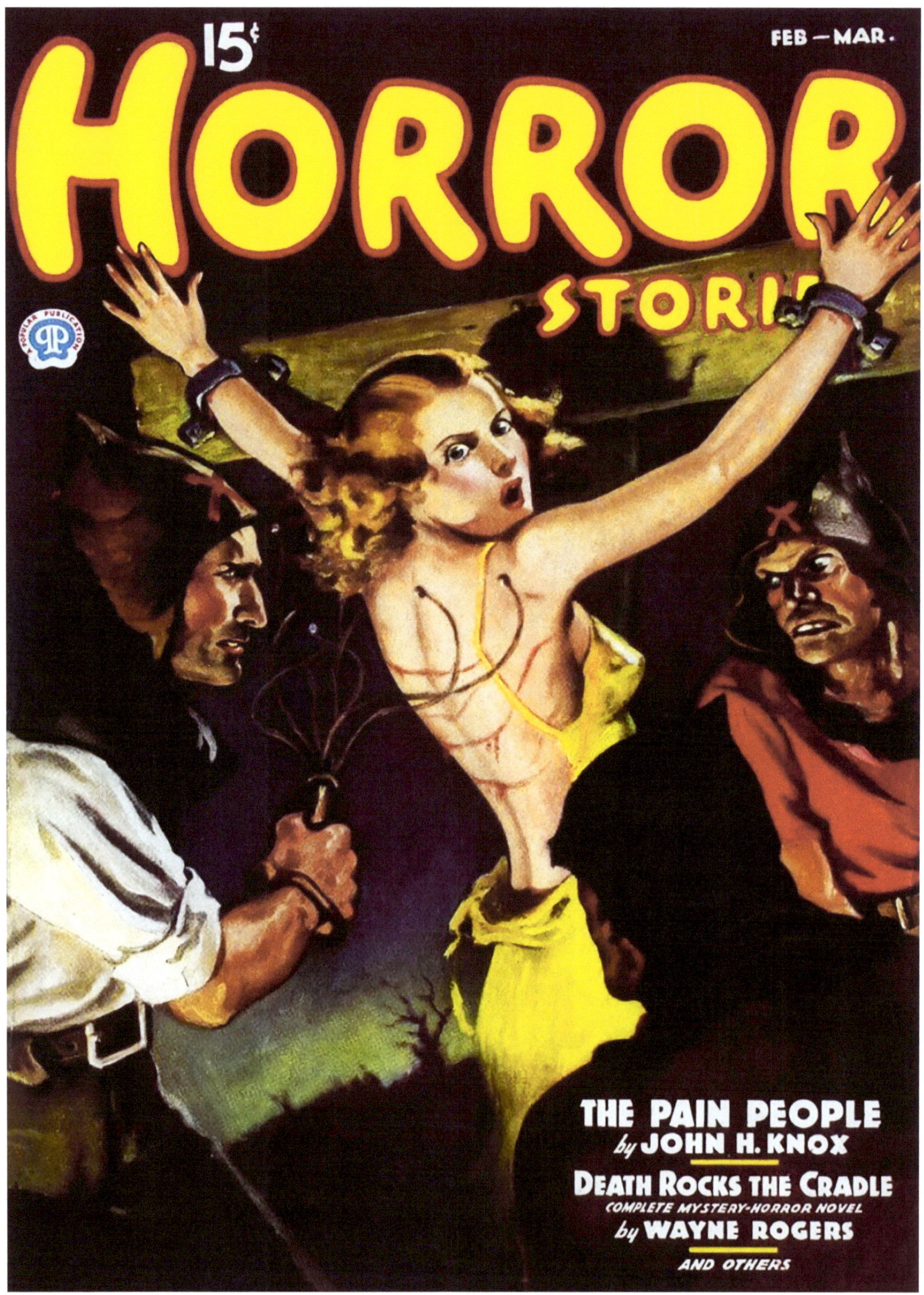

15¢
FEB — MAR.
HORROR STORIES
THE PAIN PEOPLE
by JOHN H. KNOX
DEATH ROCKS THE CRADLE
COMPLETE MYSTERY-HORROR NOVEL
by WAYNE ROGERS
AND OTHERS

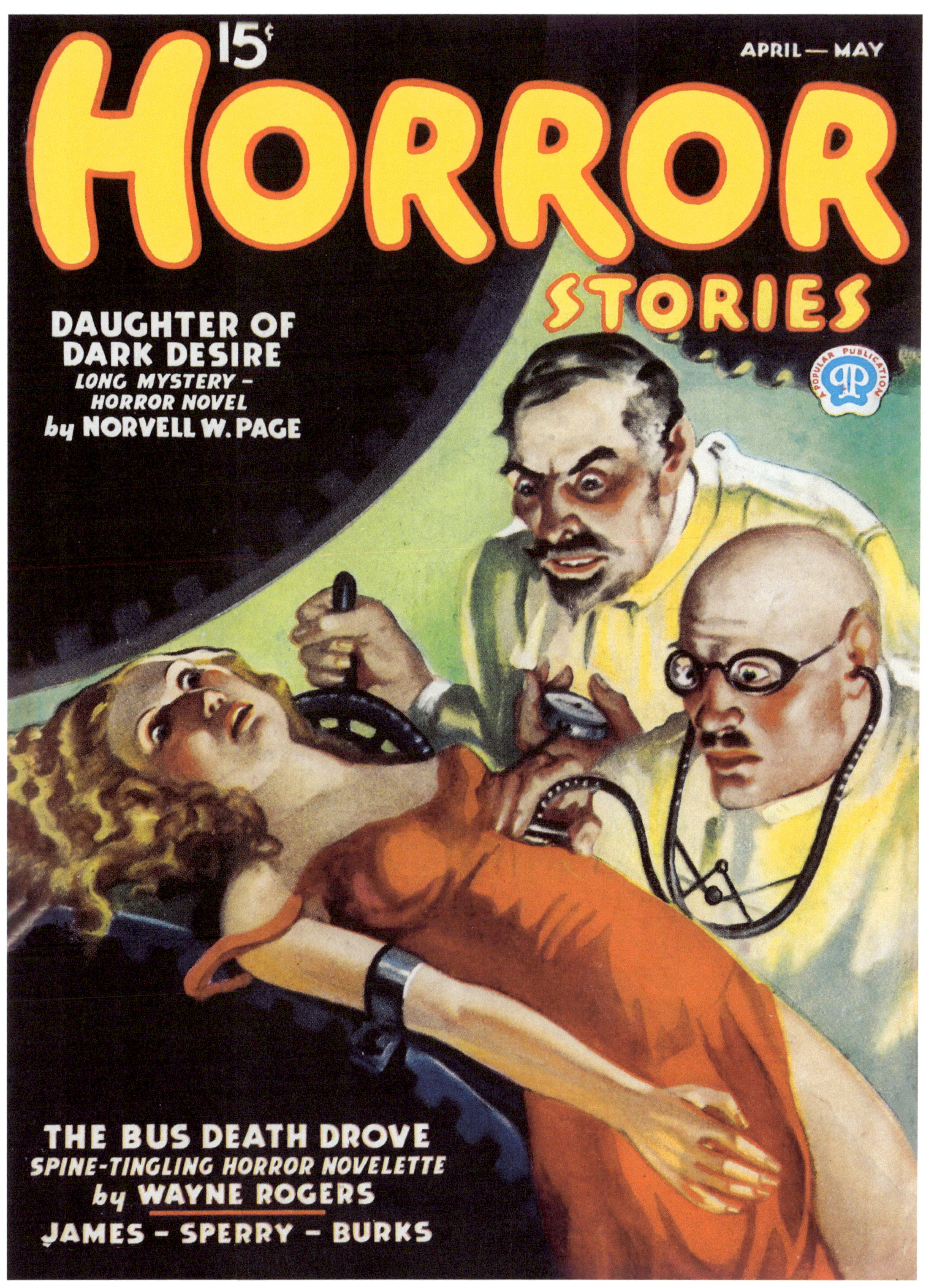

15¢
APRIL — MAY
Horror
STORIES
DAUGHTER OF DARK DESIRE
LONG MYSTERY – HORROR NOVEL
by NORVELL W. PAGE
A POPULAR PUBLICATION
THE BUS DEATH DROVE
SPINE-TINGLING HORROR NOVELETTE
by WAYNE ROGERS
JAMES - SPERRY - BURKS

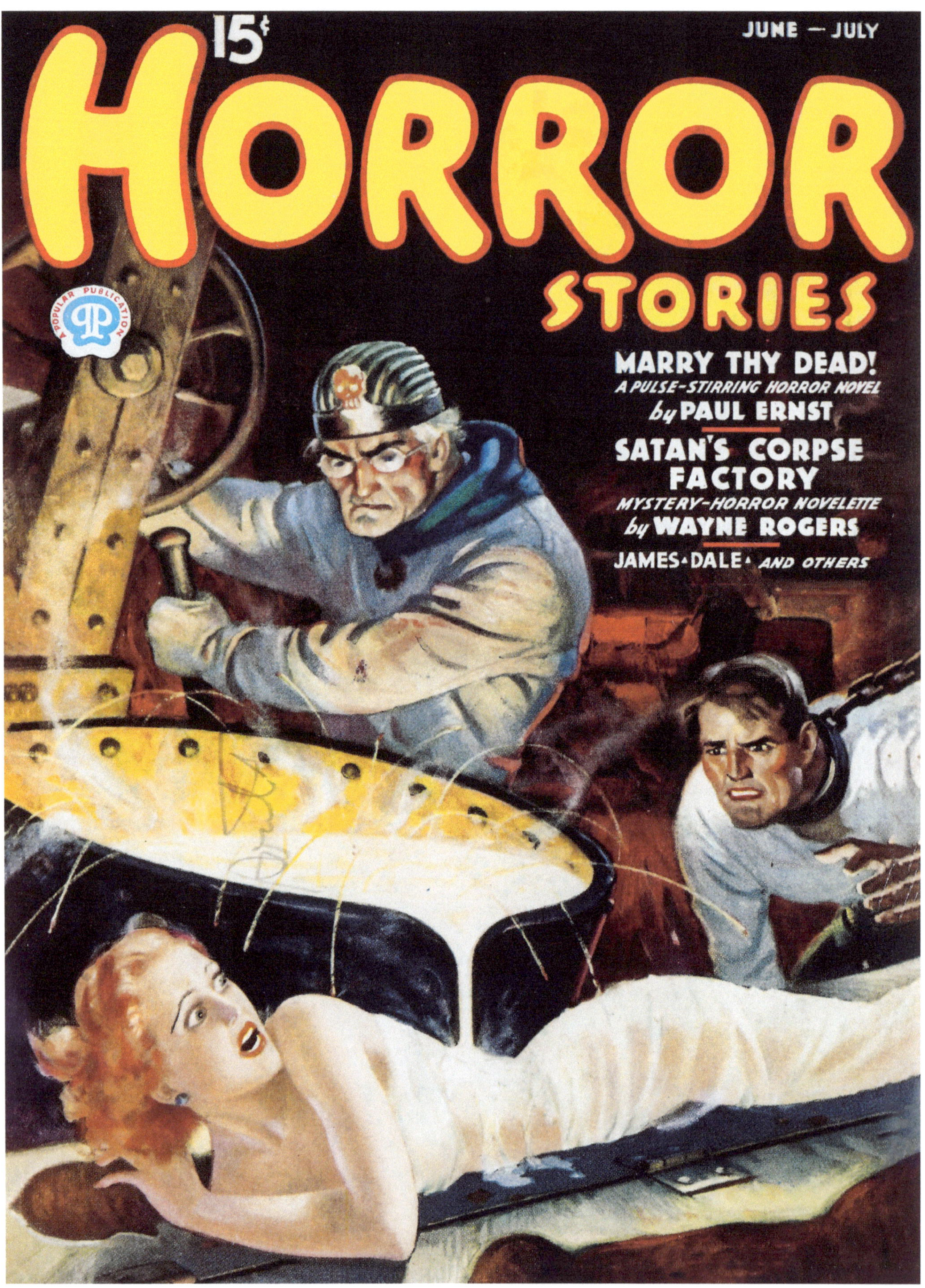

15¢
JUNE — JULY
A POPULAR PUBLICATION
HORROR STORIES
MARRY THY DEAD!
A PULSE-STIRRING HORROR NOVEL
by PAUL ERNST
SATAN'S CORPSE FACTORY
MYSTERY-HORROR NOVELETTE
by WAYNE ROGERS
JAMES DALE AND OTHERS

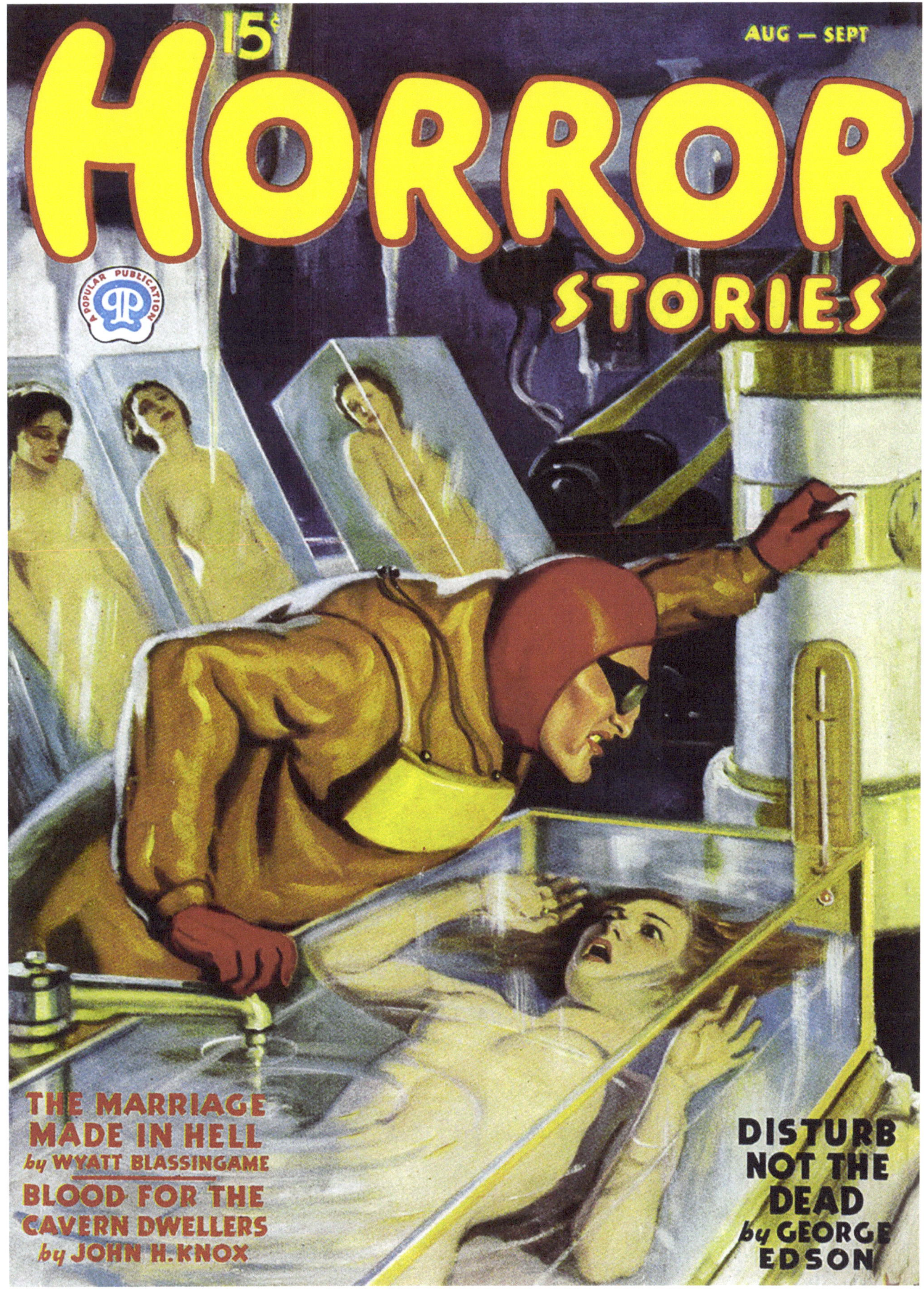

15¢
AUG — SEPT
HORROR STORIES
A POPULAR PUBLICATION
THE MARRIAGE MADE IN HELL
by WYATT BLASSINGAME
BLOOD FOR THE CAVERN DWELLERS
by JOHN H. KNOX
DISTURB NOT THE DEAD
by GEORGE EDSON

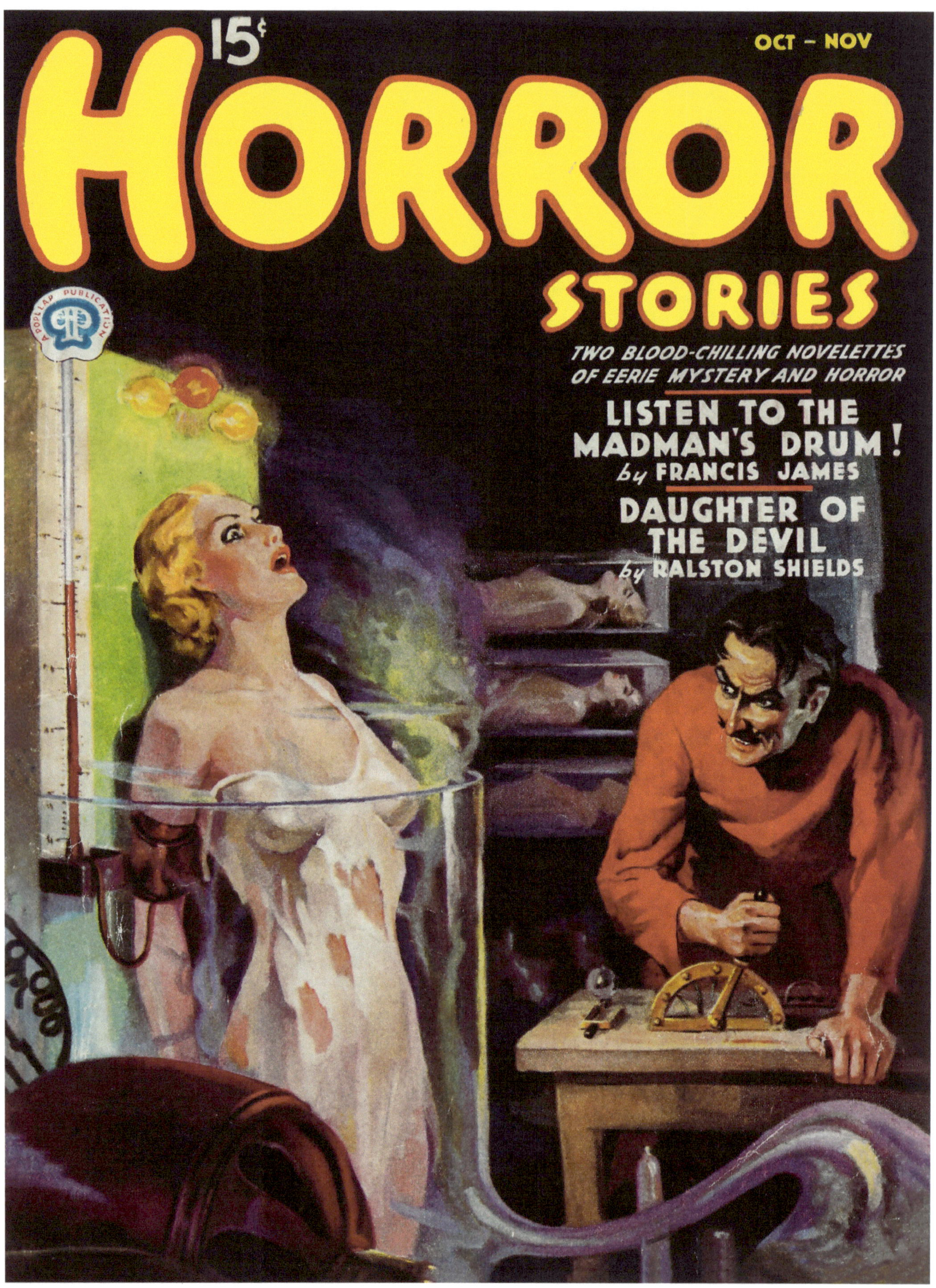

15¢
OCT – NOV
HORROR
STORIES
TWO BLOOD-CHILLING NOVELETTES
OF EERIE MYSTERY AND HORROR
LISTEN TO THE
MADMAN'S DRUM!
by FRANCIS JAMES
DAUGHTER OF
THE DEVIL
by RALSTON SHIELDS

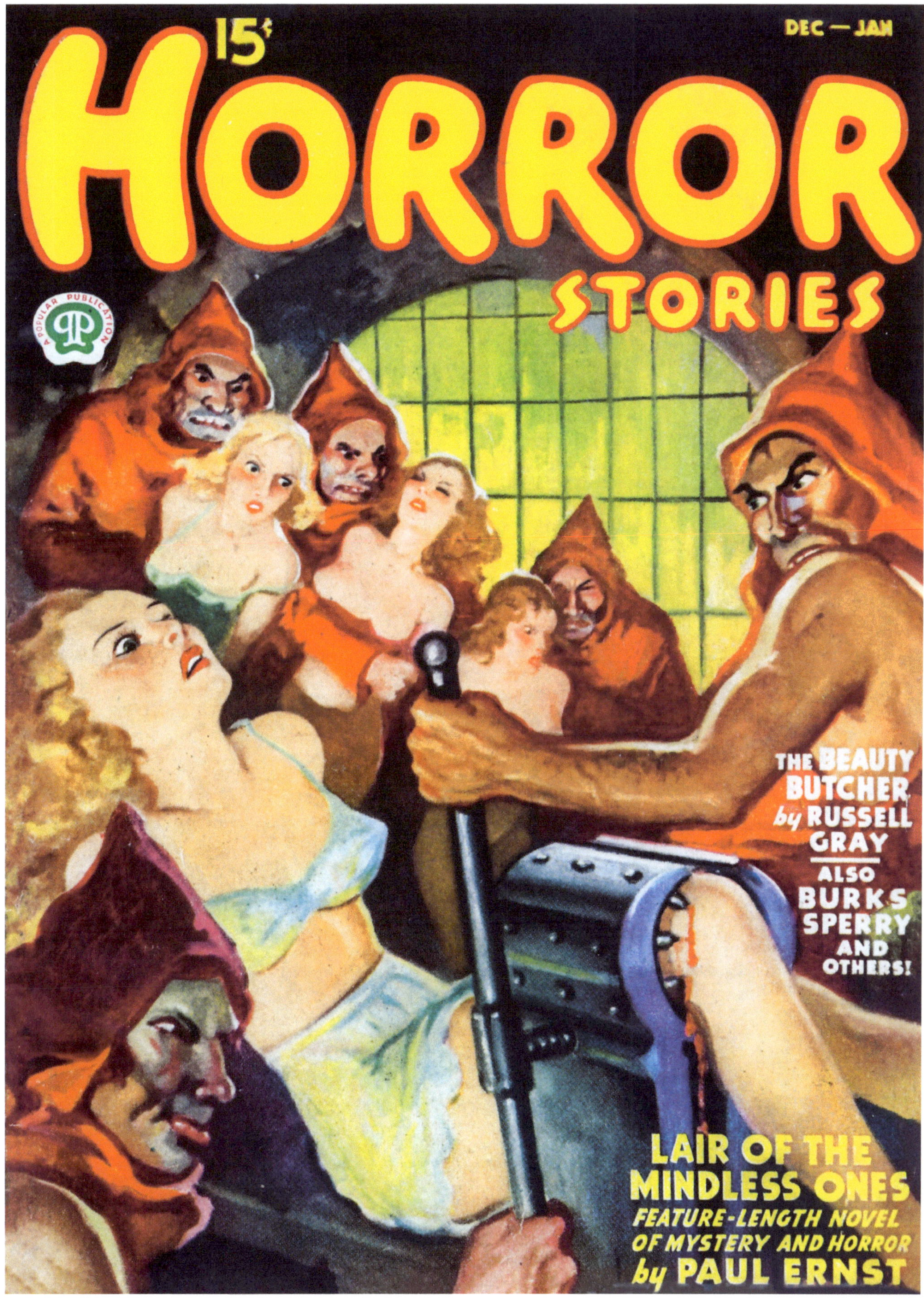

15¢
DEC — JAN
HORROR
STORIES
A POPULAR PUBLICATION
THE BEAUTY BUTCHER by RUSSELL GRAY
ALSO BURKS SPERRY AND OTHERS!
LAIR OF THE MINDLESS ONES
FEATURE-LENGTH NOVEL OF MYSTERY AND HORROR by PAUL ERNST

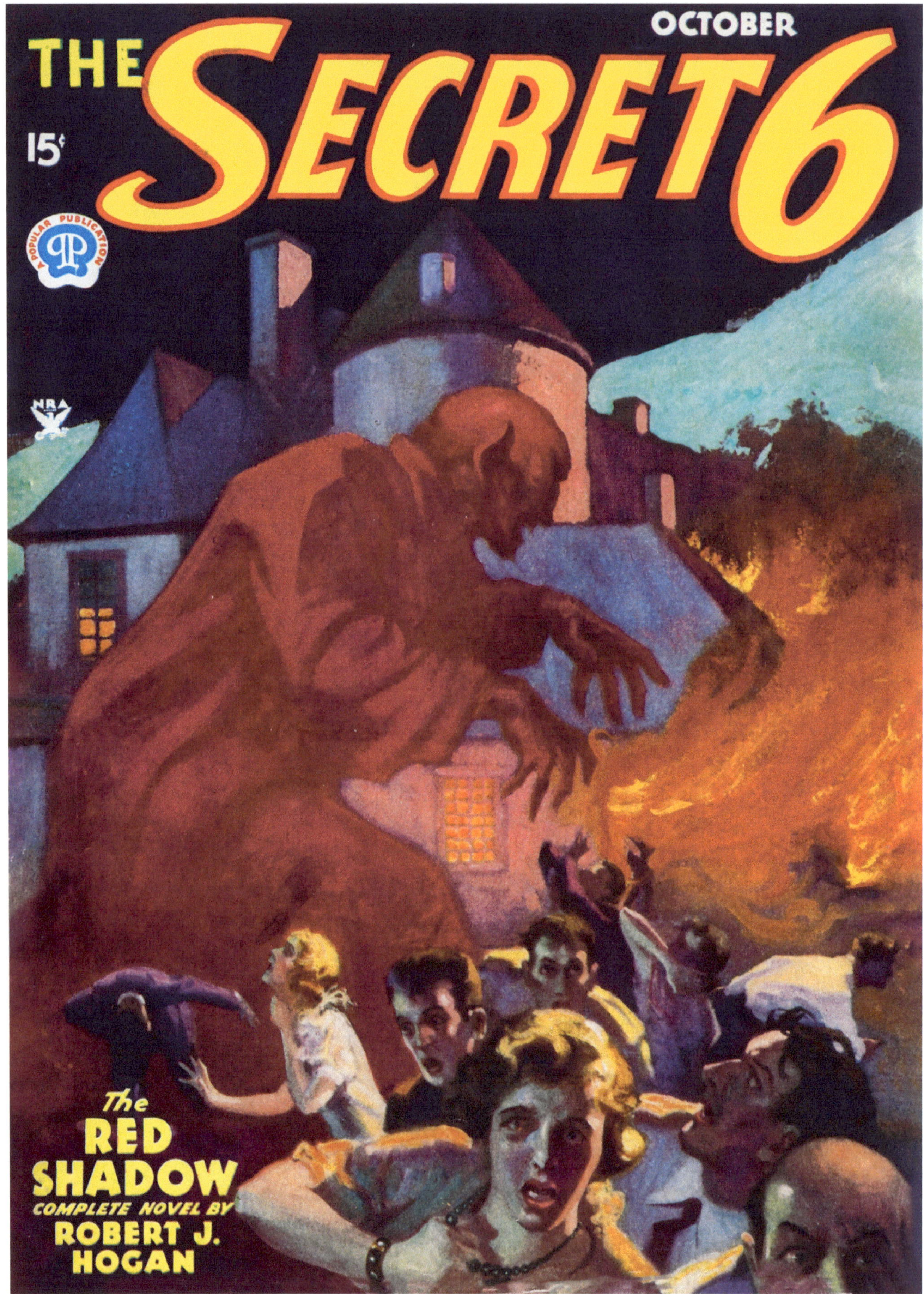

THE SECRET 6

OCTOBER 1934

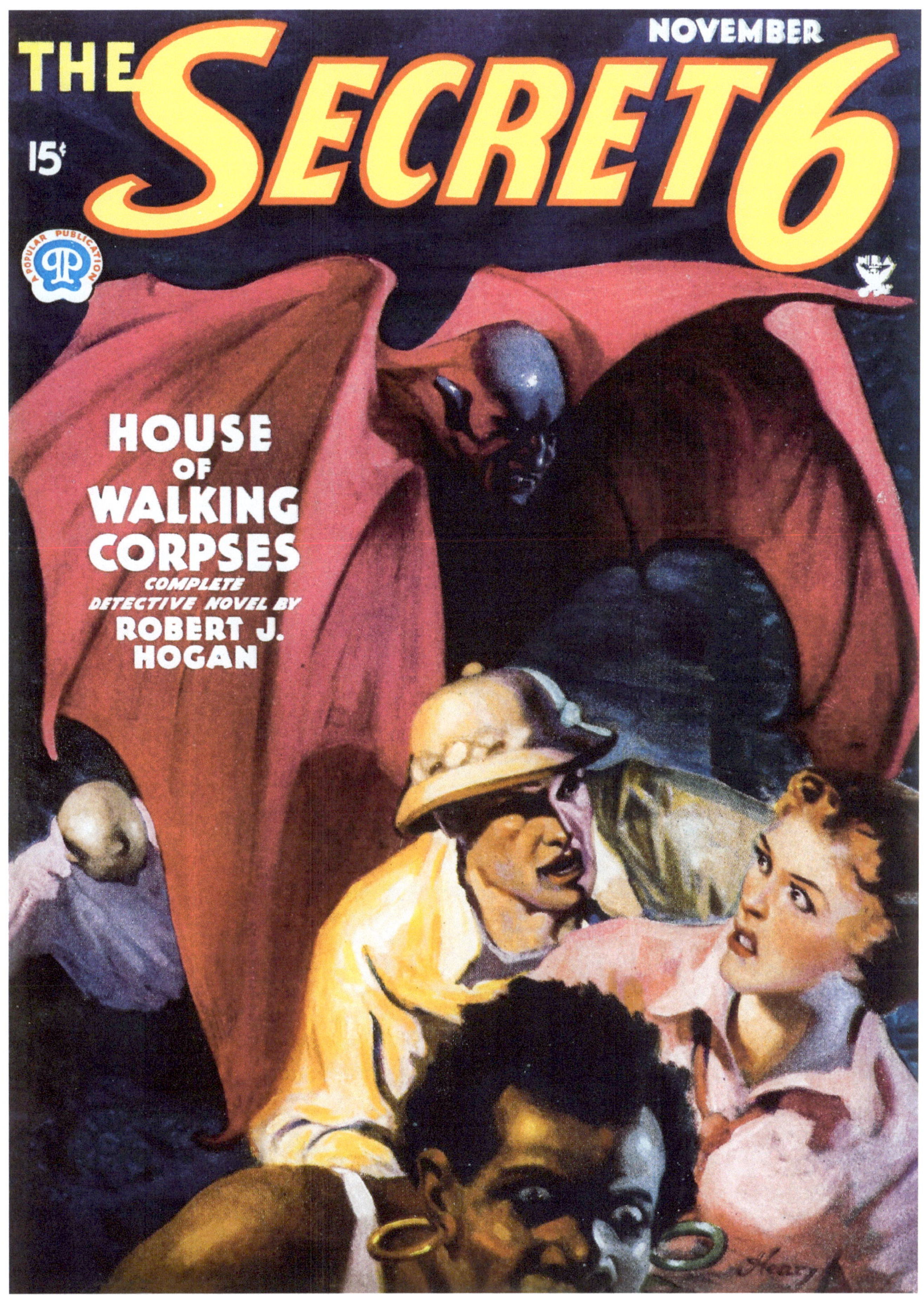

NOVEMBER
THE Secret 6
15¢
A POPULAR PUBLICATION
HOUSE OF WALKING CORPSES
COMPLETE DETECTIVE NOVEL BY
ROBERT J. HOGAN

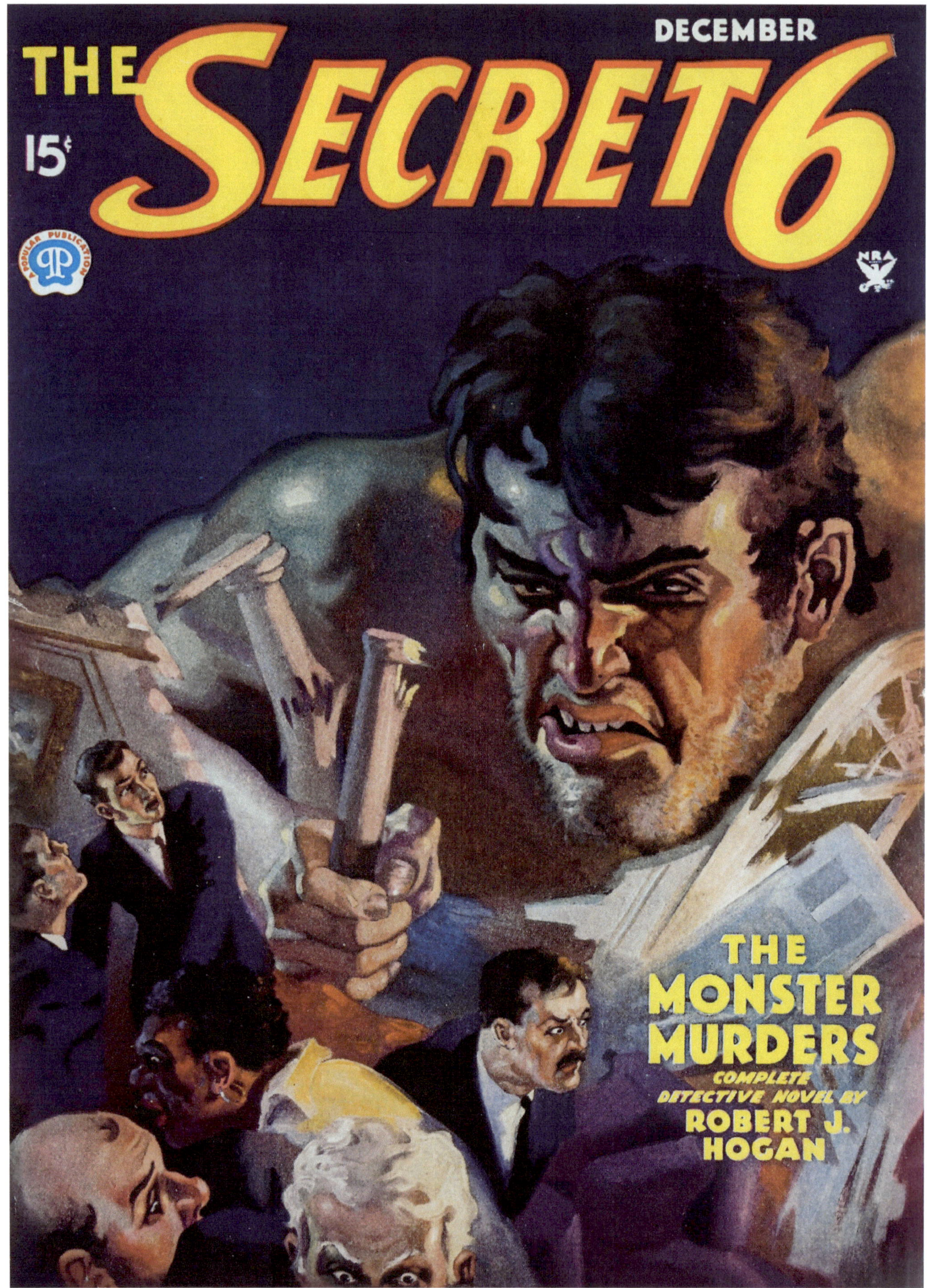

THE SECRET 6

DECEMBER 1934

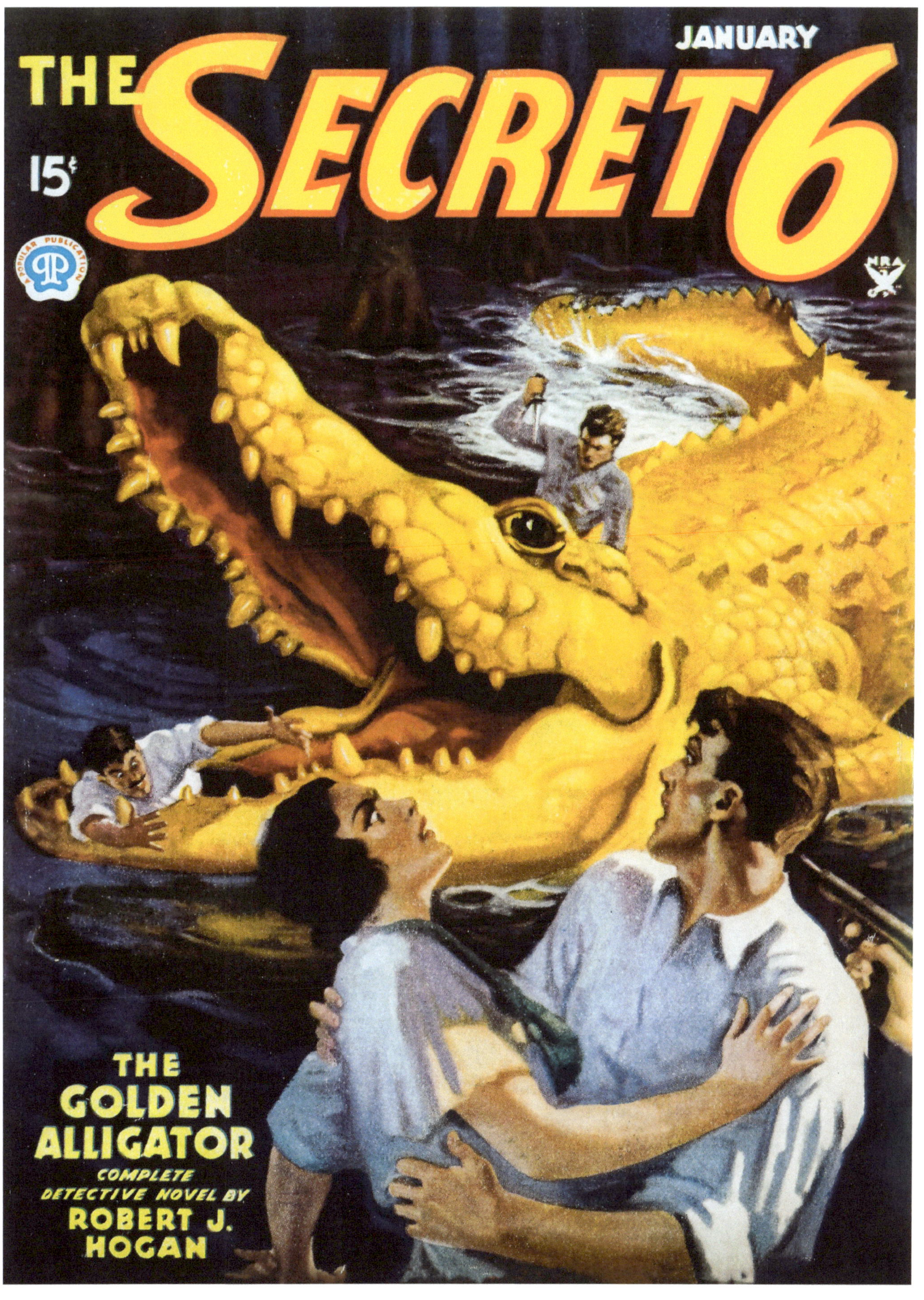

JANUARY
THE SECRET 6
15¢
A POPULAR PUBLICATION
NRA
THE
GOLDEN
ALLIGATOR
COMPLETE
DETECTIVE NOVEL BY
ROBERT J.
HOGAN

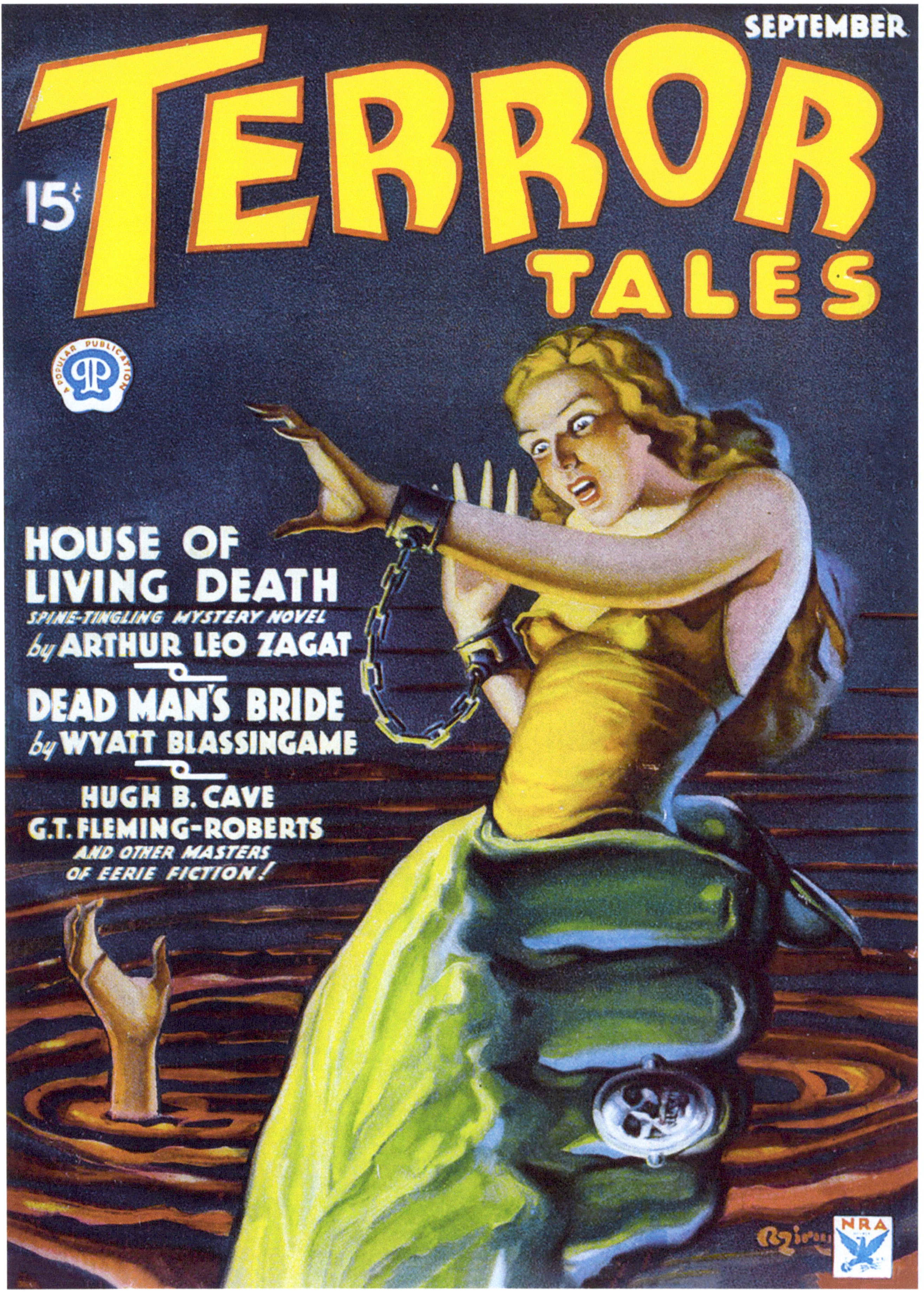

TERROR TALES

SEPTEMBER 1934

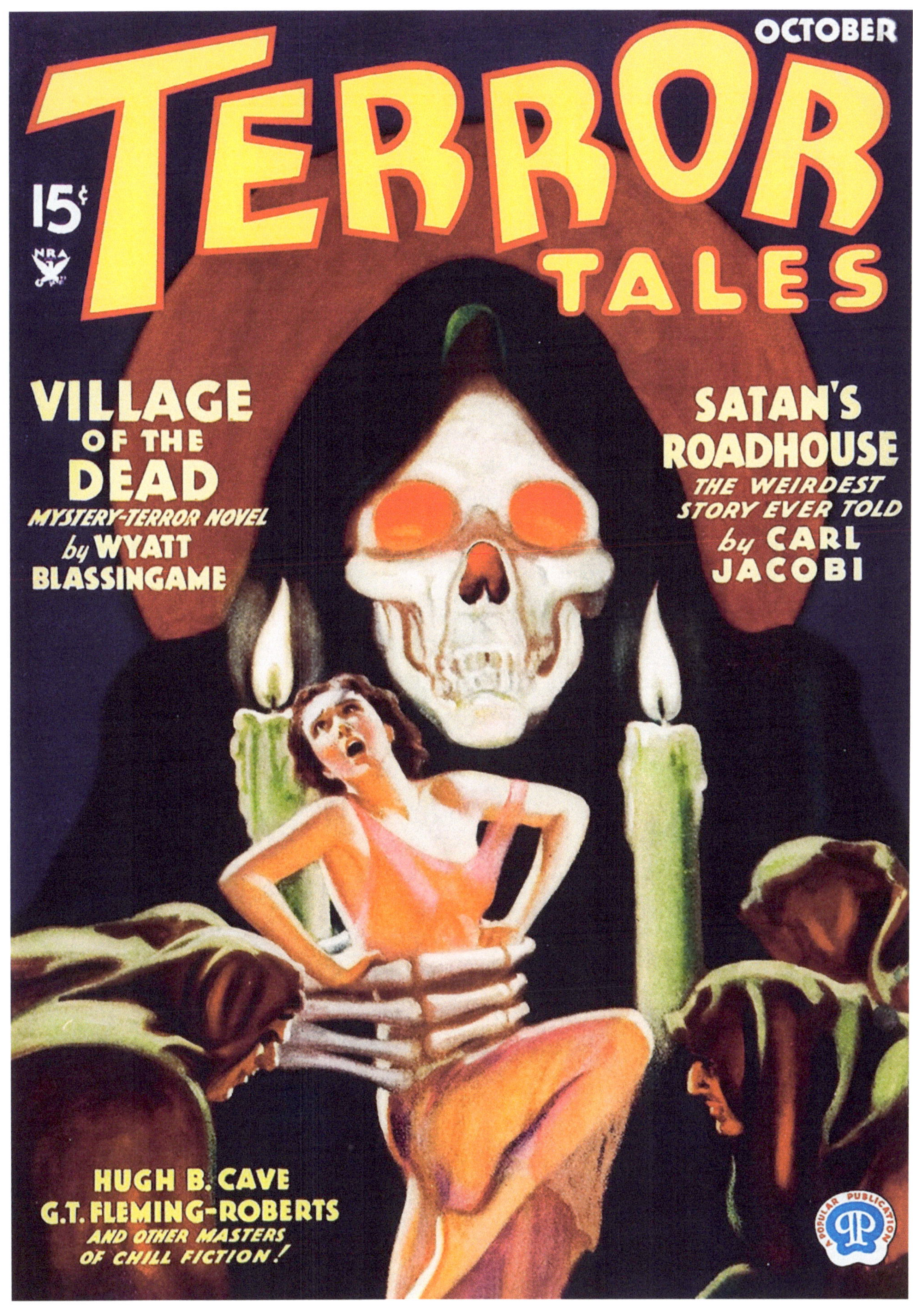

OCTOBER
15¢
TERROR TALES
VILLAGE OF THE DEAD
MYSTERY-TERROR NOVEL
by WYATT BLASSINGAME
SATAN'S ROADHOUSE
THE WEIRDEST STORY EVER TOLD
by CARL JACOBI
HUGH B. CAVE
G.T. FLEMING-ROBERTS
AND OTHER MASTERS OF CHILL FICTION!
A POPULAR PUBLICATION

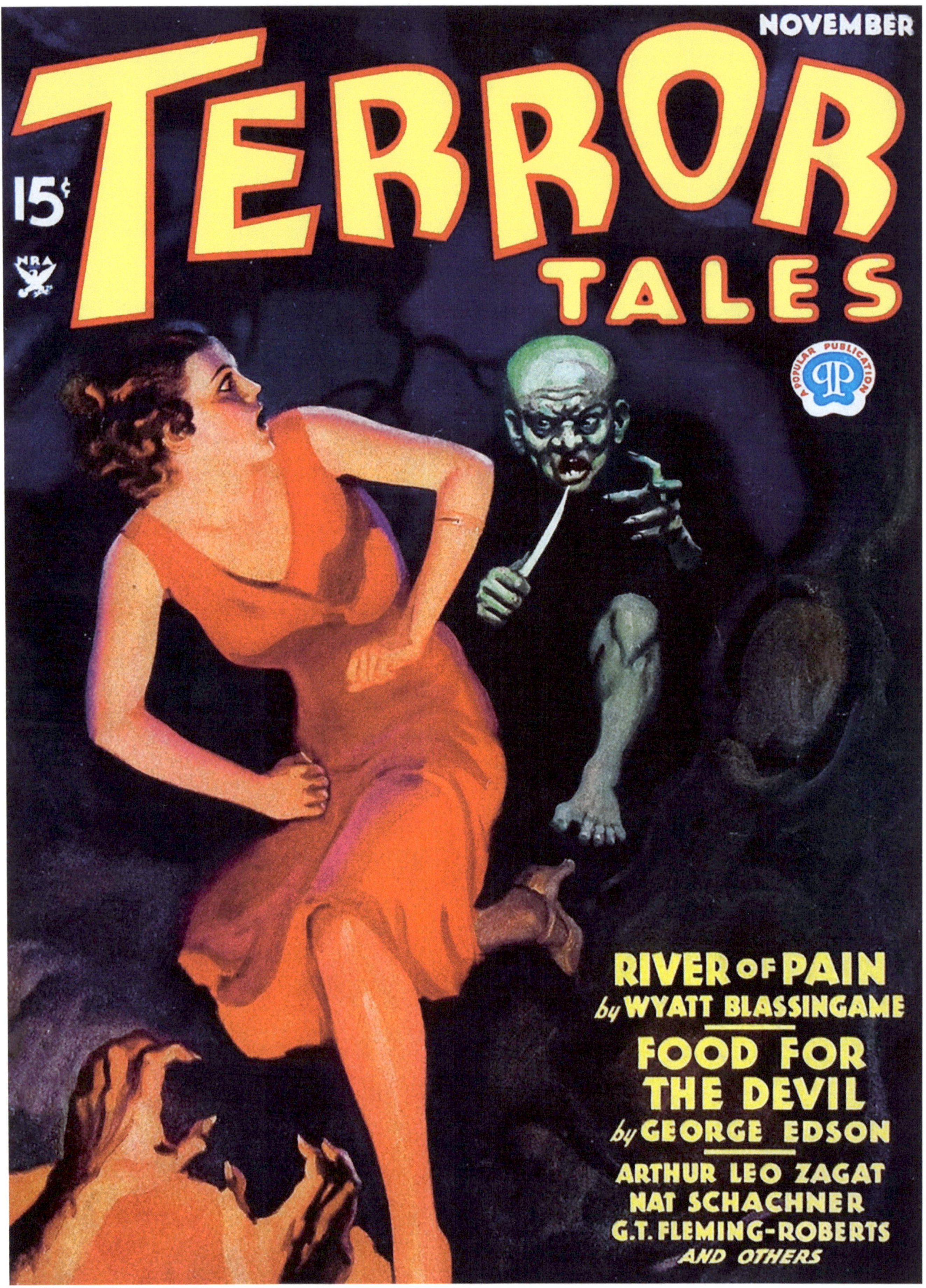
NOVEMBER
15¢
NRA
TERROR
TALES
A POPULAR PUBLICATION
PP
RIVER OF PAIN
by WYATT BLASSINGAME
FOOD FOR THE DEVIL
by GEORGE EDSON
ARTHUR LEO ZAGAT
NAT SCHACHNER
G.T. FLEMING-ROBERTS
AND OTHERS

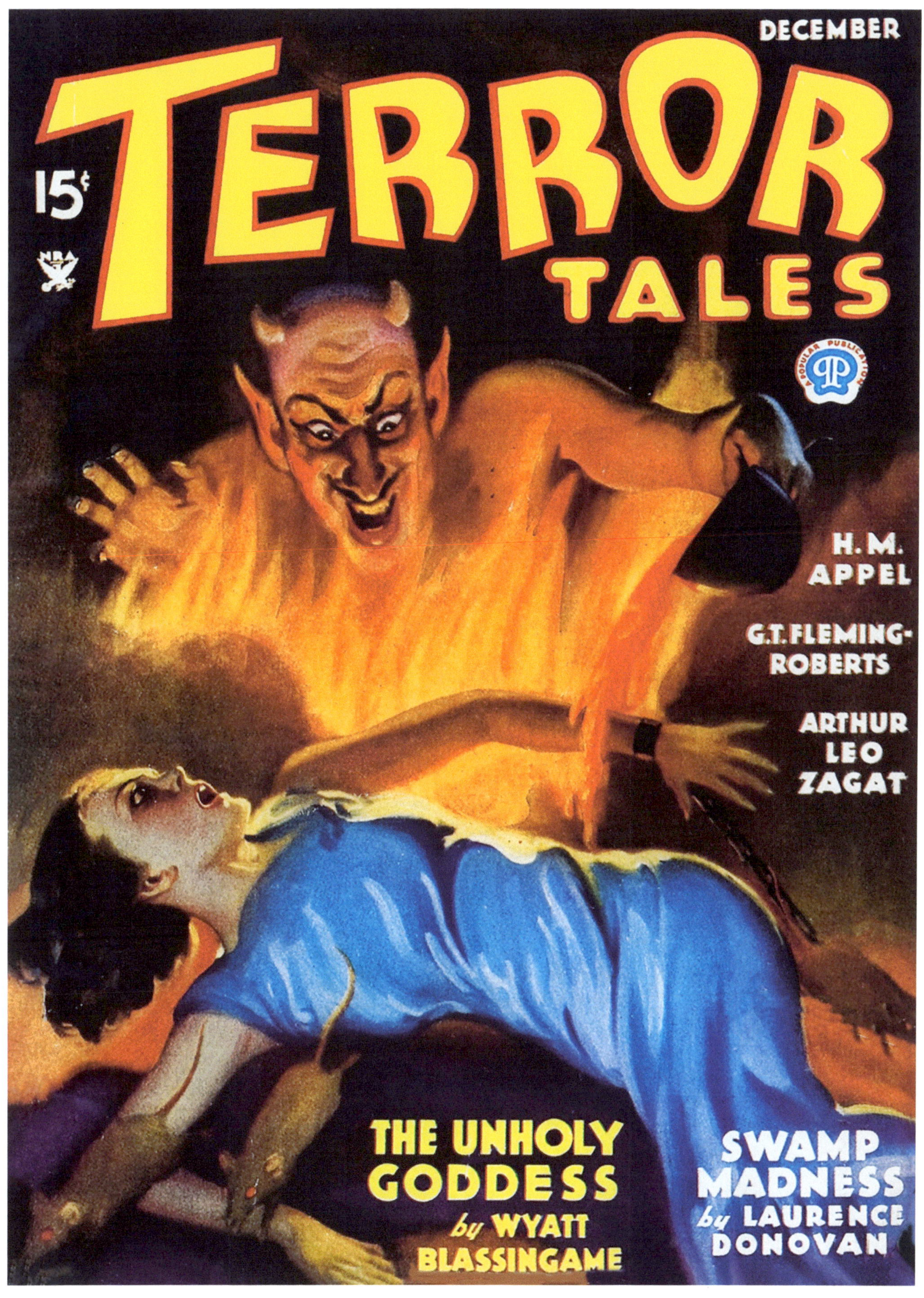

DECEMBER
15¢
TERROR TALES
H. M. APPEL
G.T. FLEMING-ROBERTS
ARTHUR LEO ZAGAT
THE UNHOLY GODDESS
by WYATT BLASSINGAME
SWAMP MADNESS by LAURENCE DONOVAN

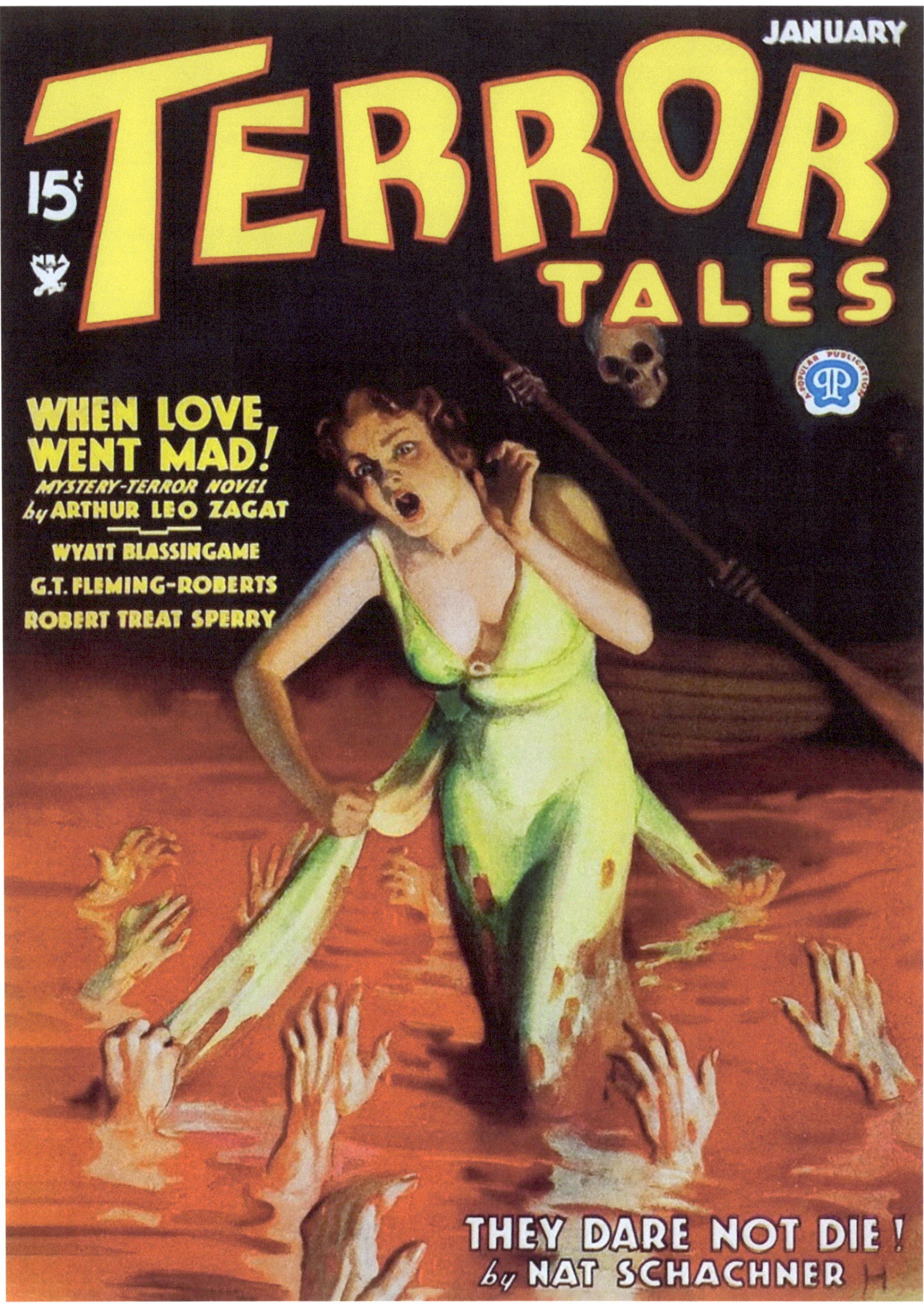

TERROR TALES

JANUARY 1935

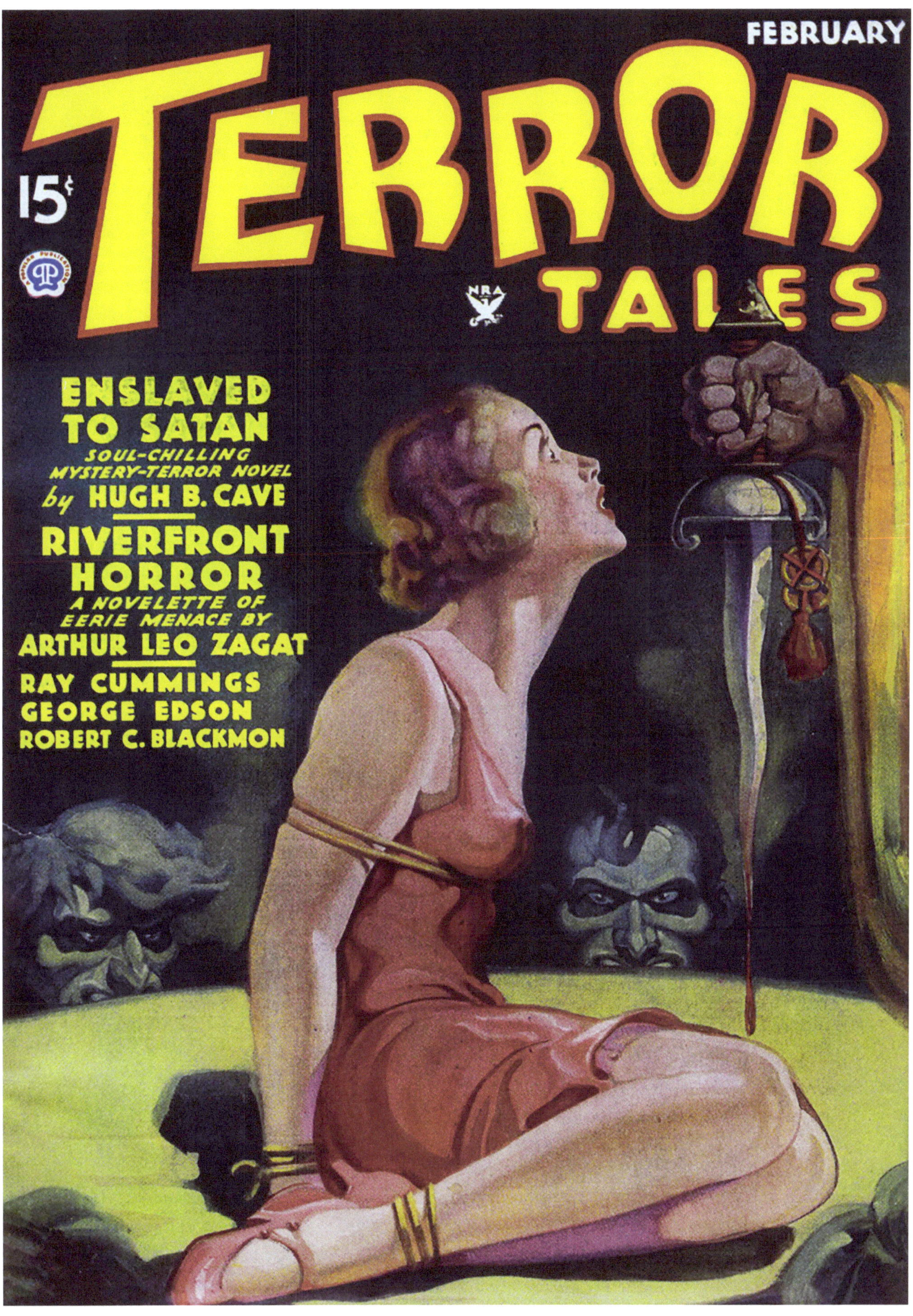

FEBRUARY
15¢
TERROR TALES
ENSLAVED TO SATAN
SOUL-CHILLING MYSTERY-TERROR NOVEL
by HUGH B. CAVE
RIVERFRONT HORROR
A NOVELETTE OF EERIE MENACE BY
ARTHUR LEO ZAGAT
RAY CUMMINGS
GEORGE EDSON
ROBERT C. BLACKMON

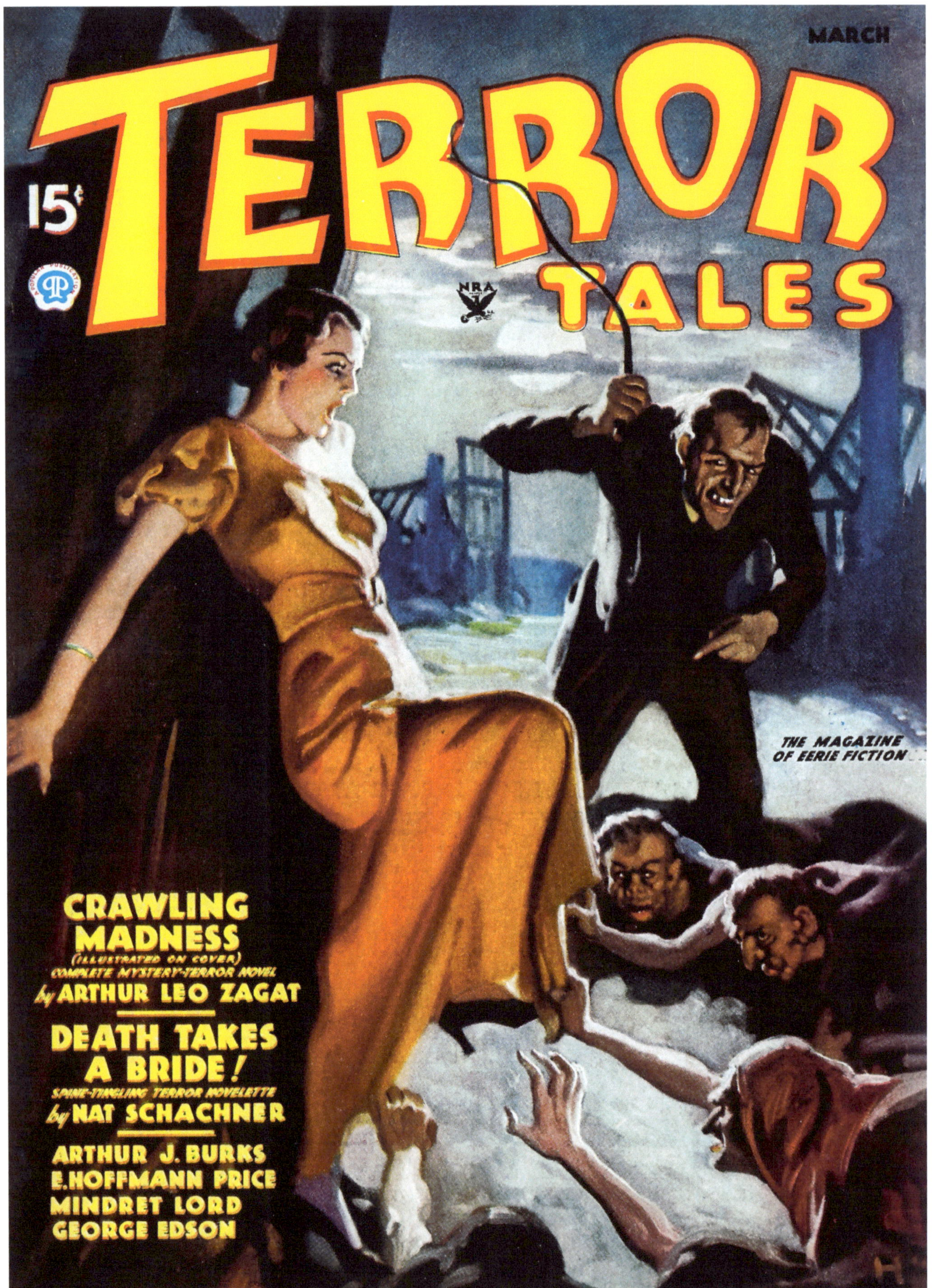

TERROR TALES

MARCH 1935

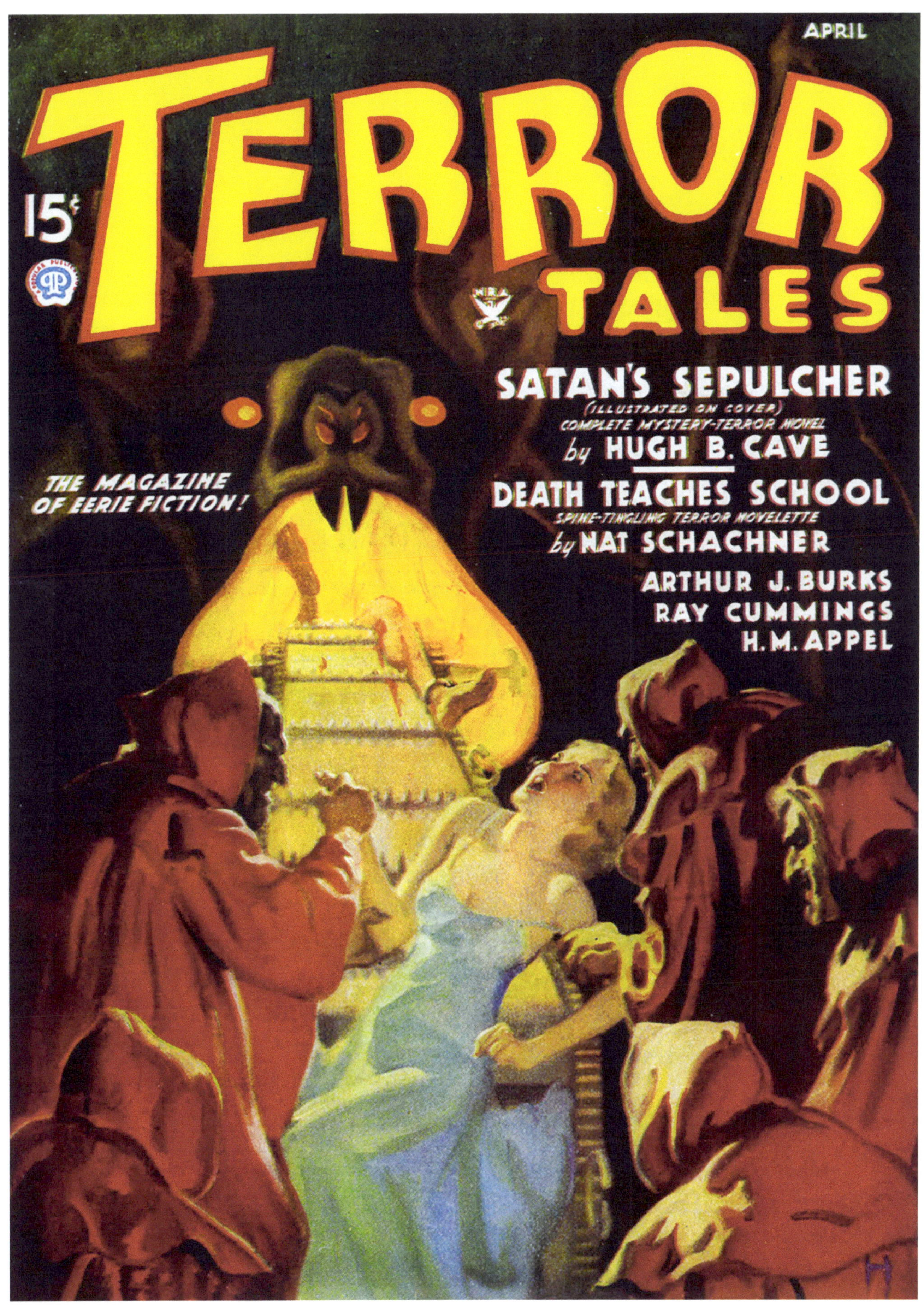

APRIL
15¢
TERROR TALES
THE MAGAZINE OF EERIE FICTION!
SATAN'S SEPULCHER
(ILLUSTRATED ON COVER)
COMPLETE MYSTERY-TERROR NOVEL
by HUGH B. CAVE
DEATH TEACHES SCHOOL
SPINE-TINGLING TERROR NOVELETTE
by NAT SCHACHNER
ARTHUR J. BURKS
RAY CUMMINGS
H. M. APPEL

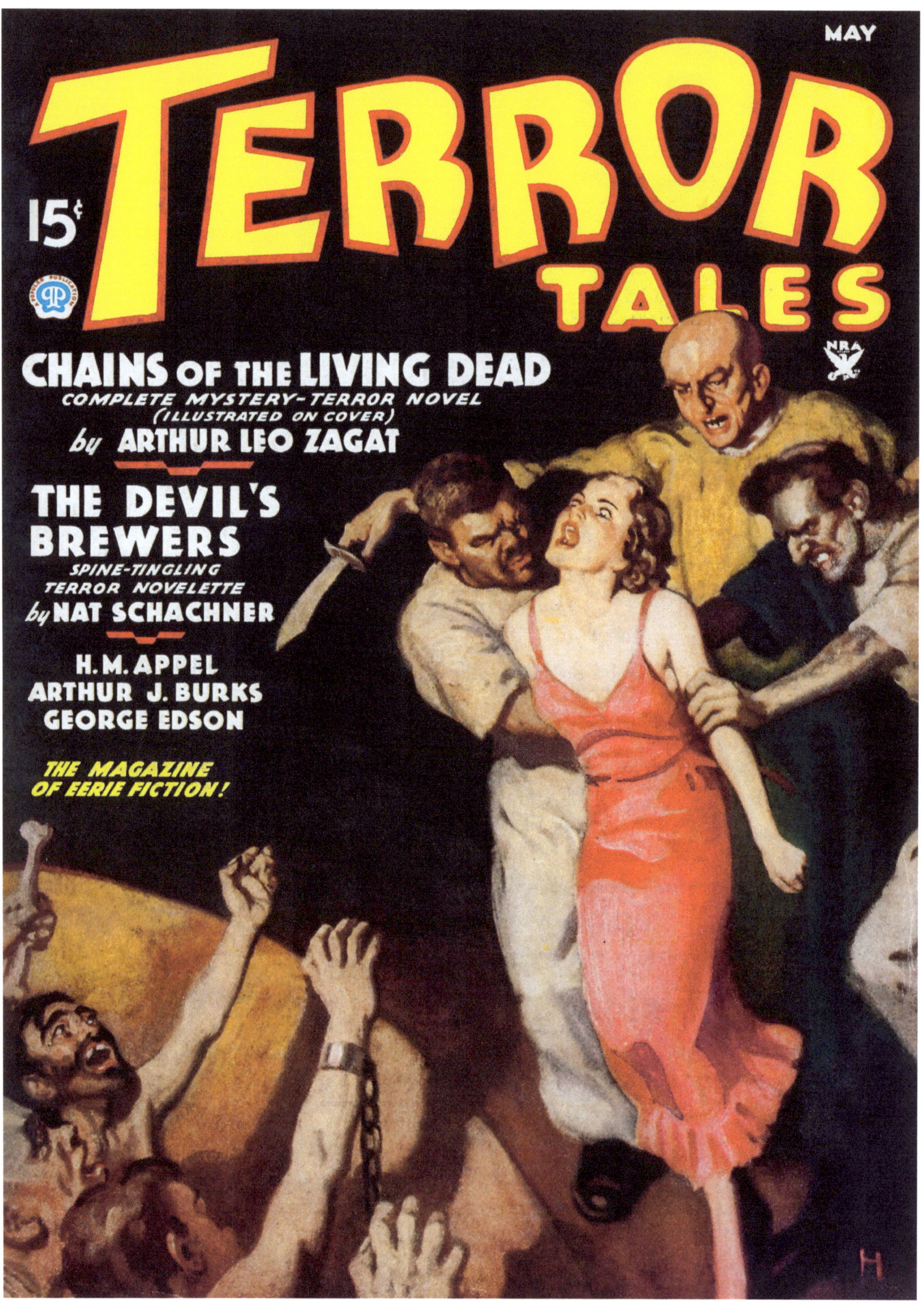

TERROR TALES

MAY 1935

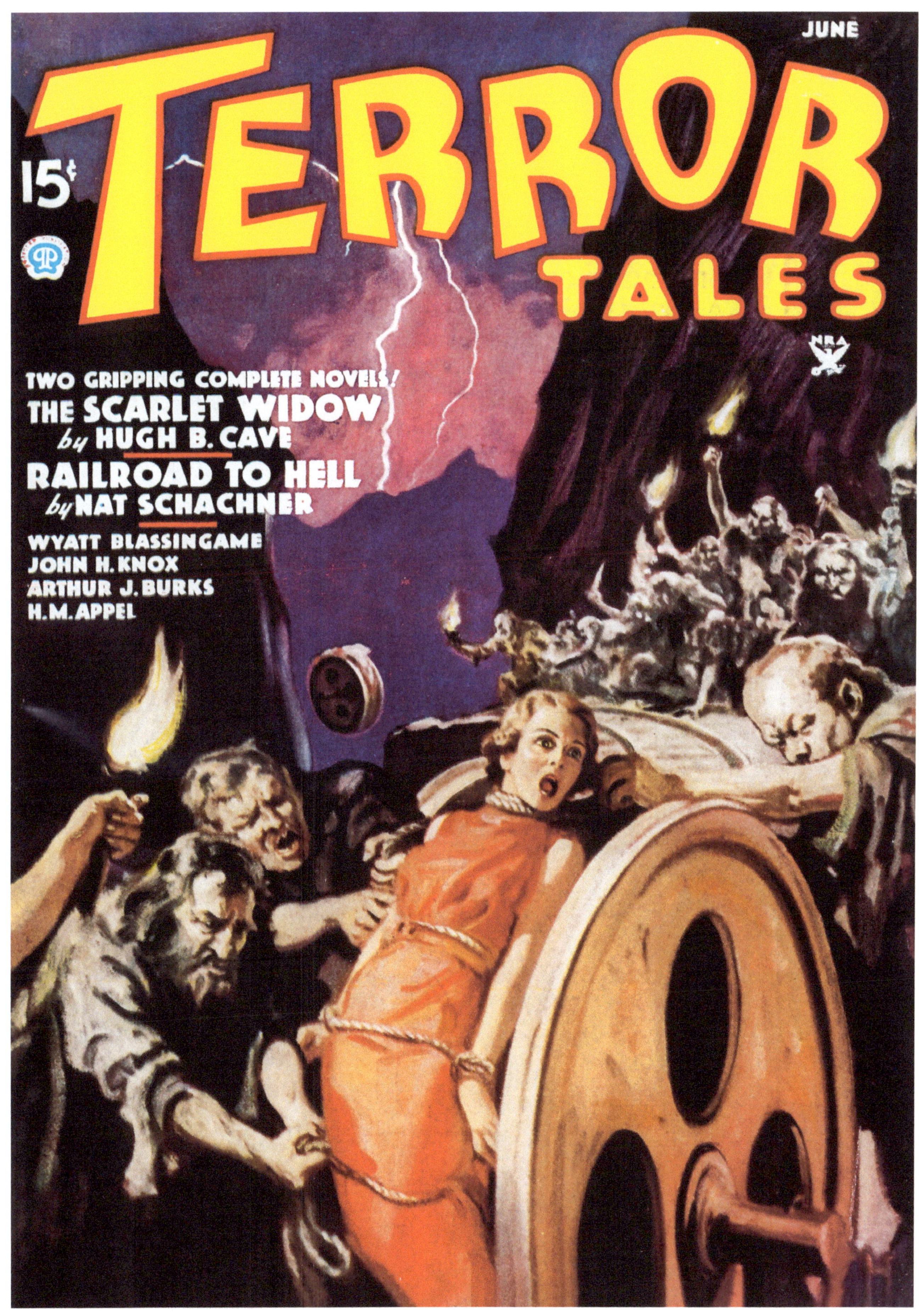

JUNE
15¢
TERROR
TALES
TWO GRIPPING COMPLETE NOVELS!
THE SCARLET WIDOW
by HUGH B. CAVE
RAILROAD TO HELL
by NAT SCHACHNER
WYATT BLASSINGAME
JOHN H. KNOX
ARTHUR J. BURKS
H. M. APPEL

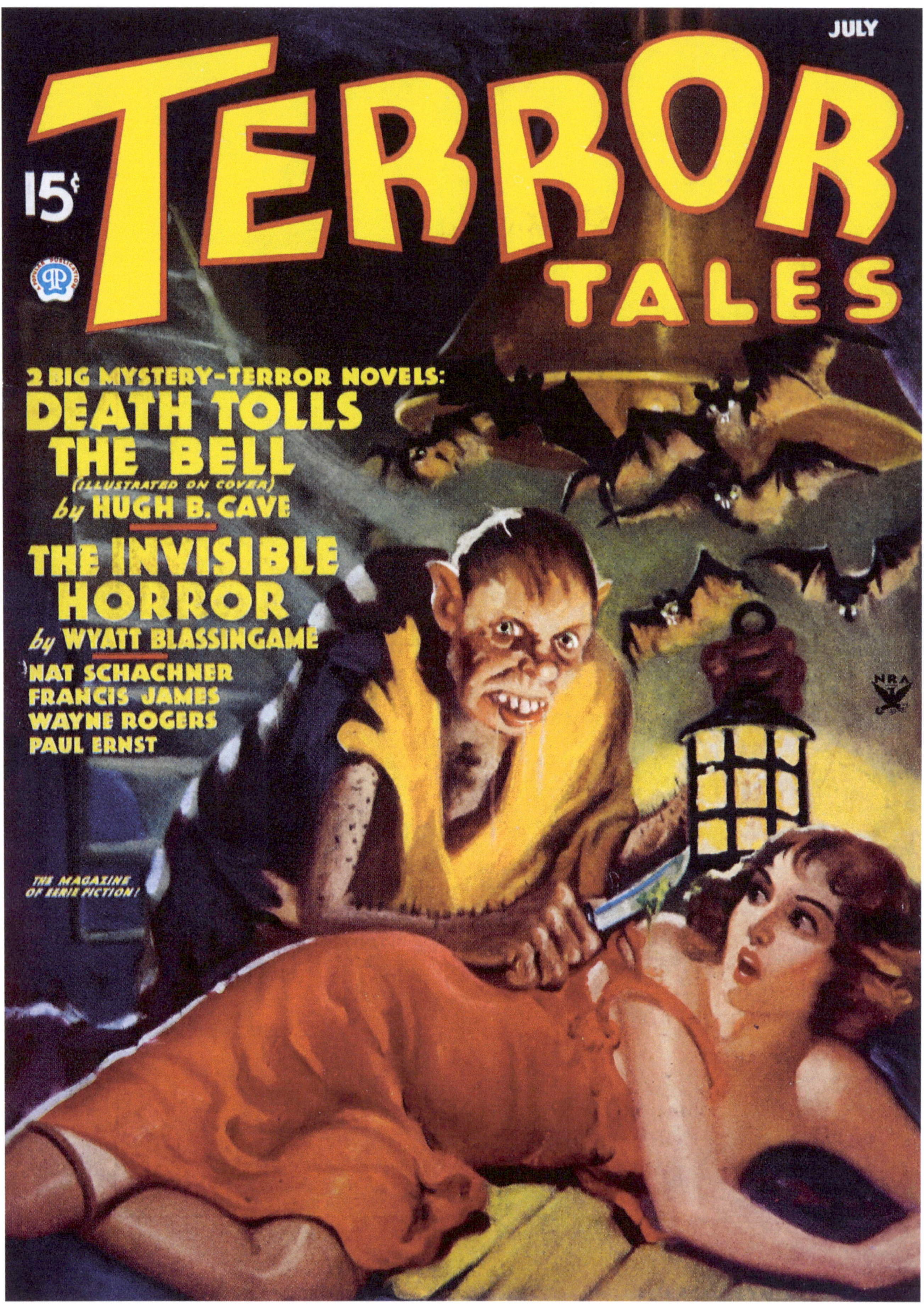

JULY
TERROR
TALES
15¢
2 BIG MYSTERY-TERROR NOVELS:
DEATH TOLLS
THE BELL
(ILLUSTRATED ON COVER)
by HUGH B. CAVE
THE INVISIBLE
HORROR
by WYATT BLASSINGAME
NAT SCHACHNER
FRANCIS JAMES
WAYNE ROGERS
PAUL ERNST
THE MAGAZINE
OF EERIE FICTION!
NRA

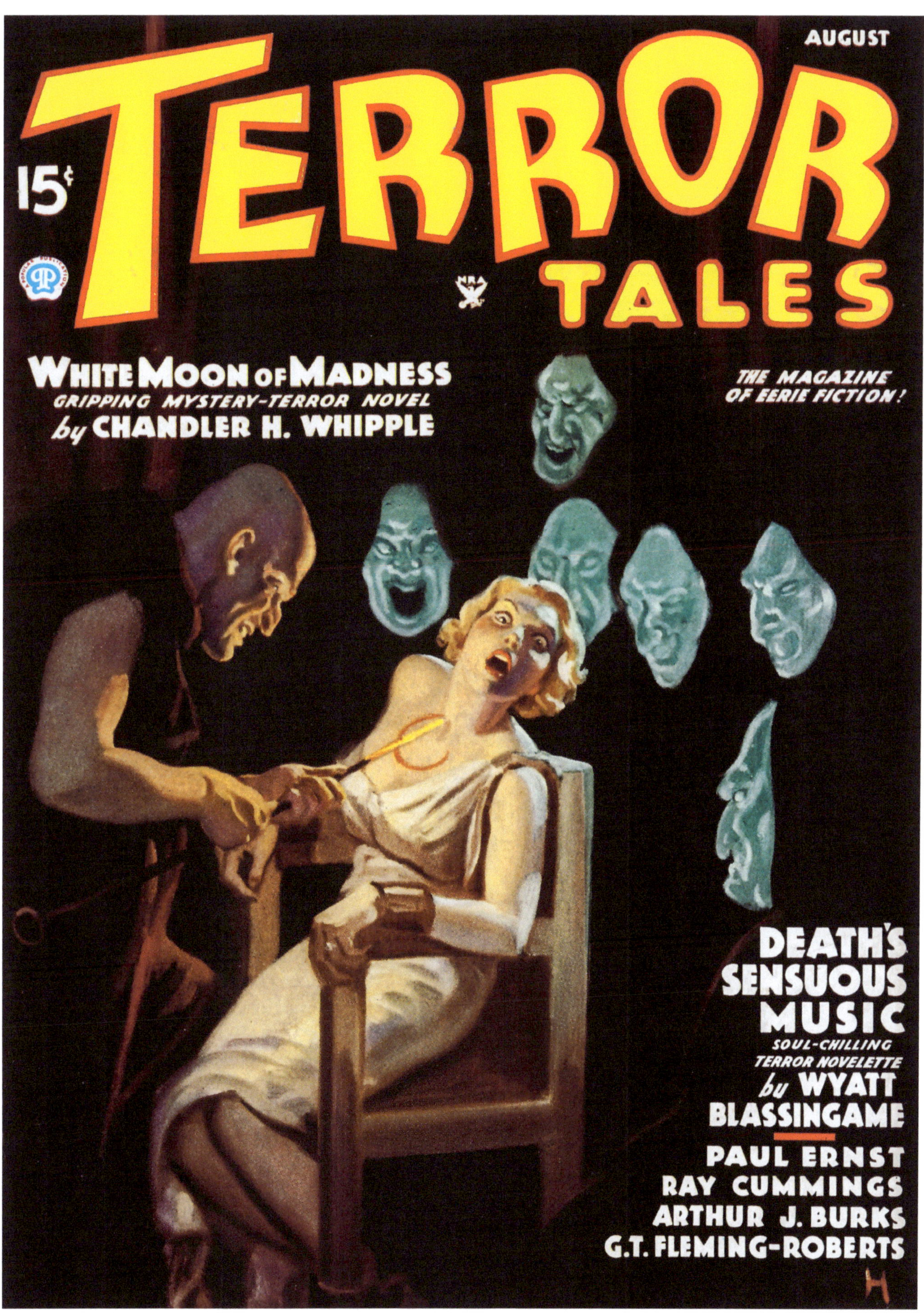

AUGUST
15¢
TERROR TALES
WHITE MOON OF MADNESS
GRIPPING MYSTERY-TERROR NOVEL
by CHANDLER H. WHIPPLE
THE MAGAZINE OF EERIE FICTION!
DEATH'S SENSUOUS MUSIC
SOUL-CHILLING TERROR NOVELETTE
by WYATT BLASSINGAME
PAUL ERNST
RAY CUMMINGS
ARTHUR J. BURKS
G.T. FLEMING-ROBERTS

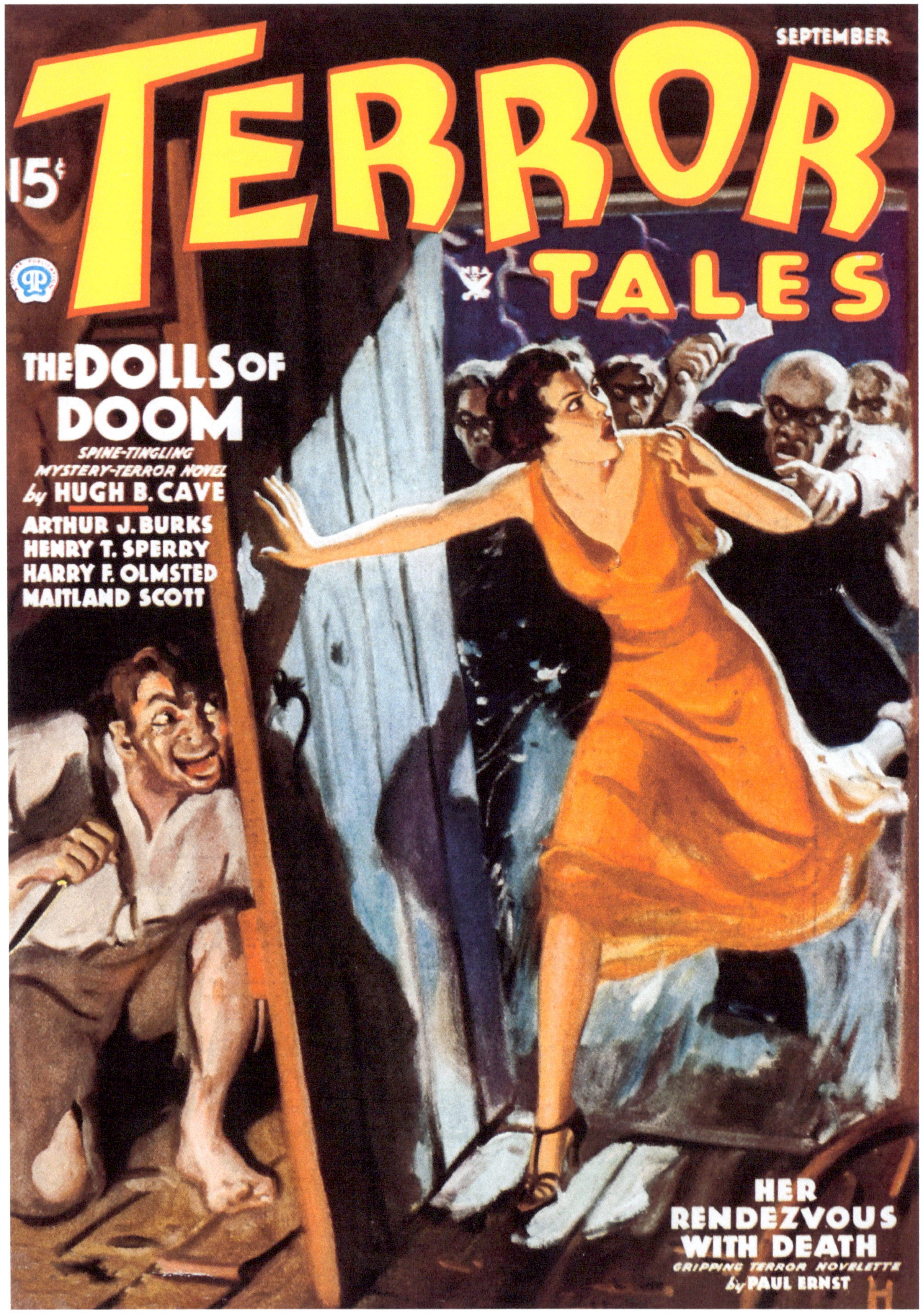

TERROR TALES

SEPTEMBER 1935

OCTOBER
15¢
TERROR
TALES
THE MAGAZINE OF EERIE FICTION!
CAVE
ERNST
MIDDLETON
WHIPPLE
DUNCAN
SATAN'S SCALPEL
GRIPPING MYSTERY-TERROR NOVEL
by ARTHUR LEO ZAGAT

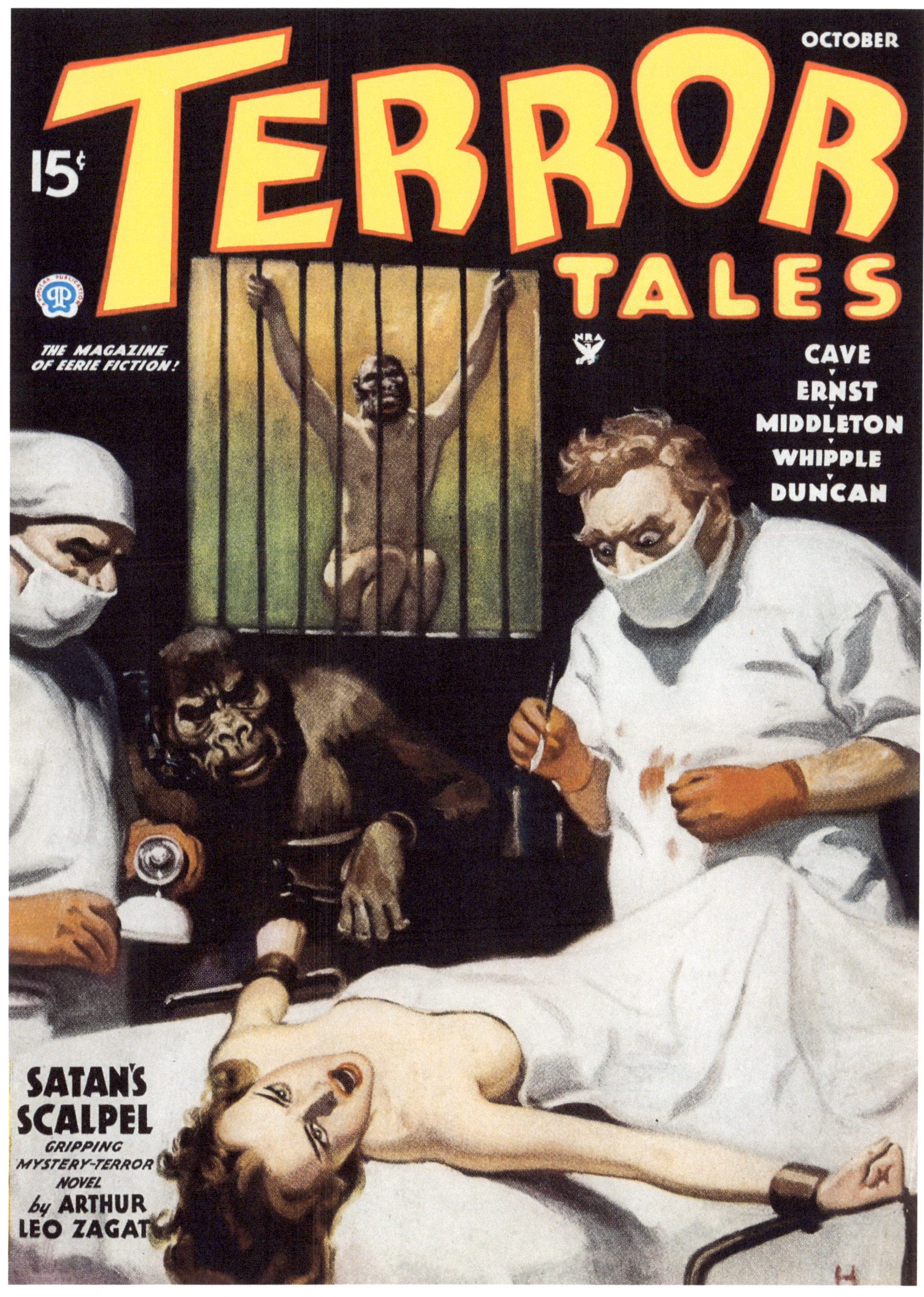

79

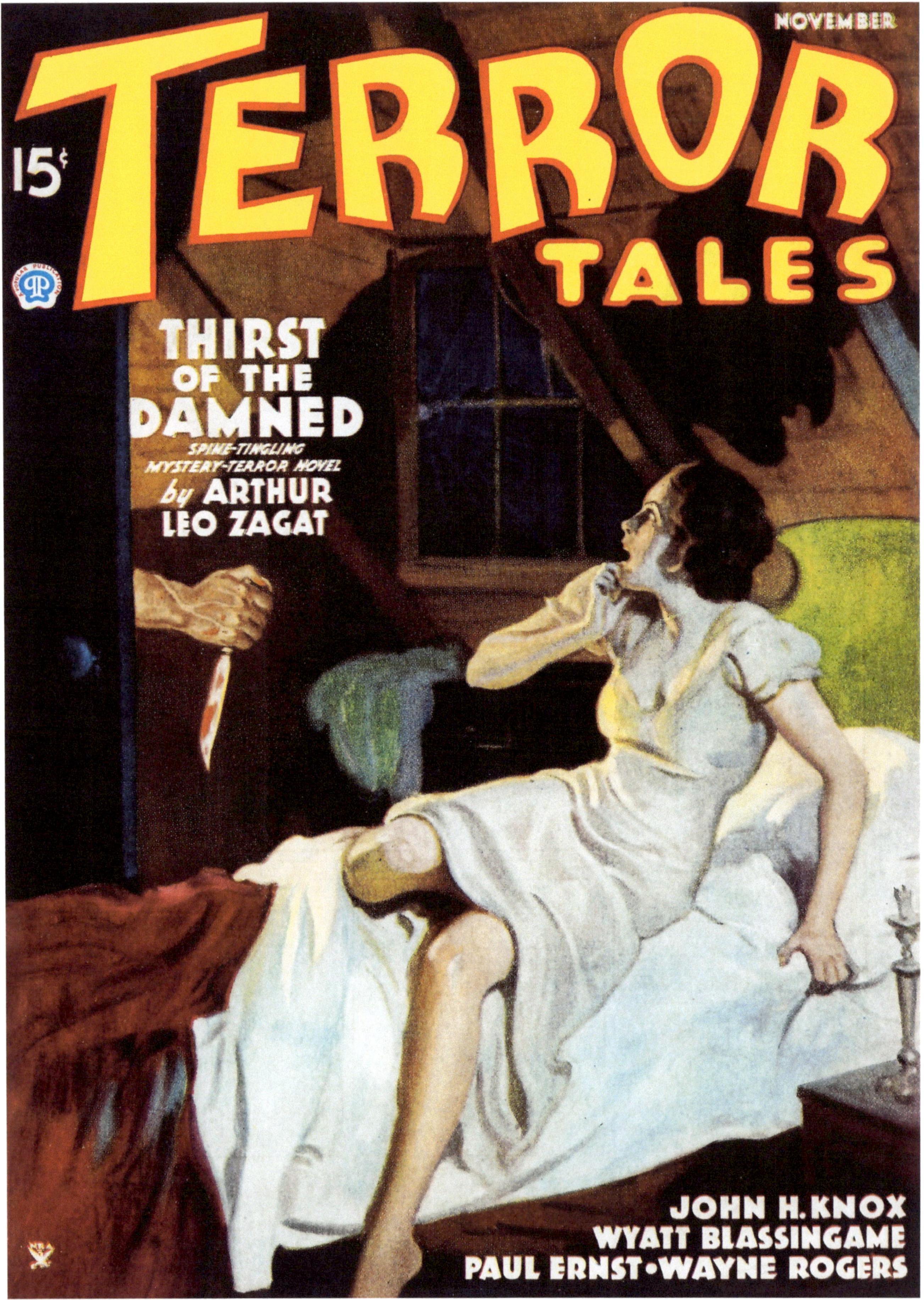

NOVEMBER
15¢
TERROR TALES
THIRST OF THE DAMNED
SPINE-TINGLING MYSTERY-TERROR NOVEL
by ARTHUR LEO ZAGAT
JOHN H. KNOX
WYATT BLASSINGAME
PAUL ERNST • WAYNE ROGERS

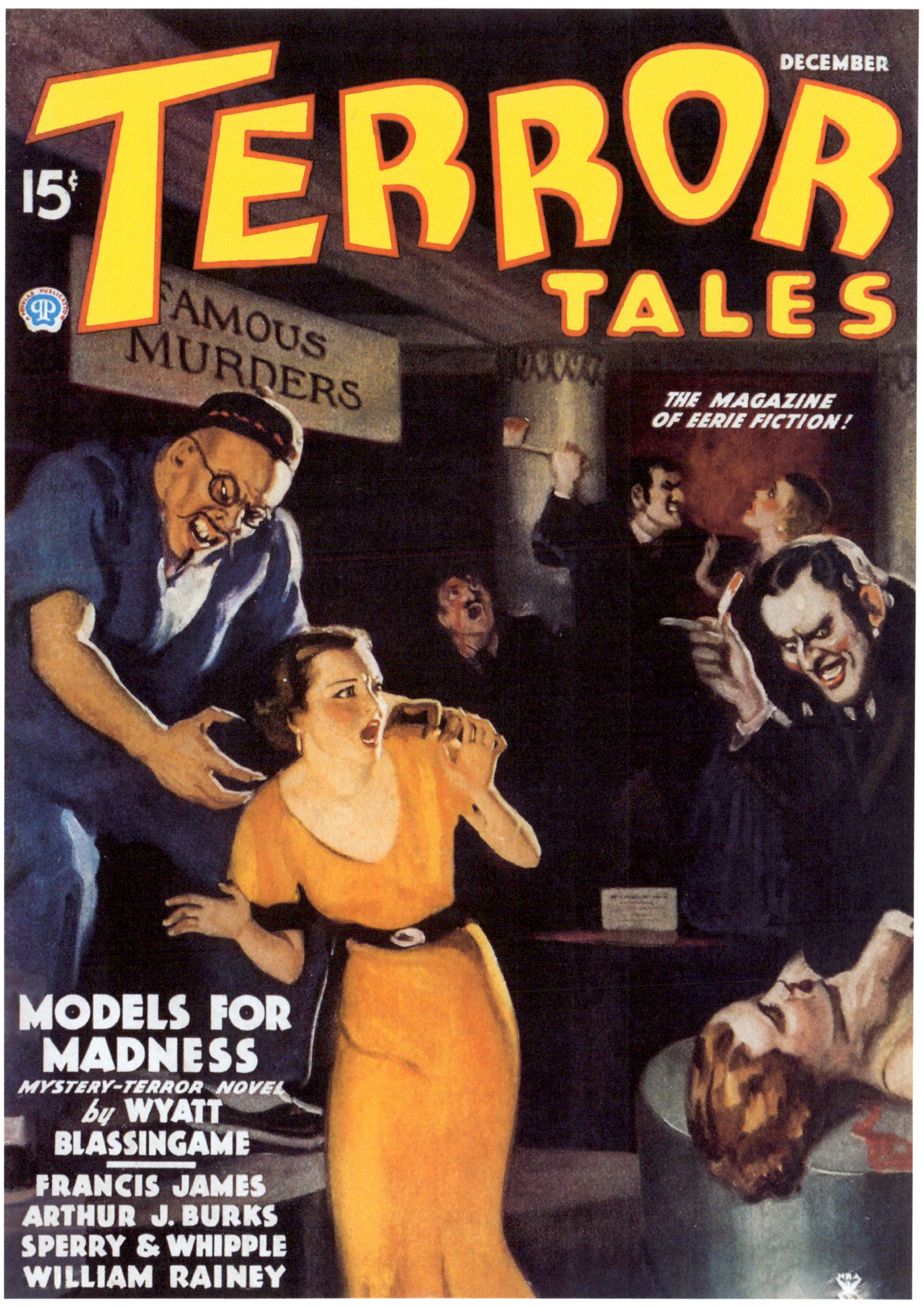

DECEMBER
15¢
TERROR
TALES
FAMOUS MURDERS
THE MAGAZINE OF EERIE FICTION!
MODELS FOR MADNESS
MYSTERY-TERROR NOVEL
by WYATT BLASSINGAME
FRANCIS JAMES
ARTHUR J. BURKS
SPERRY & WHIPPLE
WILLIAM RAINEY

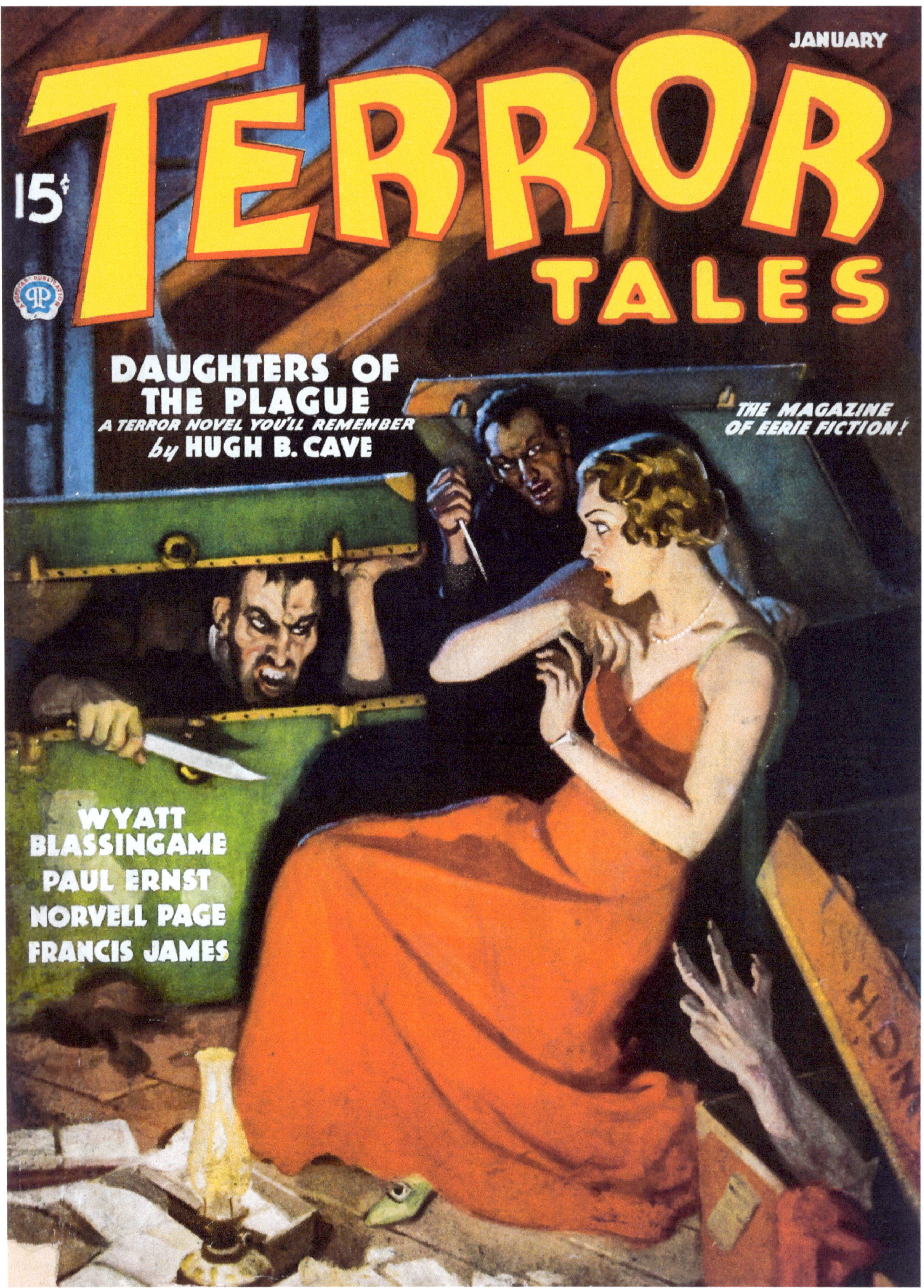

JANUARY
15¢
TERROR
TALES
DAUGHTERS OF THE PLAGUE
A TERROR NOVEL YOU'LL REMEMBER
by HUGH B. CAVE
THE MAGAZINE OF EERIE FICTION!
WYATT BLASSINGAME
PAUL ERNST
NORVELL PAGE
FRANCIS JAMES

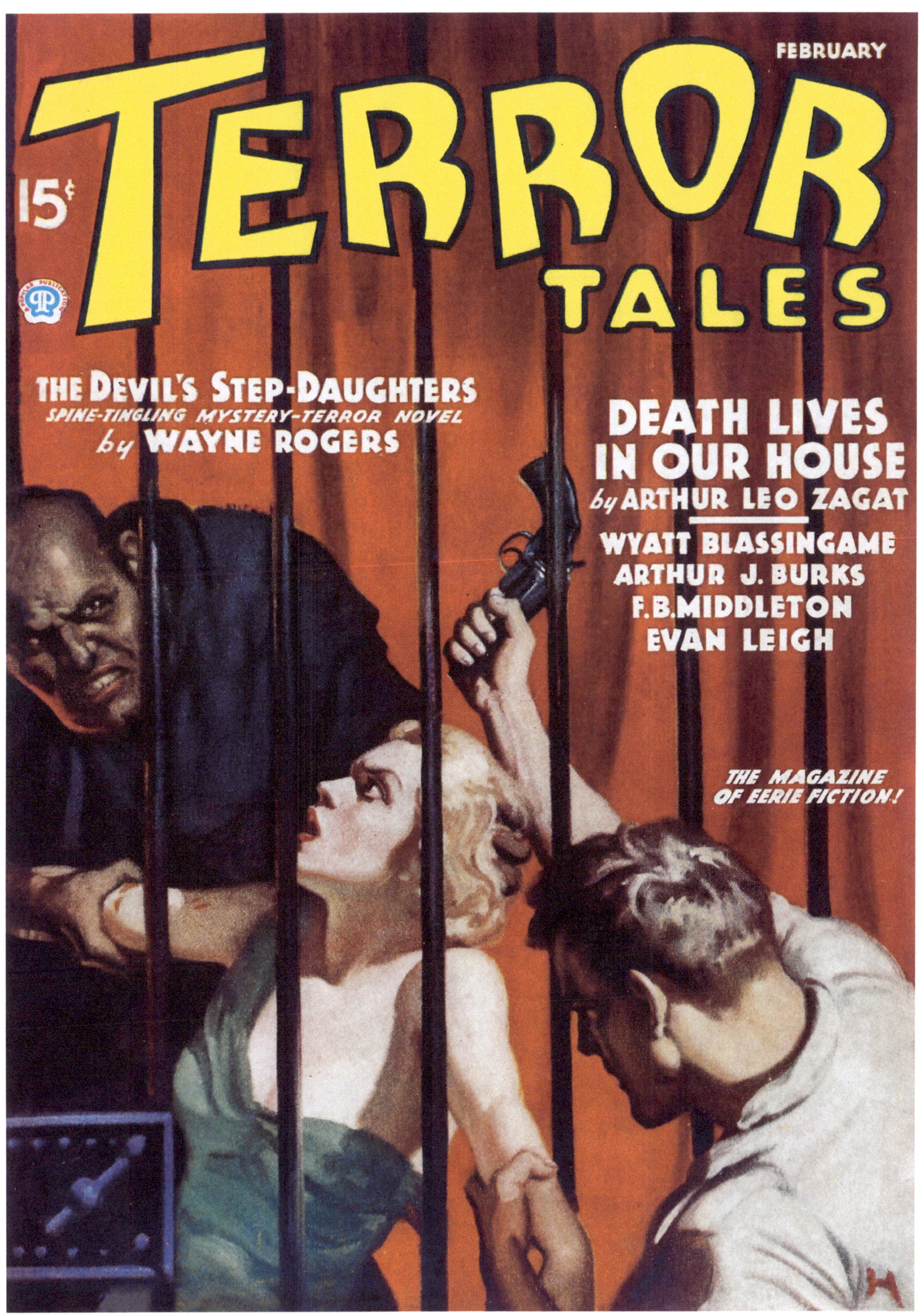

FEBRUARY
15¢
TERROR
TALES
THE DEVIL'S STEP-DAUGHTERS
SPINE-TINGLING MYSTERY-TERROR NOVEL
by WAYNE ROGERS
DEATH LIVES
IN OUR HOUSE
by ARTHUR LEO ZAGAT
WYATT BLASSINGAME
ARTHUR J. BURKS
F. B. MIDDLETON
EVAN LEIGH
THE MAGAZINE
OF EERIE FICTION!

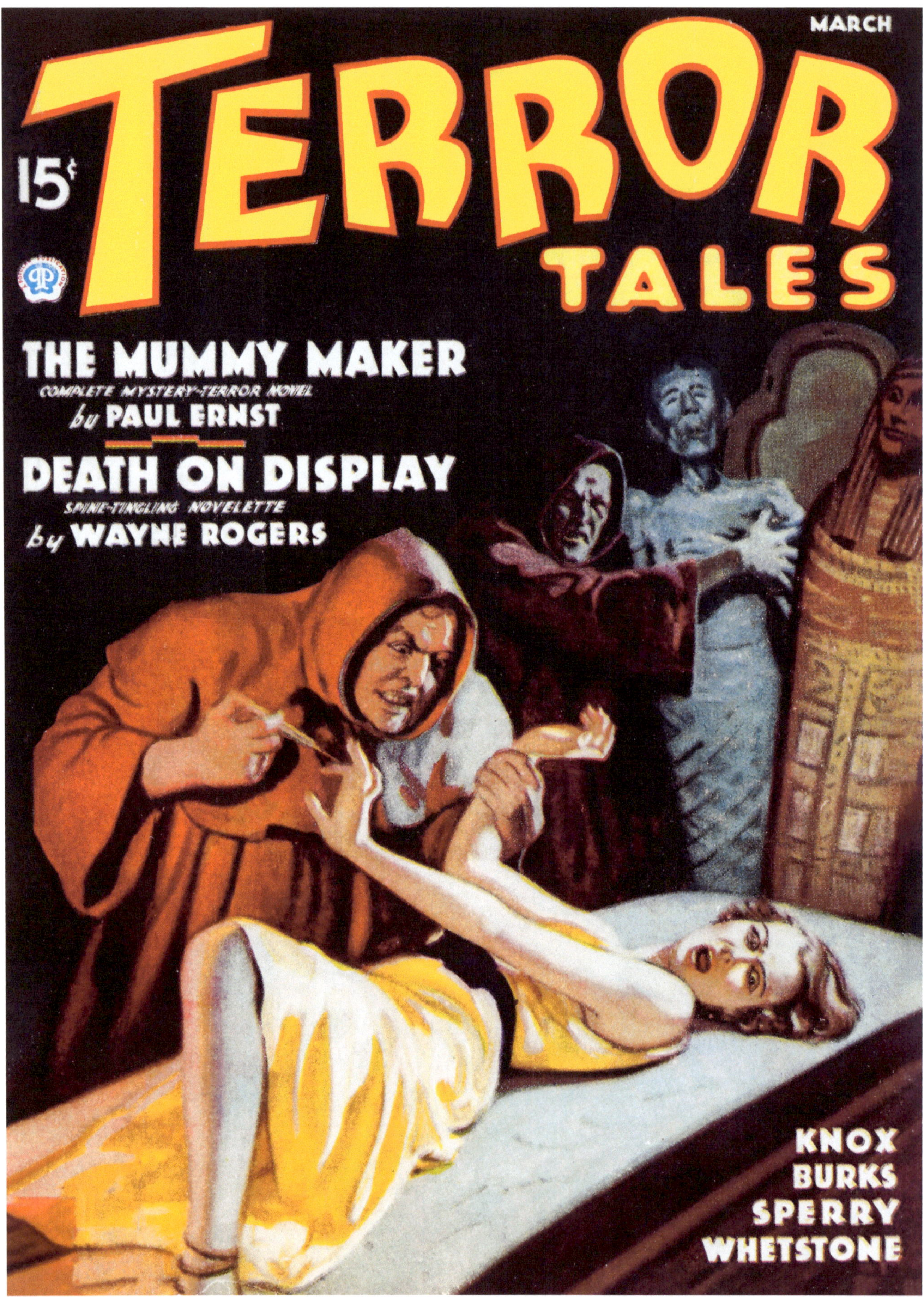

TERROR TALES

MARCH 1936

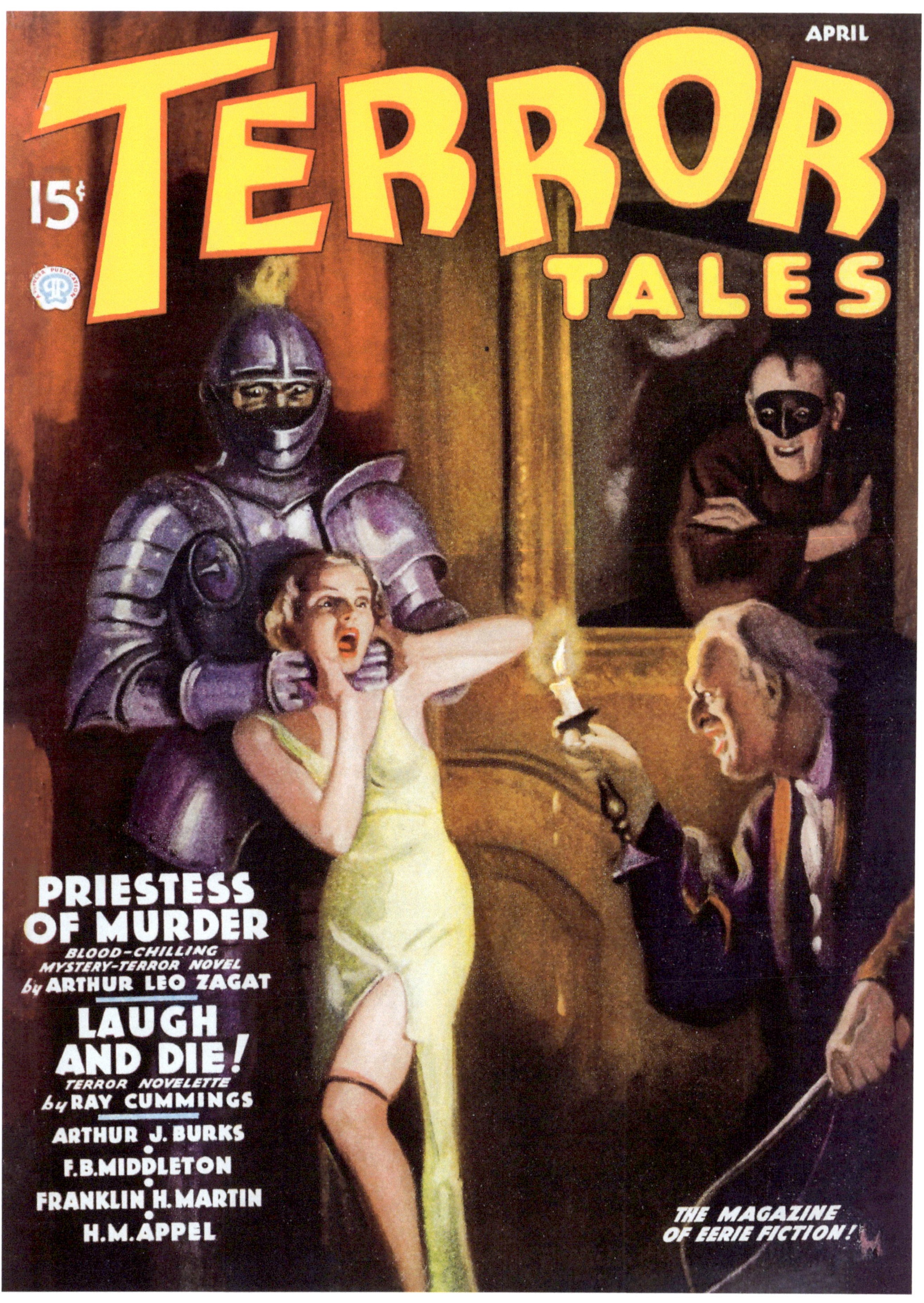

TERROR TALES
APRIL 1936

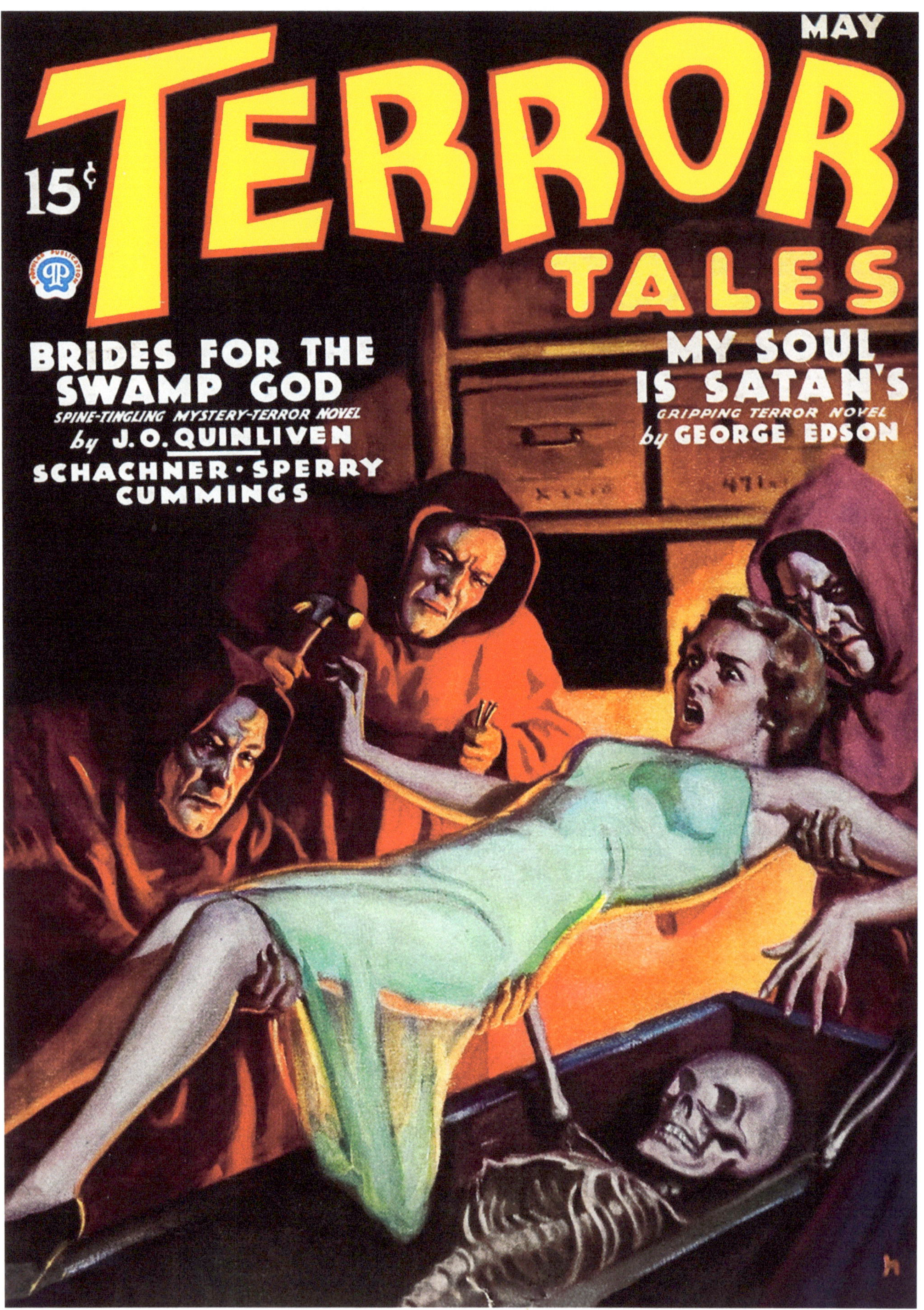

MAY
15¢
TERROR TALES
BRIDES FOR THE SWAMP GOD
SPINE-TINGLING MYSTERY-TERROR NOVEL
by J. O. QUINLIVEN
SCHACHNER · SPERRY
CUMMINGS
MY SOUL IS SATAN'S
GRIPPING TERROR NOVEL
by GEORGE EDSON

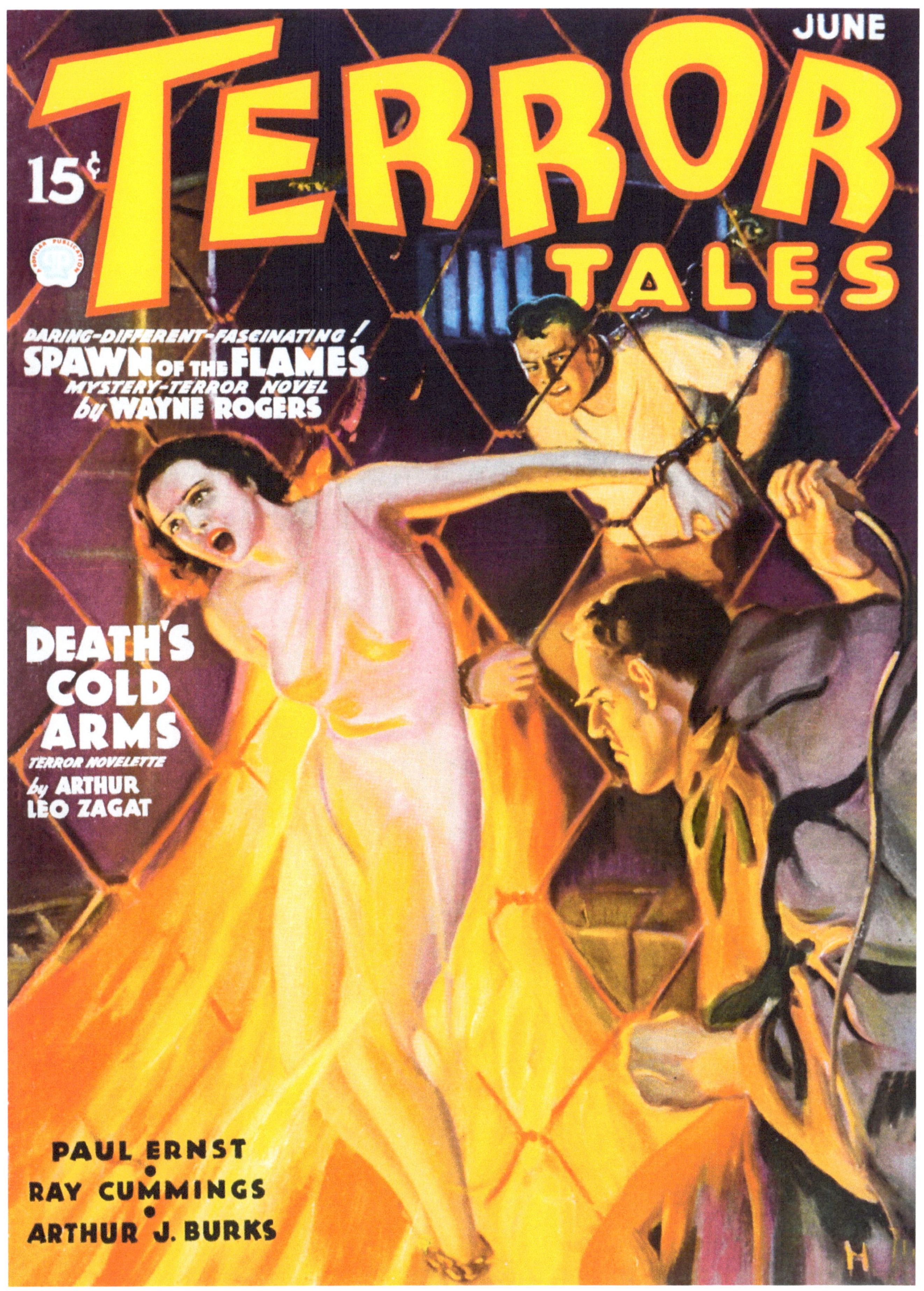

JUNE
15¢
TERROR TALES
DARING-DIFFERENT-FASCINATING!
SPAWN of the FLAMES
MYSTERY-TERROR NOVEL
by WAYNE ROGERS
DEATH'S COLD ARMS
TERROR NOVELETTE
by ARTHUR LEO ZAGAT
PAUL ERNST
RAY CUMMINGS
ARTHUR J. BURKS

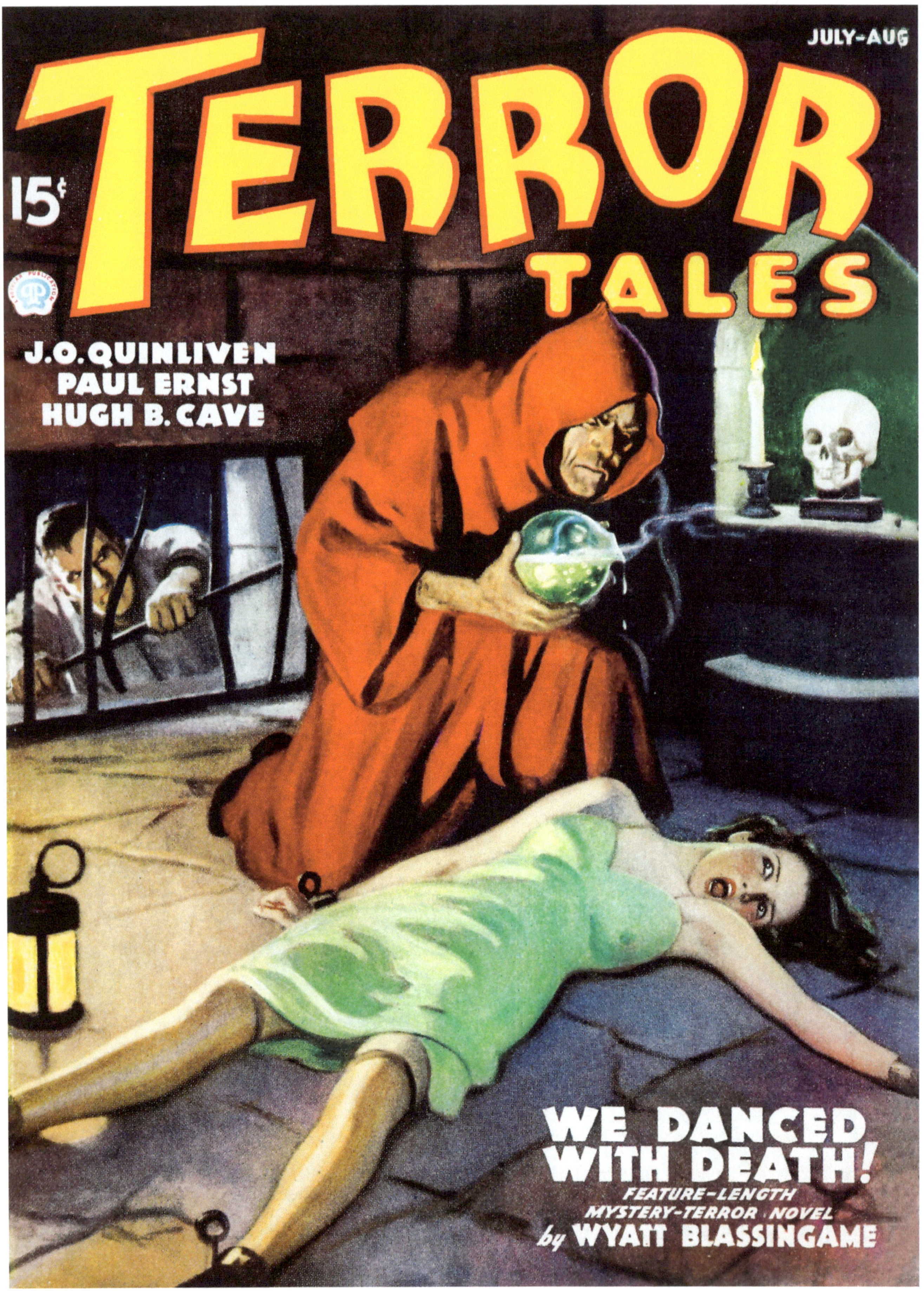

JULY-AUG
15¢
TERROR
TALES
J.O. QUINLIVEN
PAUL ERNST
HUGH B. CAVE
WE DANCED WITH DEATH!
FEATURE-LENGTH MYSTERY-TERROR NOVEL
by WYATT BLASSINGAME

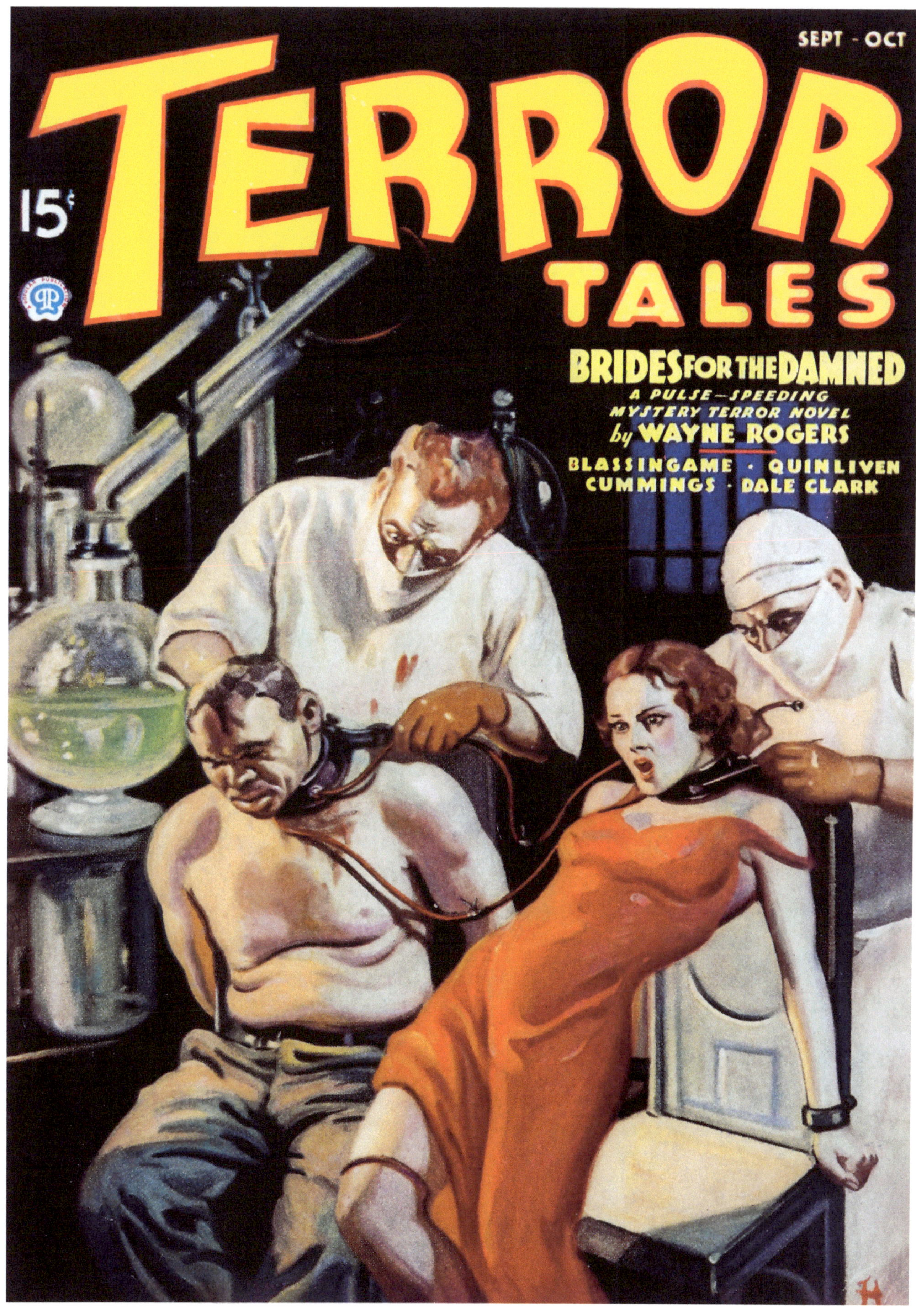

SEPT - OCT
15¢
TERROR
TALES
BRIDES FOR THE DAMNED
A PULSE—SPEEDING
MYSTERY TERROR NOVEL
by WAYNE ROGERS
BLASSINGAME · QUINLIVEN
CUMMINGS · DALE CLARK

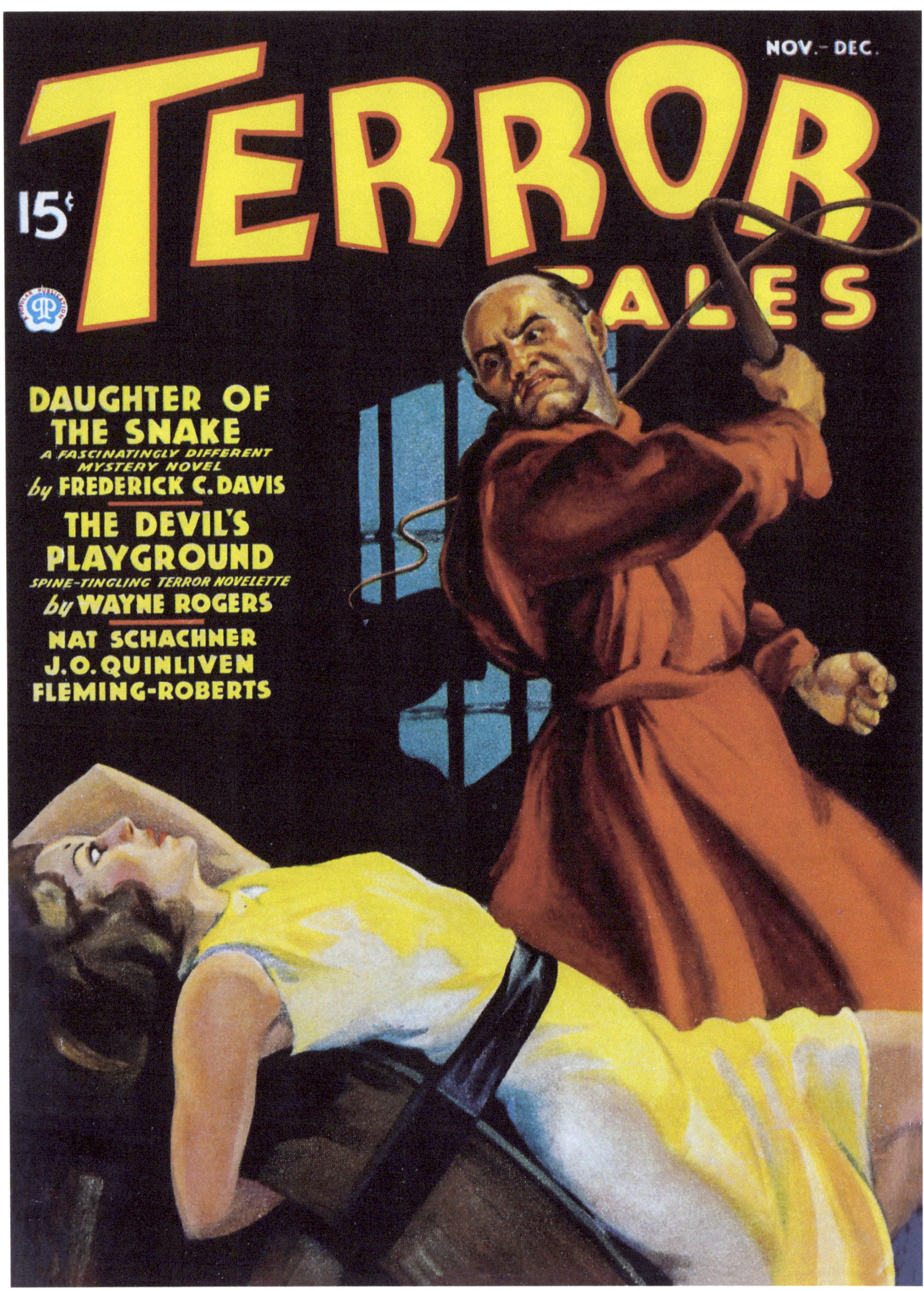

TERROR TALES

NOVEMBER-DECEMBER 1936

90

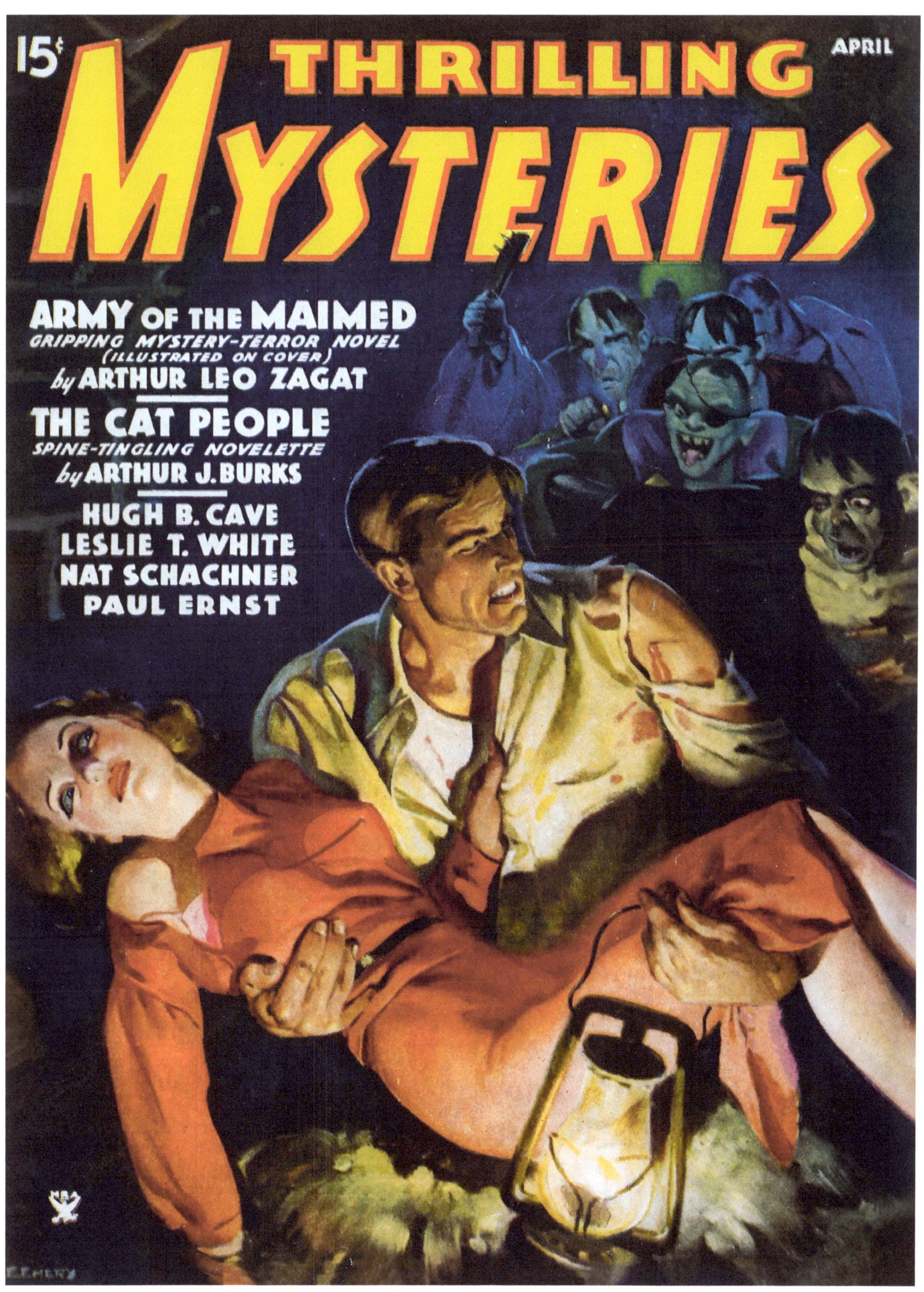

15¢
APRIL
THRILLING MYSTERIES
ARMY OF THE MAIMED
GRIPPING MYSTERY-TERROR NOVEL
(ILLUSTRATED ON COVER)
by ARTHUR LEO ZAGAT
THE CAT PEOPLE
SPINE-TINGLING NOVELETTE
by ARTHUR J. BURKS
HUGH B. CAVE
LESLIE T. WHITE
NAT SCHACHNER
PAUL ERNST

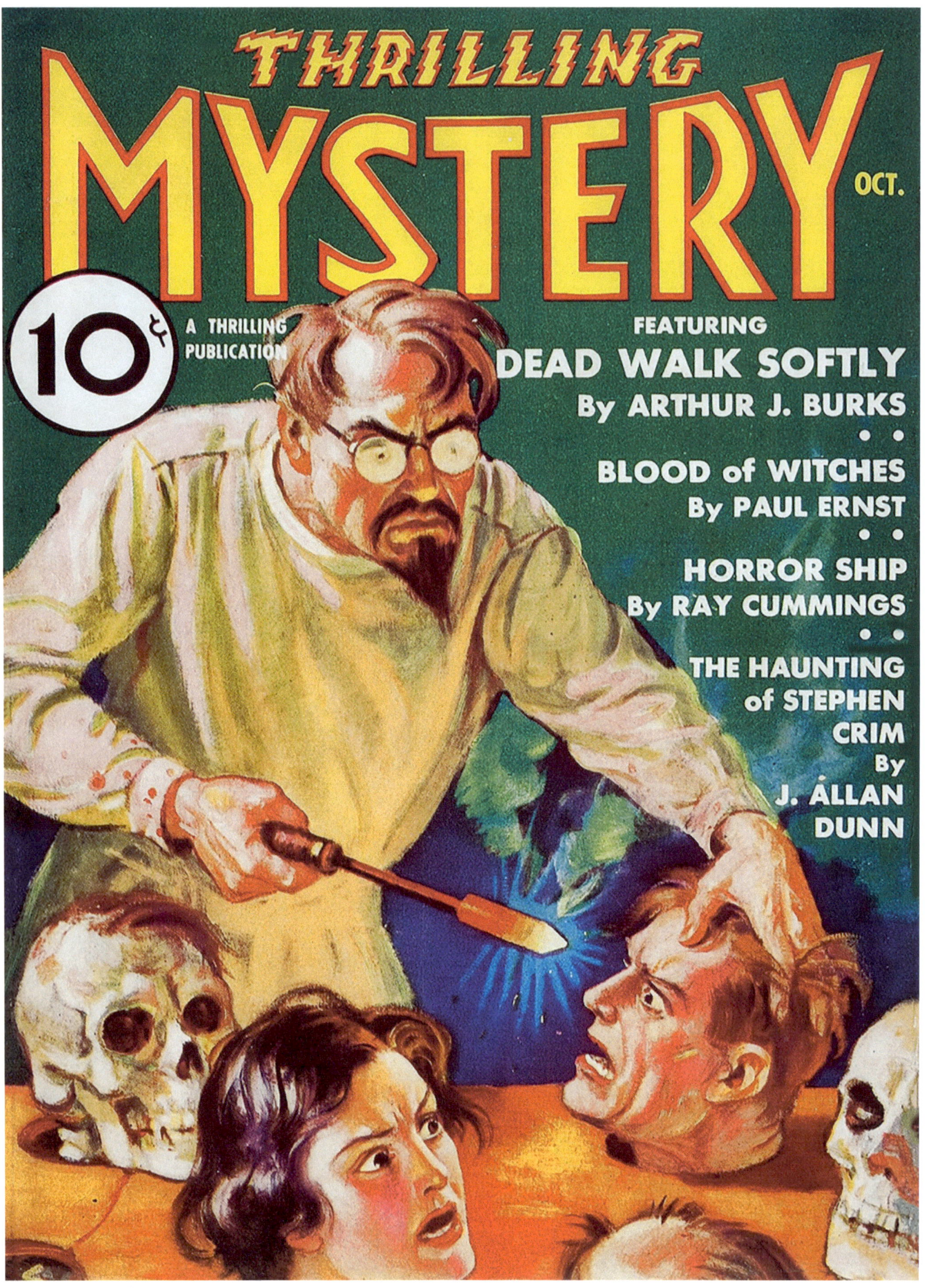

THRILLING MYSTERY

OCTOBER 1935

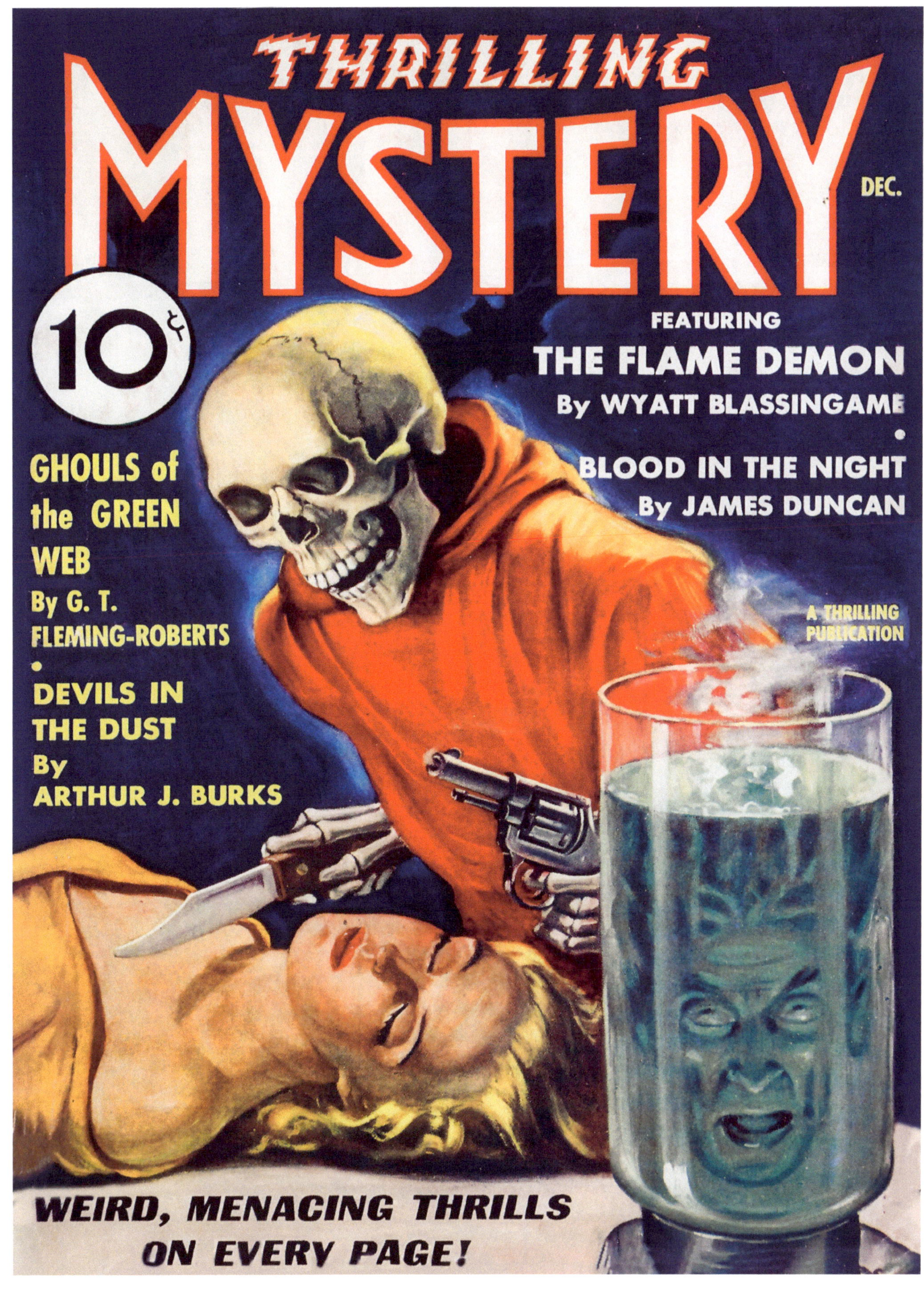

THRILLING MYSTERY
DEC.
10¢
FEATURING
THE FLAME DEMON
By WYATT BLASSINGAME
BLOOD IN THE NIGHT
By JAMES DUNCAN
A THRILLING PUBLICATION
GHOULS of the GREEN WEB
By G. T. FLEMING-ROBERTS
DEVILS IN THE DUST
By ARTHUR J. BURKS
WEIRD, MENACING THRILLS ON EVERY PAGE!

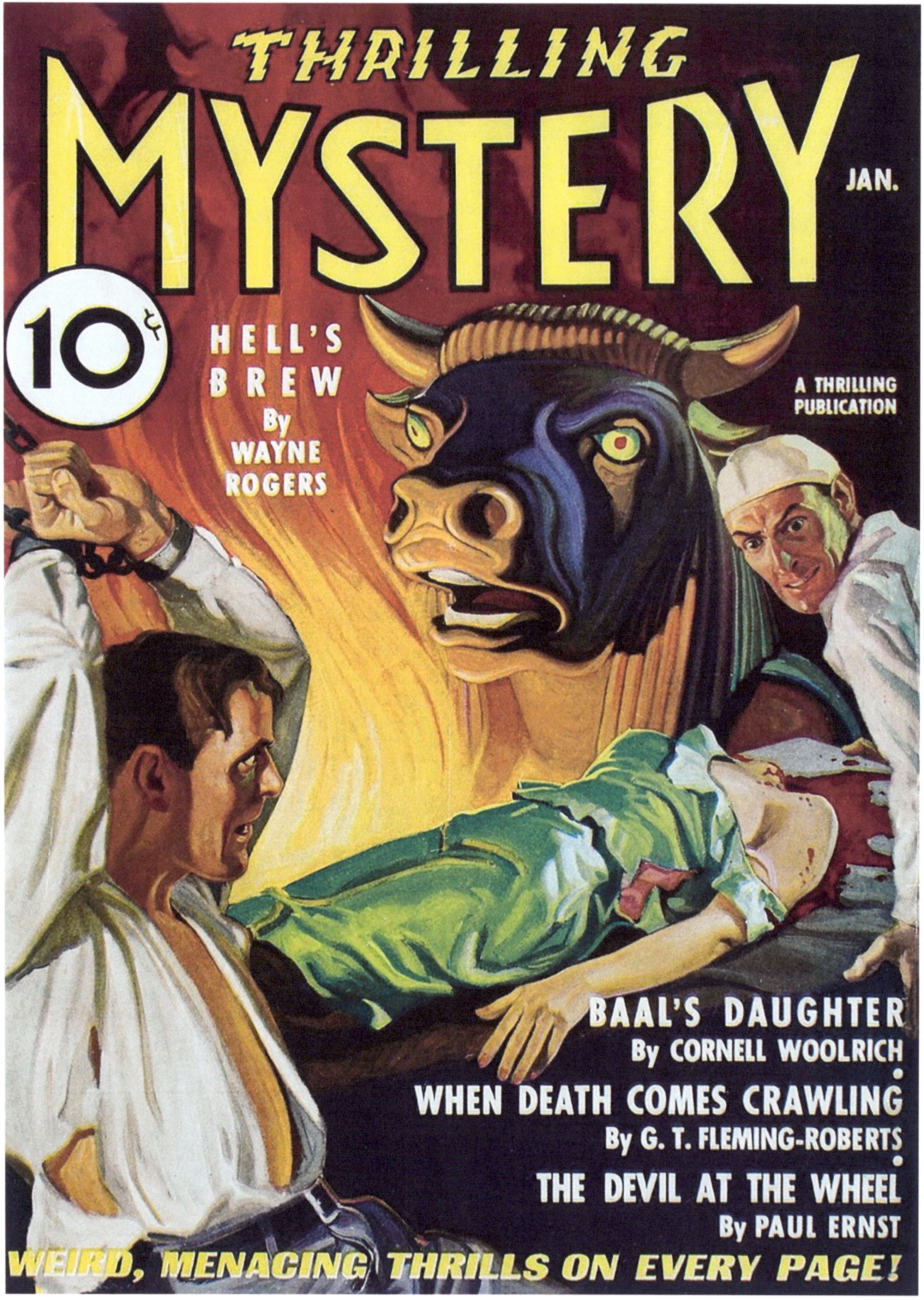

THRILLING MYSTERY

JANUARY 1936

94

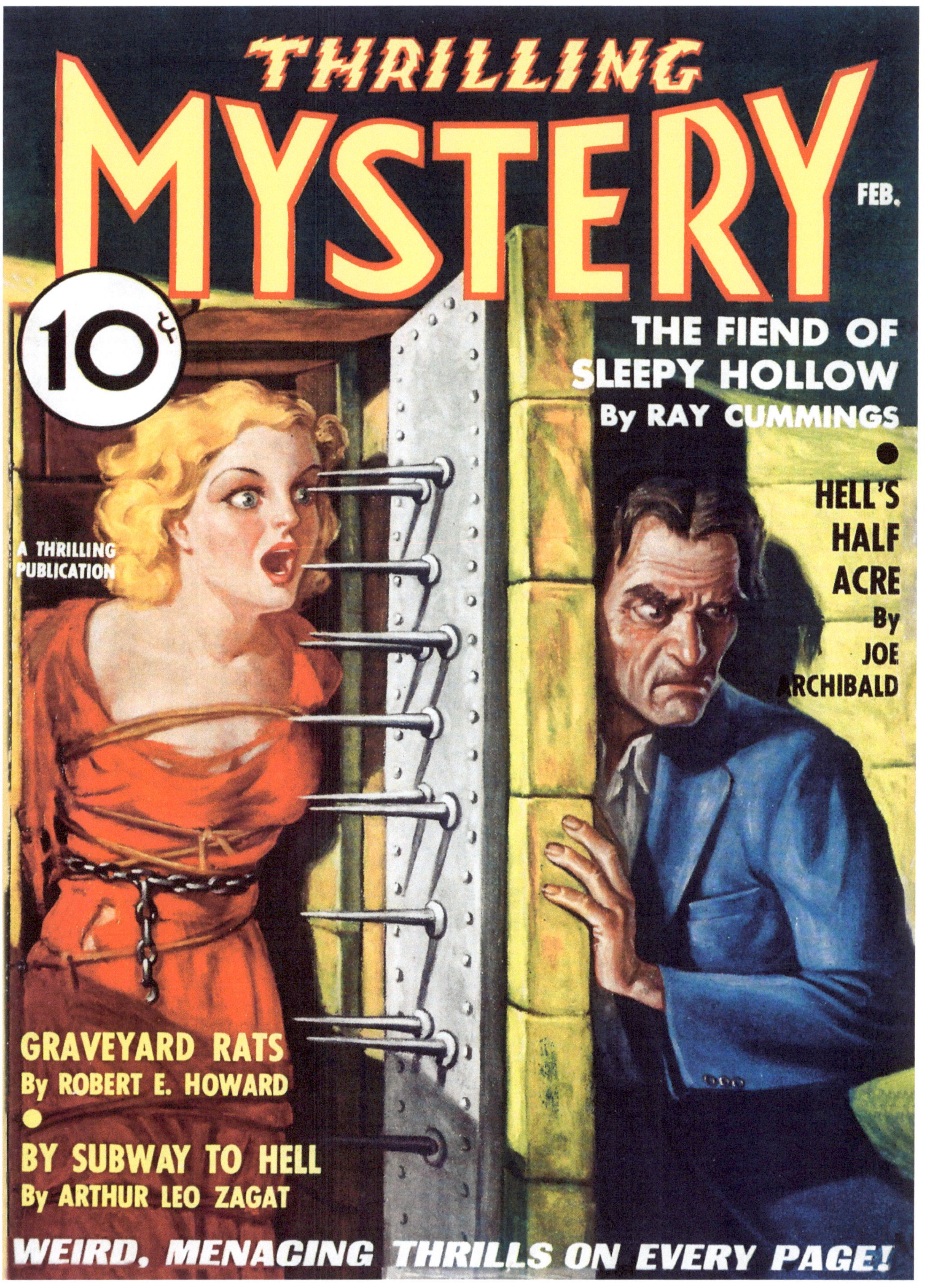

THRILLING
MYSTERY
FEB.
10¢
A THRILLING PUBLICATION
THE FIEND OF SLEEPY HOLLOW
By RAY CUMMINGS
HELL'S HALF ACRE
By JOE ARCHIBALD
GRAVEYARD RATS
By ROBERT E. HOWARD
BY SUBWAY TO HELL
By ARTHUR LEO ZAGAT
WEIRD, MENACING THRILLS ON EVERY PAGE!

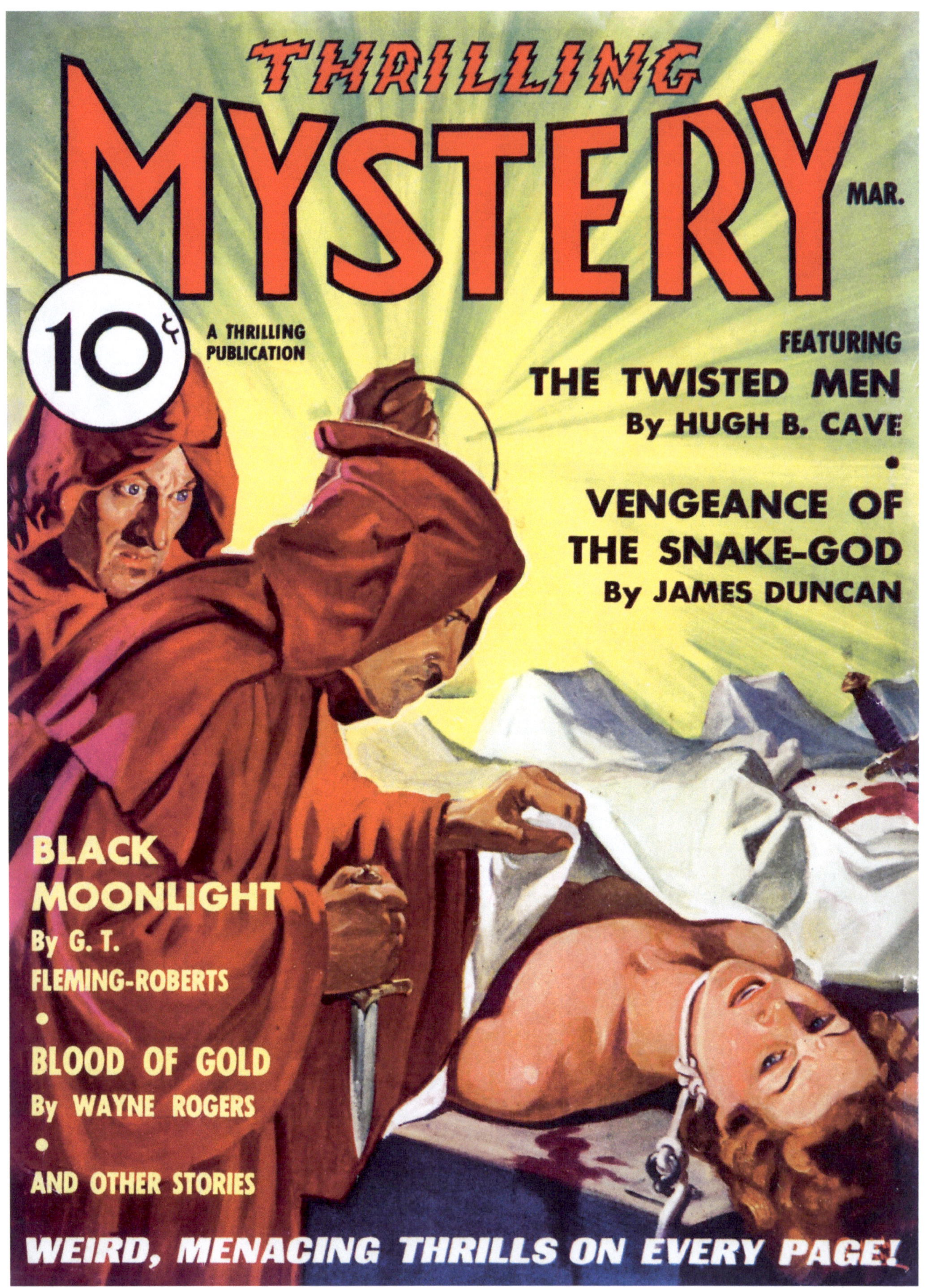

THRILLING MYSTERY

MARCH 1936

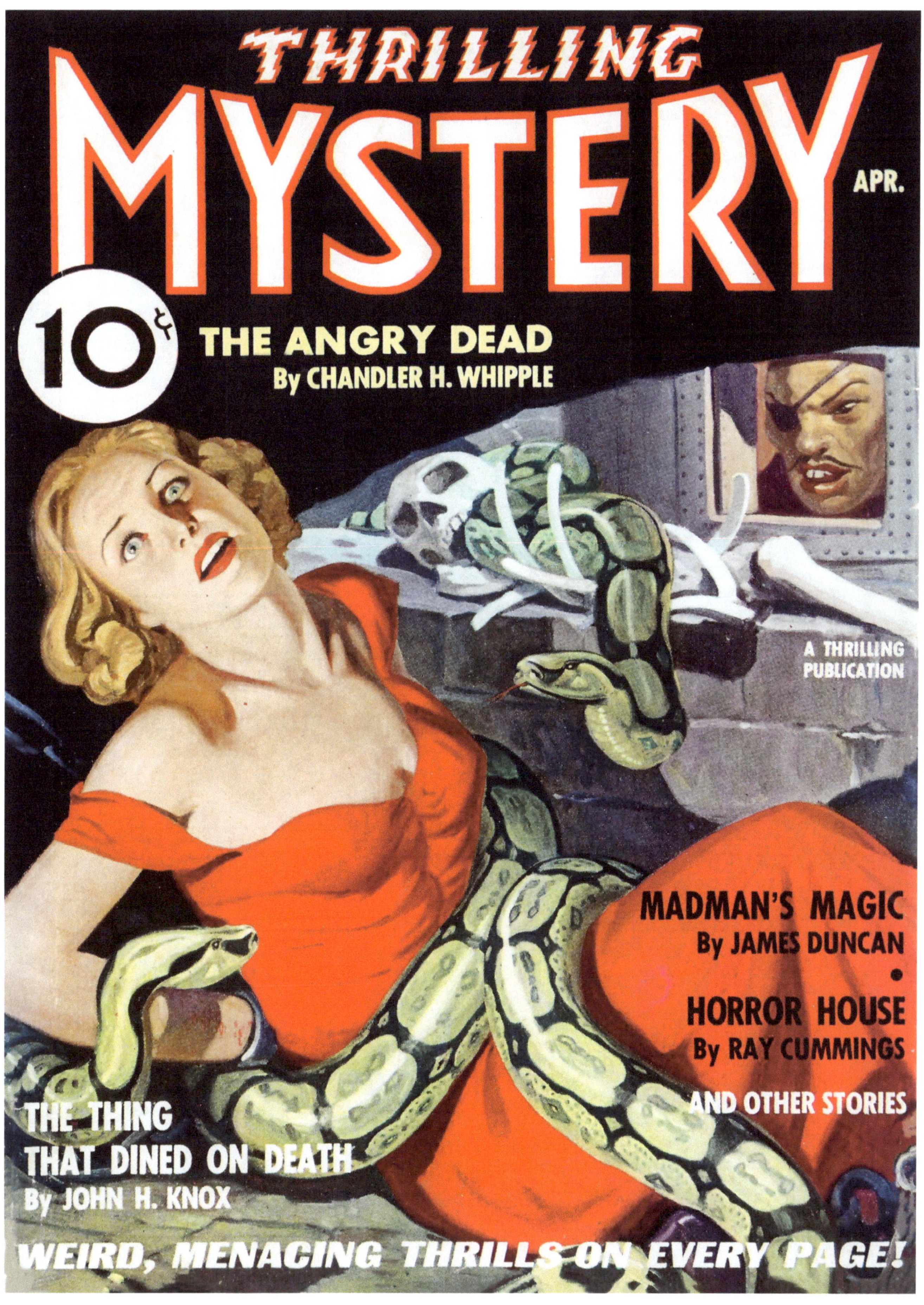

THRILLING
MYSTERY
APR.
10¢
THE ANGRY DEAD
By CHANDLER H. WHIPPLE
A THRILLING PUBLICATION
MADMAN'S MAGIC
By JAMES DUNCAN
HORROR HOUSE
By RAY CUMMINGS
AND OTHER STORIES
THE THING
THAT DINED ON DEATH
By JOHN H. KNOX
WEIRD, MENACING THRILLS ON EVERY PAGE!

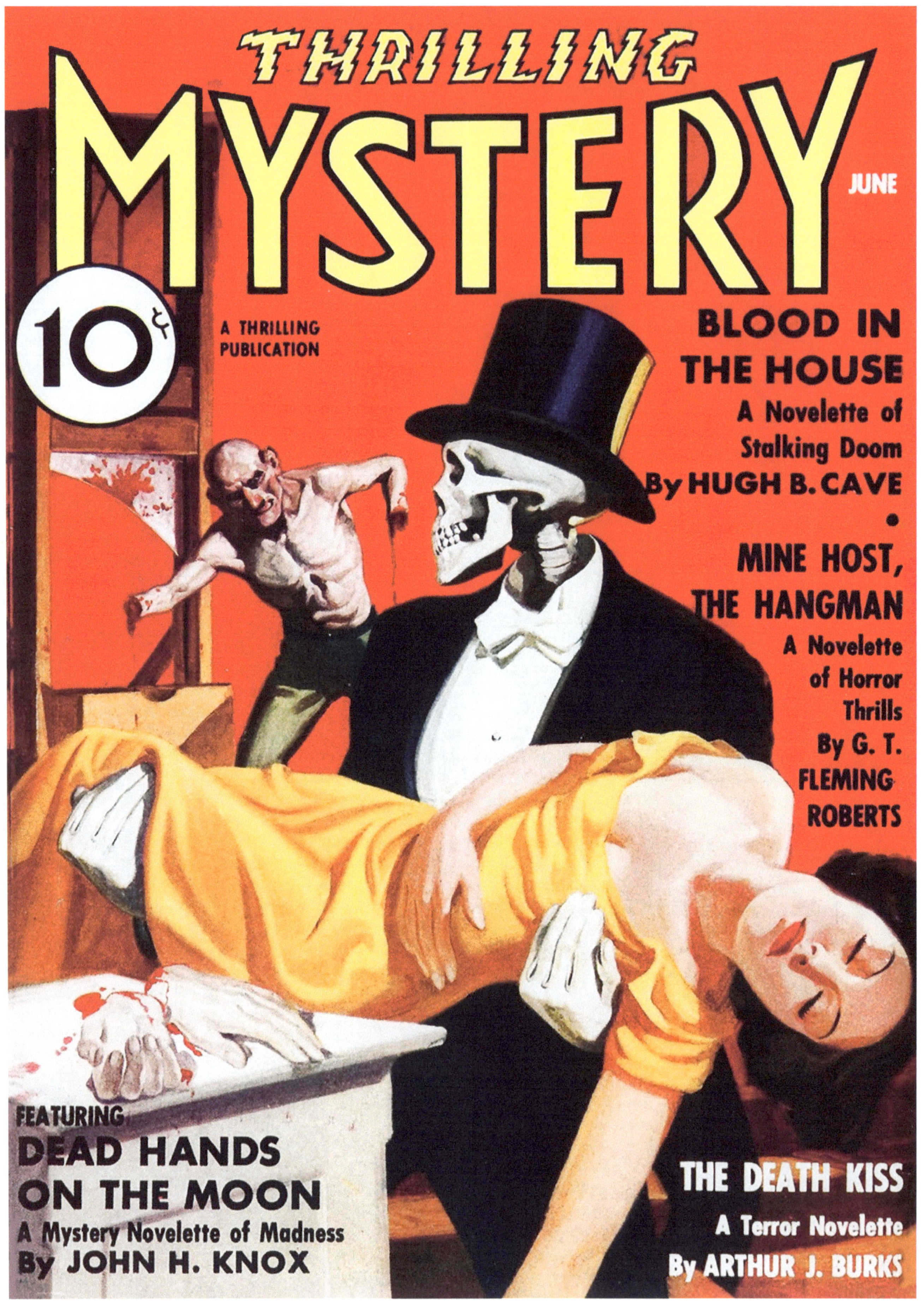

THRILLING MYSTERY
JUNE
10¢
A THRILLING PUBLICATION
BLOOD IN THE HOUSE
A Novelette of Stalking Doom
By HUGH B. CAVE
MINE HOST, THE HANGMAN
A Novelette of Horror Thrills
By G. T. FLEMING ROBERTS
FEATURING
DEAD HANDS ON THE MOON
A Mystery Novelette of Madness
By JOHN H. KNOX
THE DEATH KISS
A Terror Novelette
By ARTHUR J. BURKS

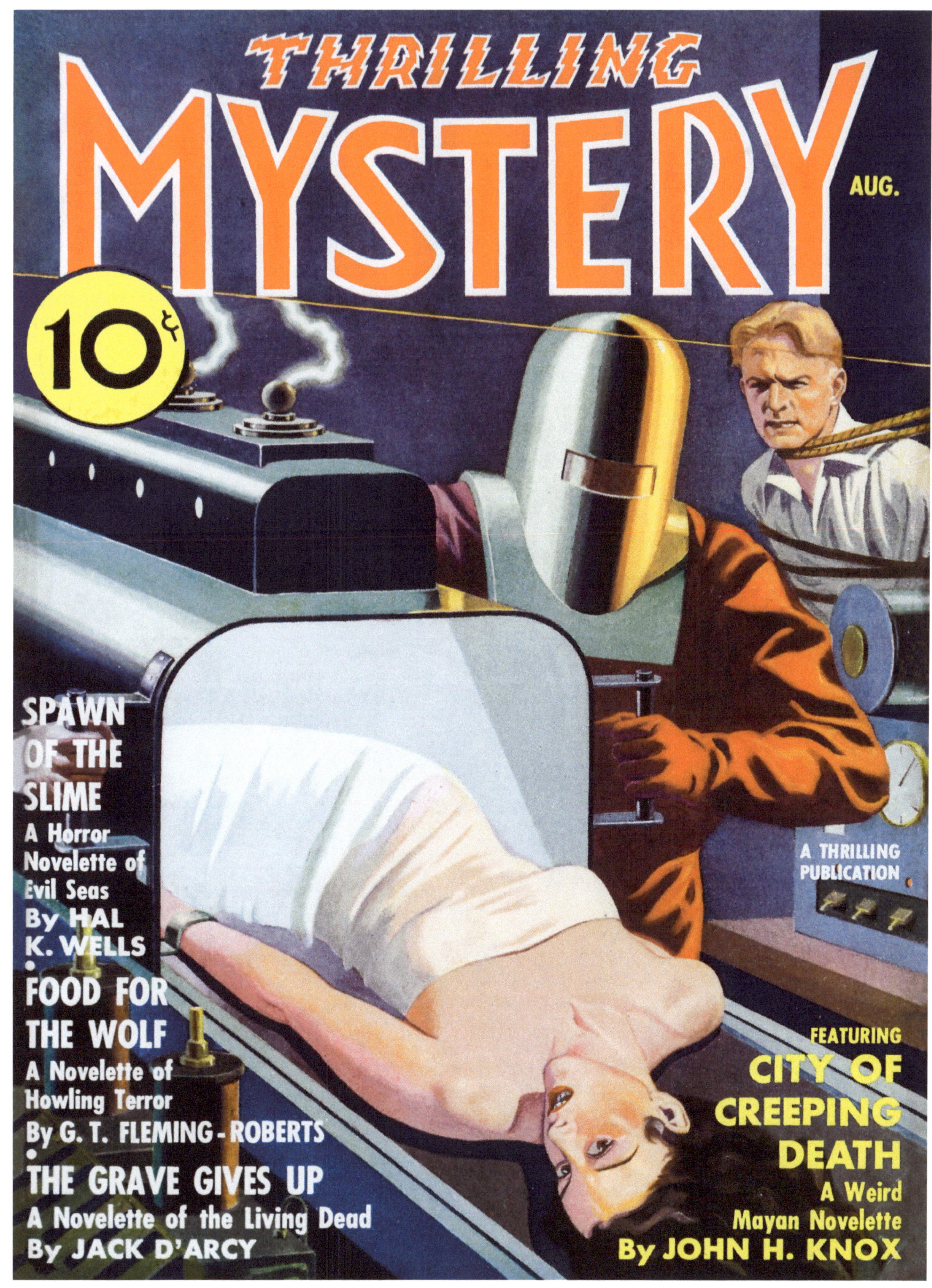

THRILLING MYSTERY
AUGUST 1936

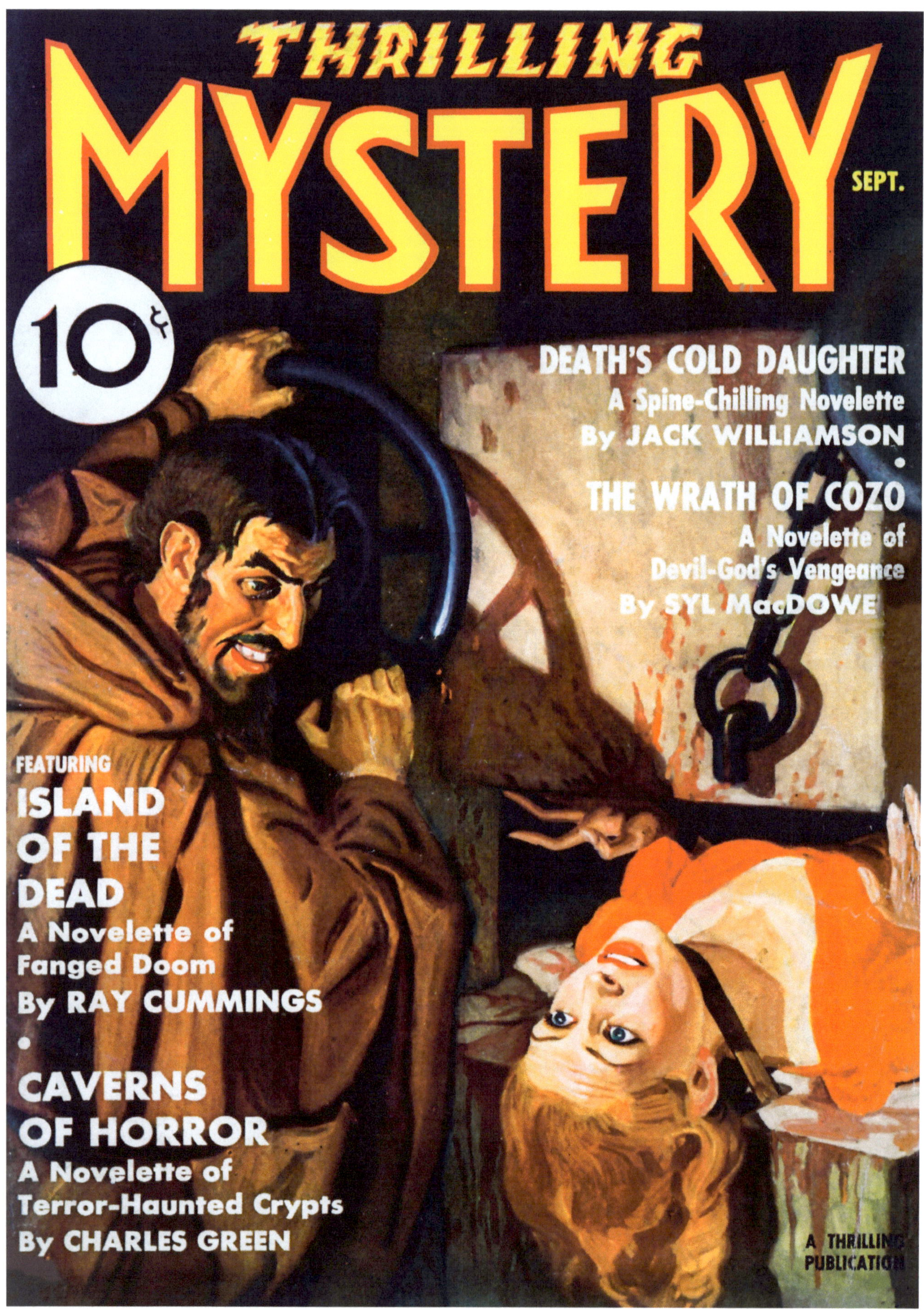

THRILLING MYSTERY

SEPTEMBER 1936

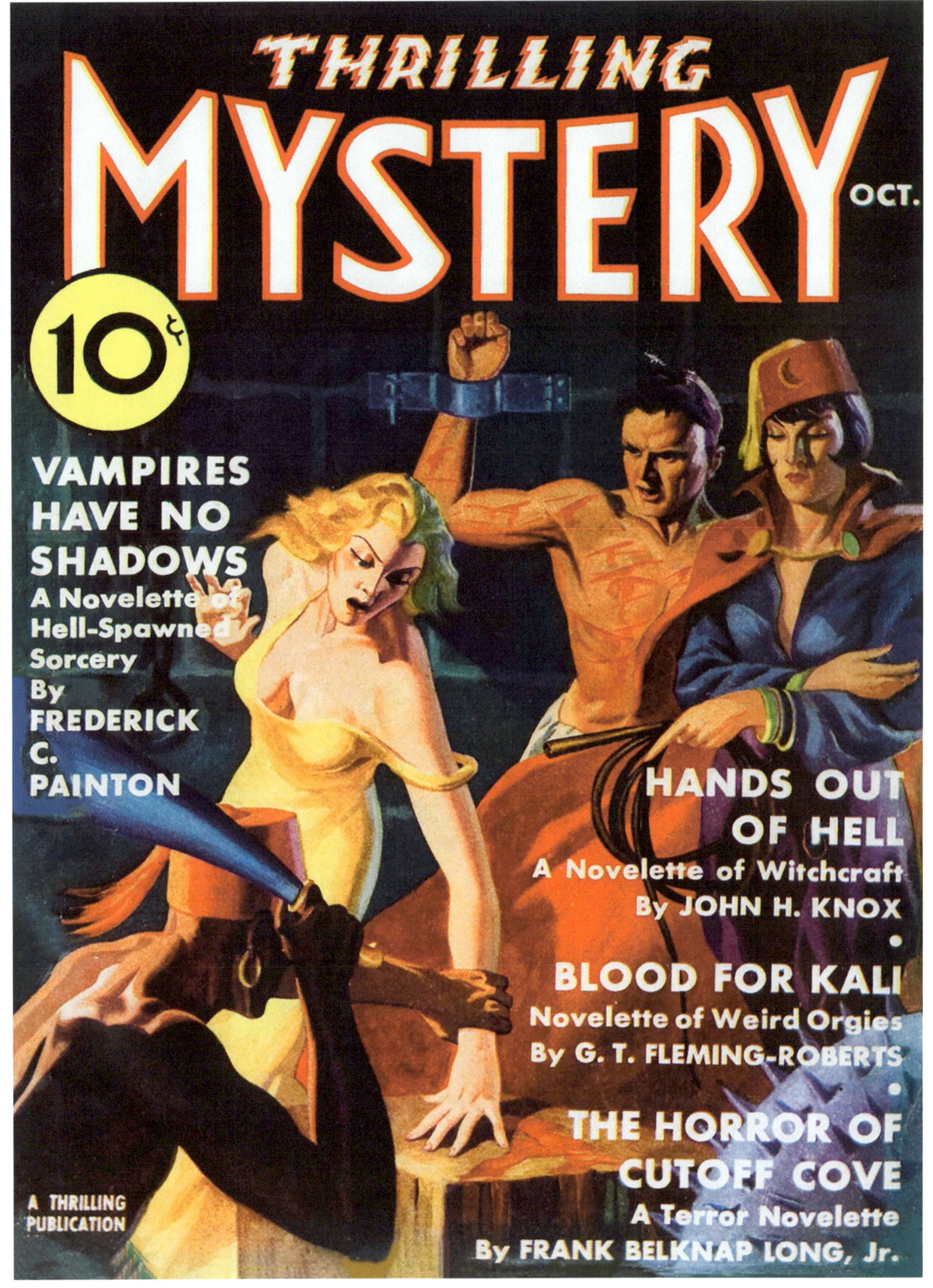

THRILLING MYSTERY
OCT.
10¢
VAMPIRES HAVE NO SHADOWS
A Novelette of Hell-Spawned Sorcery
By FREDERICK C. PAINTON
HANDS OUT OF HELL
A Novelette of Witchcraft
By JOHN H. KNOX
BLOOD FOR KALI
Novelette of Weird Orgies
By G. T. FLEMING-ROBERTS
THE HORROR OF CUTOFF COVE
A Terror Novelette
By FRANK BELKNAP LONG, Jr.
A THRILLING PUBLICATION

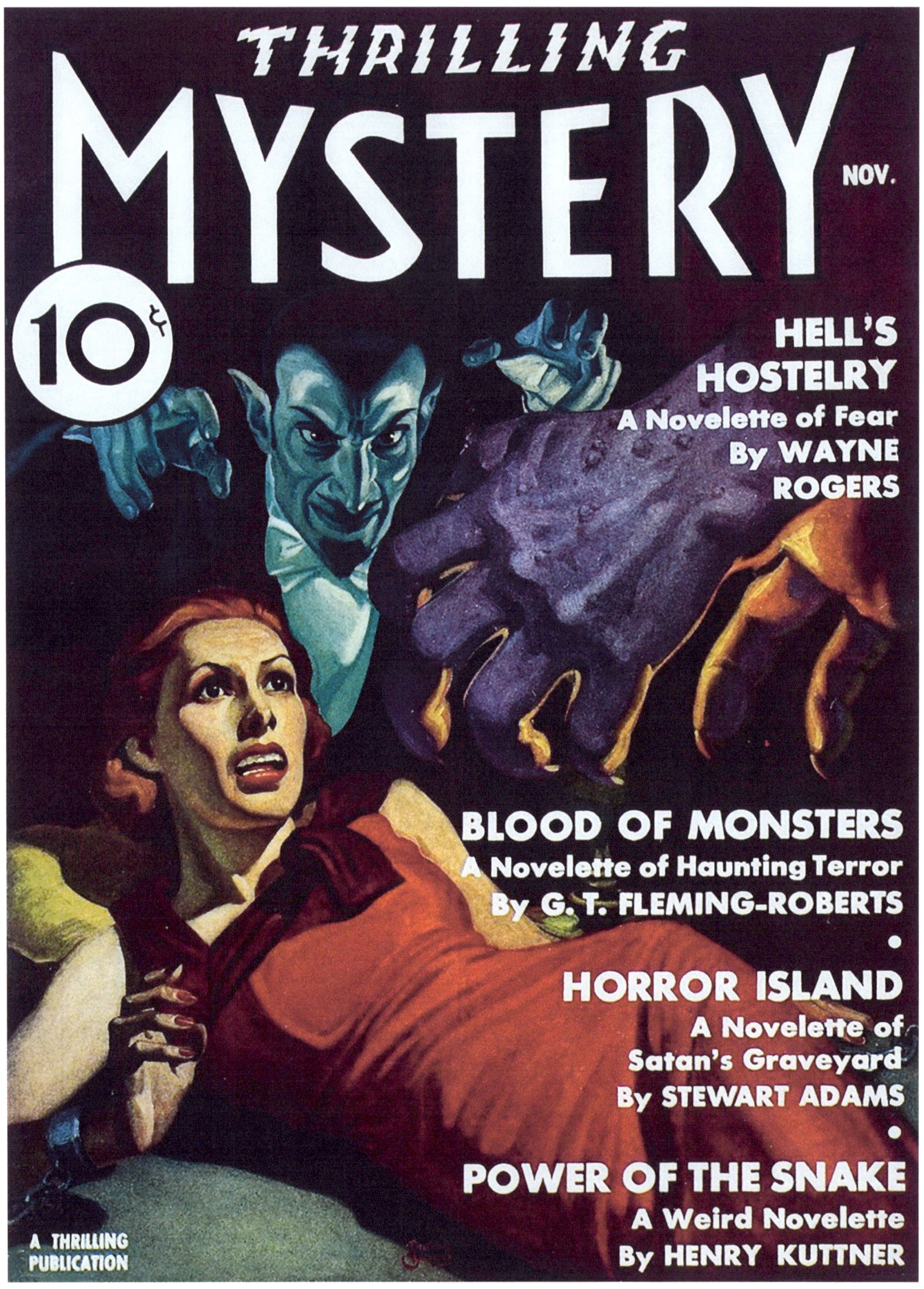

THRILLING MYSTERY

NOVEMBER 1936

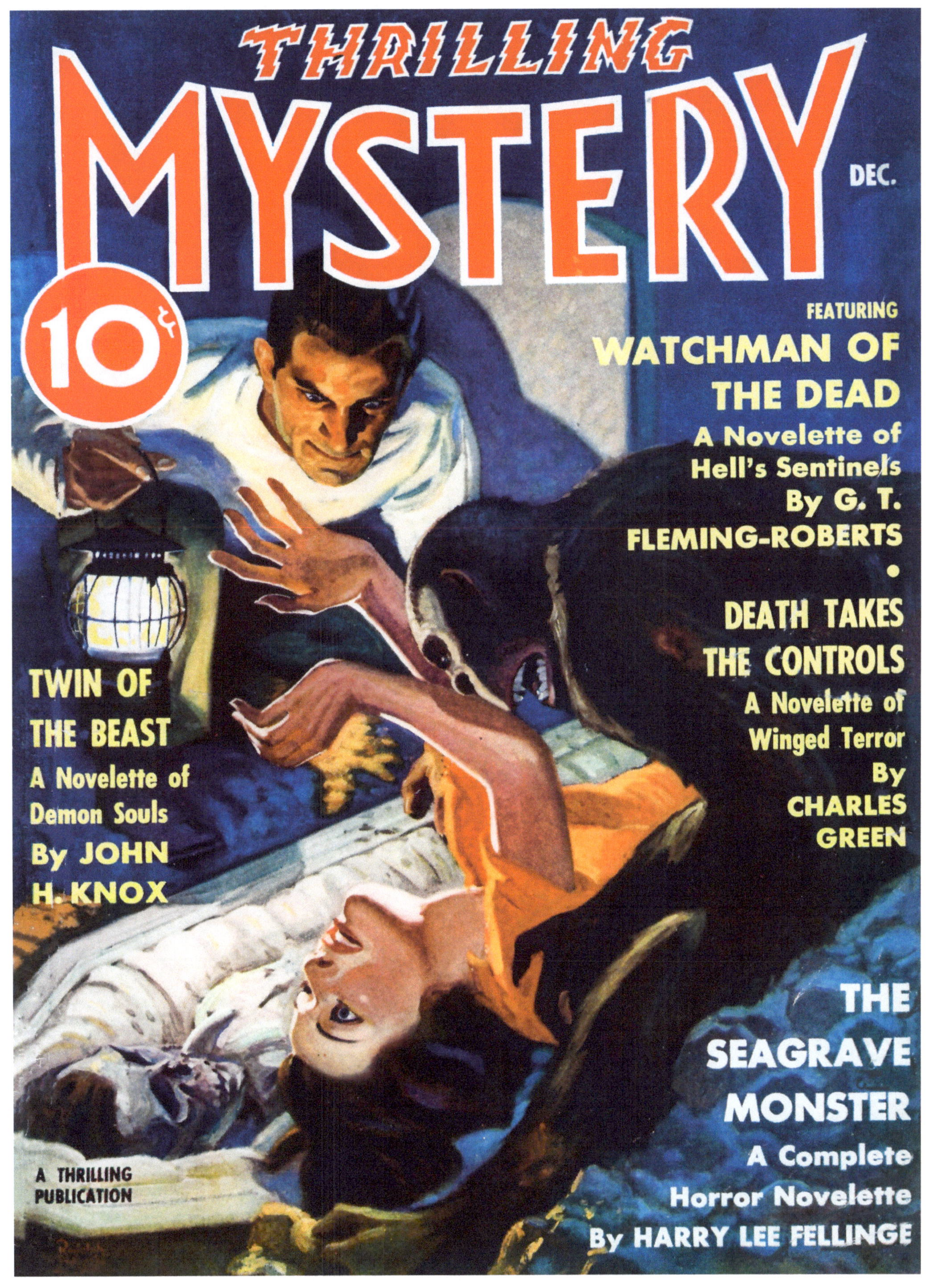

THRILLING MYSTERY

DECEMBER 1936

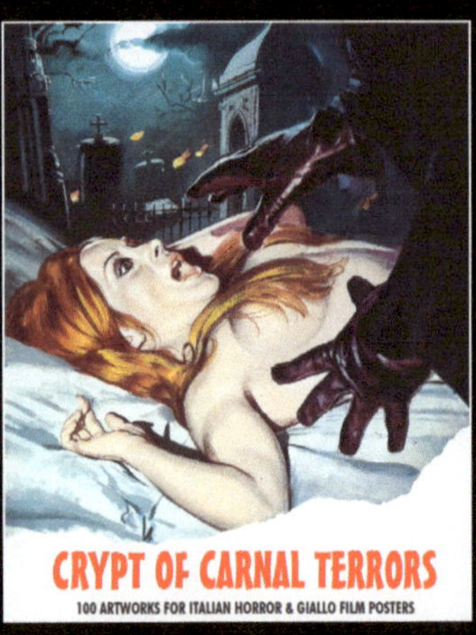
CRYPT OF CARNAL TERRORS
100 ARTWORKS FOR ITALIAN HORROR & GIALLO FILM POSTERS

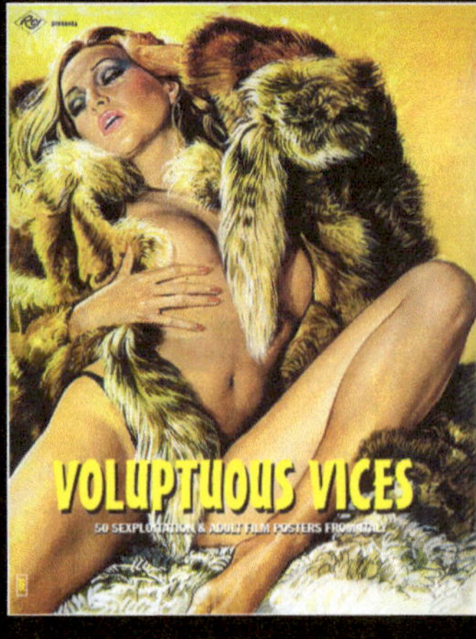
VOLUPTUOUS VICES
50 SEXPLOITATION & ADULT FILM POSTERS FROM ITALY

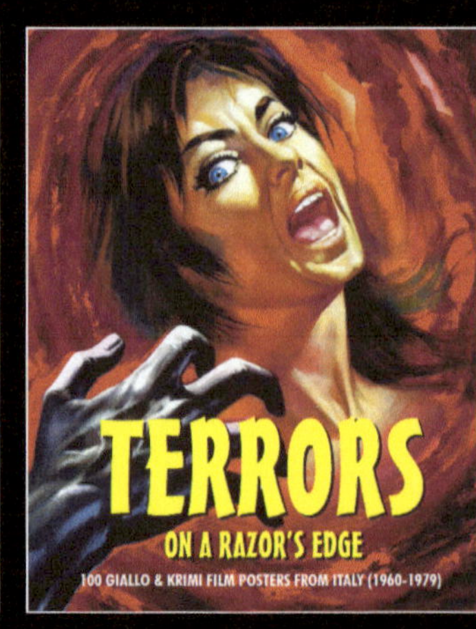
TERRORS
ON A RAZOR'S EDGE
100 GIALLO & KRIMI FILM POSTERS FROM ITALY (1960-1979)

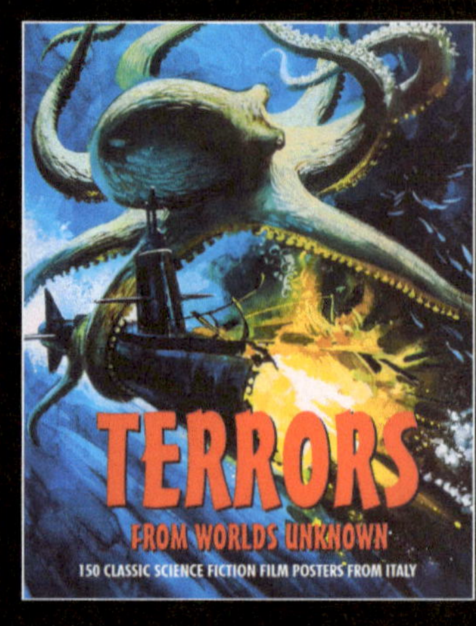
TERRORS
FROM WORLDS UNKNOWN
150 CLASSIC SCIENCE FICTION FILM POSTERS FROM ITALY

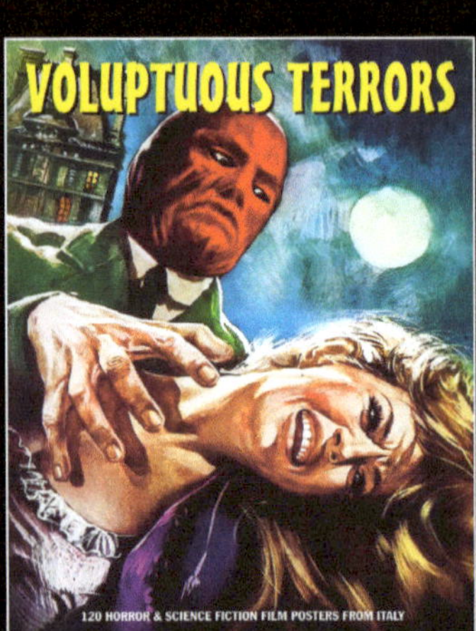
VOLUPTUOUS TERRORS
120 HORROR & SCIENCE FICTION FILM POSTERS FROM ITALY

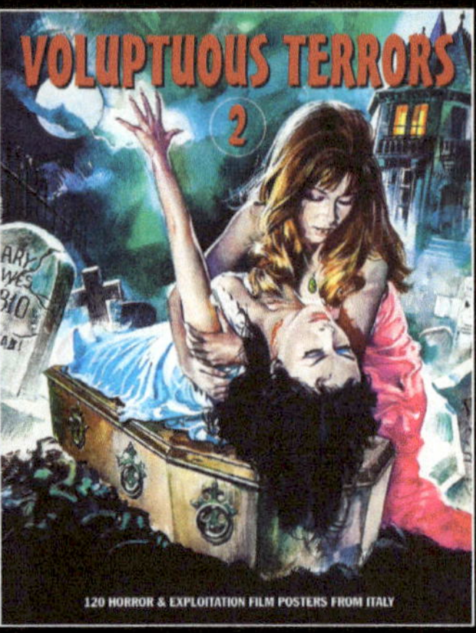
VOLUPTUOUS TERRORS
2
120 HORROR & EXPLOITATION FILM POSTERS FROM ITALY

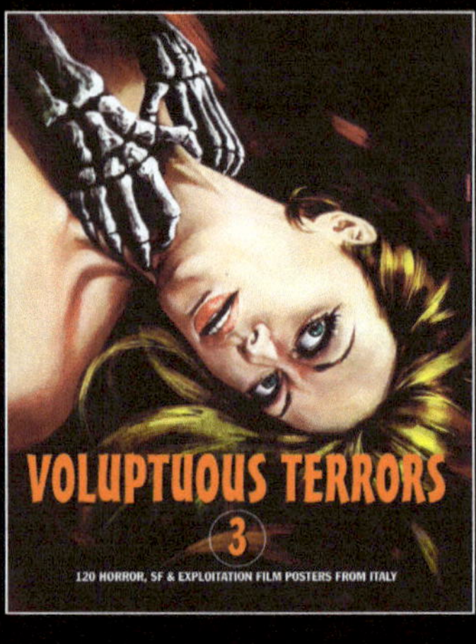
VOLUPTUOUS TERRORS
3
120 HORROR, SF & EXPLOITATION FILM POSTERS FROM ITALY

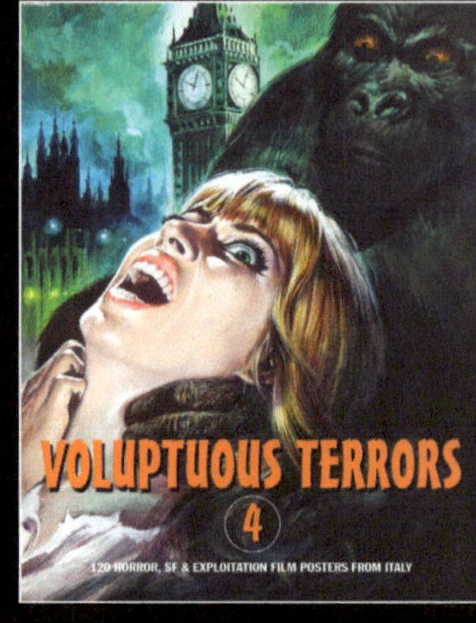
VOLUPTUOUS TERRORS
4
120 HORROR, SF & EXPLOITATION FILM POSTERS FROM ITALY

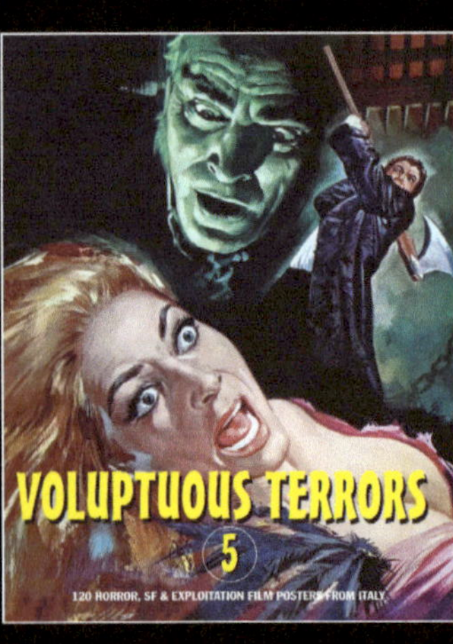
VOLUPTUOUS TERRORS
5
120 HORROR, SF & EXPLOITATION FILM POSTERS FROM ITALY

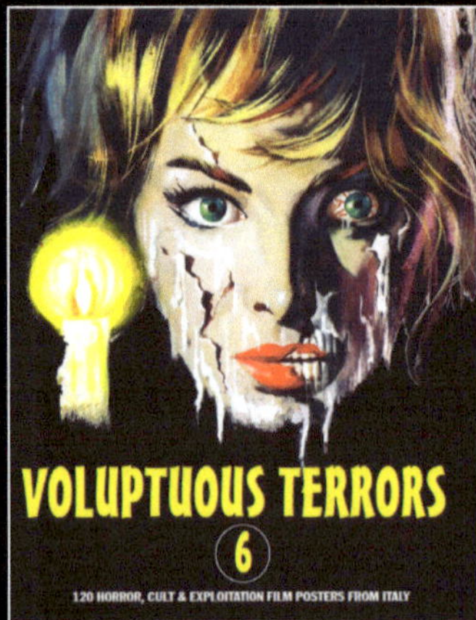
VOLUPTUOUS TERRORS
6
120 HORROR, CULT & EXPLOITATION FILM POSTERS FROM ITALY

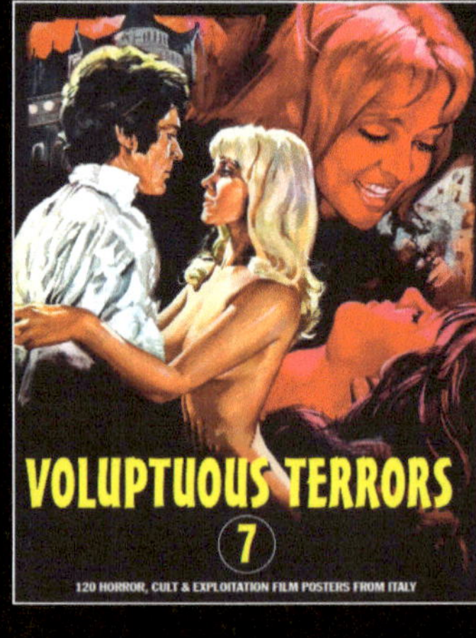
VOLUPTUOUS TERRORS
7
120 HORROR, CULT & EXPLOITATION FILM POSTERS FROM ITALY

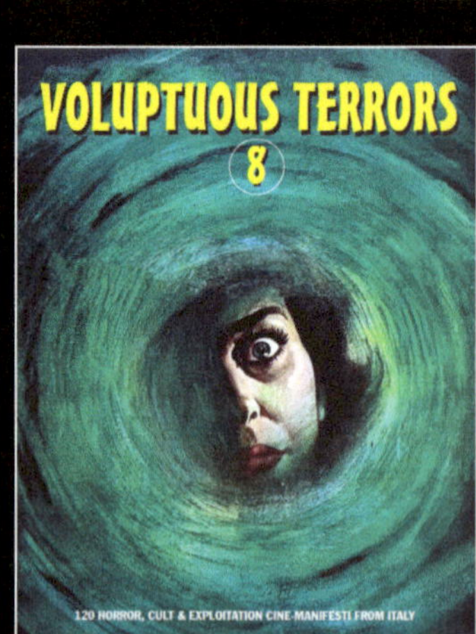
VOLUPTUOUS TERRORS
8
120 HORROR, CULT & EXPLOITATION CINE MANIFESTI FROM ITALY

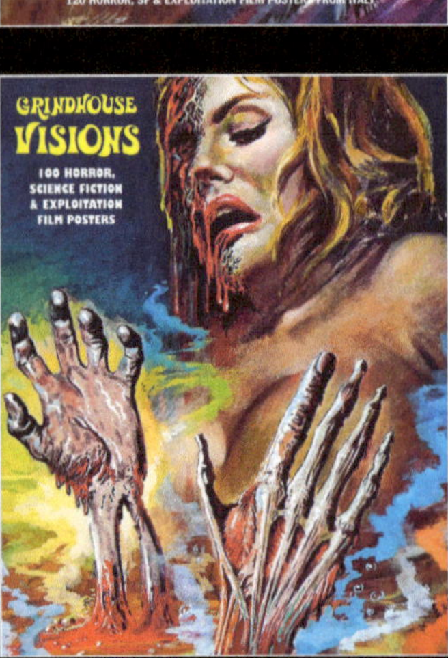
GRINDHOUSE
VISIONS
100 HORROR,
SCIENCE FICTION
& EXPLOITATION
FILM POSTERS

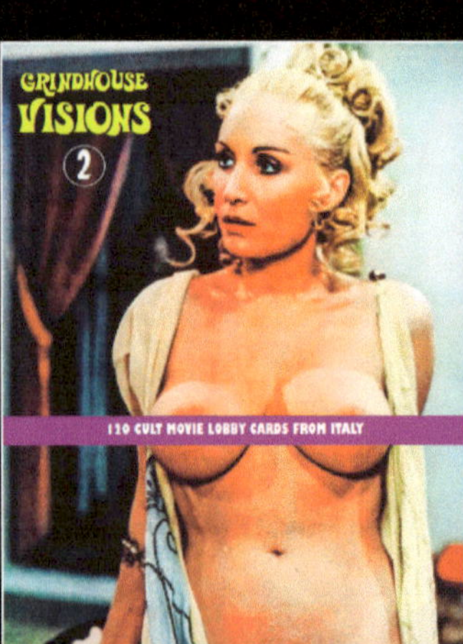
GRINDHOUSE
VISIONS
2
120 CULT MOVIE LOBBY CARDS FROM ITALY

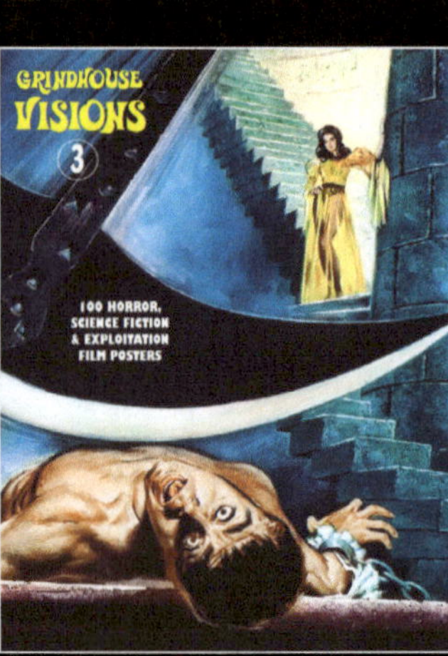
GRINDHOUSE
VISIONS
3
100 HORROR,
SCIENCE FICTION
& EXPLOITATION
FILM POSTERS